The Sanity We Are Born With

THE

Sanity We Are Born With

A BUDDHIST APPROACH TO PSYCHOLOGY

Chögyam Trungpa

Compiled and edited by Carolyn Rose Gimian
Forewords by Daniel Goleman and Kidder Smith

SHAMBHALA
Boston & London
2005

Shambhala Publications, Inc.
Horticultural Hall
300 Massachusetts Avenue
Boston, Massachusetts 02115
www.shambhala.com

9 8 7 6 5 4 3 2 1

First Edition
Printed in the United States of America

⊗ This edition is printed on acid-free paper that meets
the American National Standards Institute z39.48 Standard.
Distributed in the United States by Random House, Inc.,
and in Canada by Random House of Canada Ltd

Library of Congress Cataloging-in-Publication Data
Trungpa, Chögyam, 1939–
The sanity we are born with: a Buddhist approach to psychology /
Chögyam Trungpa;
compiled and edited by Carolyn Rose Gimian.
p. cm.
ISBN 1-59030-090-4 (pbk.: alk. paper)
1. Buddhism—Psychology. I. Gimian, Carolyn Rose. II. Title.
BQ4570.P76T78 2005
294.3'01'9—dc22
2004056509

CONTENTS

FOREWORD

Daniel Goleman

THE YEAR WAS 1975, the setting a restaurant in Cambridge, Massachusetts. Chögyam Trungpa Rinpoche had invited me out to dinner to tell me about his plans for a new educational institution he was founding, Naropa Institute. At one point in the conversation he leaned across the table toward me with a conspiratorial air, looked me straight in the eye, and said emphatically, "Buddhism will come to the West as a psychology."

That proposition made immediate sense to me. I had recently received my doctorate in psychology from Harvard, and returned there as a visiting lecturer after a year of postdoctoral study in Sri Lanka and India. My topic was abhidharma, an ancient Buddhist theory of mind that has been in continual use as an applied psychology for the last fifteen hundred years or more.

Of course, I had never heard of this system in any of my academic psychology studies. The implicit assumption (culture-bound and flavored with hubris though it may be) was that the field of psychology had begun only a century before, in Europe and America—none of my psychology professors had ever heard of abhidharma. I took Rinpoche's observation to mean that Western students of psychology would soon be hearing whispers of abhidharma that might inspire them to pursue further study of Buddhism. Indeed, he sprinkled his teachings with nuggets from this rich psychological mine, offering practical hints on everything from one's state of mind while diapering the baby to transforming aggression. Trungpa Rinpoche was among the very first to offer such glimpses to a Western audience, sometimes casually interspersing these into a discussion and sometimes discoursing on them at great length.

This volume does a great favor for Western readers who want to understand the view Buddhist psychology takes of the human condition, pulling together a lifetime of insights on the subject by one of its most articulate teachers. Buddhism, like Western thought, harbors multiple schools of philosophy and psychology of mind. Several of these are represented here, though there are still more awaiting exploration by those readers who find themselves intrigued. Chögyam Trungpa offers us a rich banquet, with many inviting, intriguing, and delicious glimpses into these Buddhist perspectives on our mind and life.

FOREWORD

Kidder Smith

PERHAPS IT'S A SHOCKING THOUGHT, that we are all born sane. But the Buddhist tradition goes further still, declaring that we are actually sane right now. Whatever confusions we experience, whatever doubts or anxieties may arise, at the base of all this, in the midst of all this, our fundamental sanity is always present. We might say that this book seeks to demonstrate how such an outrageous claim can be true. But actually this book provides a means for you, the reader, to determine its truth for yourself.

That means is meditation. As Trungpa Rinpoche says, meditation is "a way of clarifying the actual nature of mind" (page 3 below). Insofar as psychology is the study of mind, meditation offers us a psychological practice that is uniquely intimate. It is not someone else's experience we are studying, it is our own. And yet, as we will see, meditation takes us into the same intimacy with other beings that we have with ourselves.

What is mind? Everything. We get a hint of that in the way our experience is continuous. Even in deepest sleep our mind is active, aware, processing. When we meditate, attending consciously to mind, it never abandons us, never runs out or expires. Not only is our consciousness abundantly wall-to-wall, it actually *is* those walls, and everything imaginable or unimaginable lying beyond them. There is no end to this, nor exit from it. When we plan our escape, it is already taking place in mind. When we reach our destination, we are here in mind as well.

All we know is mind. It creates our world. "By meditating, we are dealing with the very mind that devised our eyeglasses and put the lenses in the rims, and the very mind that put up this tent. Our coming here is the product of our minds. . . . So this is a living world, mind's world. Realizing this, working with mind is no longer a remote or mysterious thing to do. It is no longer dealing with something that is hidden or somewhere else. Mind is right here. Mind is hanging out in the world. It is an open secret" (page 68).

Unhidden, omnipresent, not elsewhere, endless, that's quite a lot. So when we seek to work with mind, we need a discipline that is equally vast—and utterly simple. Otherwise it's like trying to devise an elaborate set of china platters, pewter flagons, and silver utensils for serving up the whole world. There would never be enough of them the right shape, nor could the world ever fit comfortably inside. Actually, all we need is one very, very big flat plate. Meditation is that open plate; it accommodates everything. Thus in chapter after chapter, Trungpa Rinpoche returns us to simplicity. All we need to do is just sit here on the earth. We breathe. We give bare attention to that breath.

As we settle into doing nothing much, we start bumping into our thought processes. At first we may notice only their valences of like, dislike, or neutrality. But as we become more familiar with this way of attending, we begin to sense the subtler and more complex dynamics of mind. Several chapters in Part Two of this book address these matters: the eight consciousnesses, the six realms, the five buddha families, and so on. Here the practice of psychology means recognizing these patterns as they begin to show themselves, like seascapes at the bottom of an ocean when the winds subside.

Even before we start noticing that clarity, Trungpa Rinpoche urges us further into the ungainly: "Don't be afraid of being a fool; start as a fool. The techniques of meditation practice are not designed to reduce active thoughts at all. They provide a way of coming to terms with everything that goes on inside. . . . When we begin to find the spiky quality in ourselves, we see it as antispirituality and try to push it away. This is the biggest mistake of all in working with our basic psychological patterns" (pages 47–48). Here the psychotherapist meets her first client: herself. In the practice of sitting meditation, she has no compulsion to reduce, alter, or reject anything or anyone. All are welcome. All are simply thoughts. They manifest in varying intensity or appeal, and end-less flavors, but their nature is always the same. They are only "*that, that, that*" (page 34).

Sitting with this nameless "that," doing nothing whatsoever, allow-ing the mystery that we are to arise, arise, arise, something finally be-comes obvious. The thoughts that seem to perpetuate our existence and define our being are pretty flimsy things. When we peer directly at them, trying to catch hold for a closer look, they melt right out from under us, evaporate into nothing. We have accomplished nothing: the thoughts dissolve on their own, without our even looking at them. We could not preserve them even if we wished. But now that we have experienced their utter transitoriness, they have yielded up the secret of their instan-taneous mortality. Their persuasiveness is never quite the same.

From that recognition it is possible to relax into our native gentle-ness. Since we do not experience our mind as threatening, we can, as Trungpa Rinpoche often says, make friends with ourselves. That friend-ship is the basis for all relatedness. In particular, it is the model for the conduct of psychotherapy:

"This means working first of all with our natural capacity for warmth. To begin with, we can develop warmth toward ourselves, which then expands to others. This provides the ground for relating with dis-turbed people, with one another, and with ourselves, all within the same framework. . . . Patients should experience a sense of wholesomeness vibrating from you. . . . Therapy has to be based on mutual appreciation. . . . You have to cut your own impatience and learn to love people. That is how to cultivate basic healthiness in others" (pages 138, 140, 141, and 142).

This recognition of our basic healthiness is what distinguishes Bud-dhist psychology from all others I have encountered. Through the prac-tice of sitting meditation, kerplunk in the midst of watching our thoughts dissolve, in our very inability to sustain a storyline about our-selves or anything else, we come, obliquely or directly, to something that was always there. Trungpa Rinpoche calls it basic goodness. It is also known as buddha nature, primordial purity, the true nature of mind, the essence of dharma. It is the sanity we are born with.

I think many of us come to psychology because we feel that something, somehow, must be wrong. Our curiosity about the human mind is not unmotivated. Though we may be repelled by the concept of original sin, the experience of our own mental states has not yet conclusively ruled it out. But the practice of meditation, with its fearless investigation and unconditional acceptance of all forms of consciousness, carries us ineluctably to a deeper knowledge. We actually experience the fundamental purity of mind, of *our* minds. This is not faith or doctrine, nor can we produce it if we try. But neither can we miss it when it rises up within our experience. And gradually we may develop confidence in its constant presence, the way we know our lungs will find air to breathe, in and out, in and out. It requires no thought of us.

At this point we can no longer maintain that we, or any others, are wounded at our core. Indeed, "the world that we live in is fabulous. It is utterly workable. . . . We should realize that there is no passion, aggression, or ignorance existing in what we see. . . . Whatever we do is sacred" (page 17–18).

This fabulous sacredness means that Buddhist psychology has no sense of cure or healing. In fairy tales the kissed frog transforms into a prince. But in Buddhism the frog is crowned as a frog. Our lily pad is a royal seat. "You realize that you are capable of sitting like a king or queen on a throne. The regalness of that situation shows you the dignity that comes from being still and simple" (page 21). "One begins to feel, without egotism, that one is the king of the universe. Because you have achieved an understanding of impersonality, you can become a person. . . . This stage is called enlightenment" (page 60).

At that point our approach to existence inverts. We no longer start with experience and peer through its confusing folds in search of depth, clarity, or Buddha. Instead we find ourselves resting in basic goodness, and our experiences arise continuously out of that, folding and unfolding as they will. There is no need to pry loose grasping fingers, or a grasping heart. We can begin with an open love that knows when to hold, when to let go. Because this is so intimately impersonal, we can become, and unbecome, a person.

Thus, when asked about the difference between meditation and psychotherapy, Trungpa Rinpoche replied: "The difference is in the individual's attitude toward undergoing the disciplines of meditation and psychotherapy. In the popular therapeutic style, the individual's attitude is one of trying to recover from something. He looks for a technique to help him get rid of, or overcome, his complaint. The meditative attitude accepts, in some sense, that you are what you are" (page 176). "From that point of view," he says elsewhere, "we could say that meditation is not therapy. If there is any notion of therapy involved in the spiritual journey, or in any kind of spiritual discipline, then it becomes conditional. . . . The practice of meditation is the experience of totality. You can't regard it as anything at all, but it is completely universal" (pages 184 and 186).

So should an authentic psychologist become a Buddhist? Of course not. We could go further: the authentic psychologist must *cease* being Buddhist or Western, or anything that is based on concept, doctrine, or design. "Buddhist psychology," then, is a funny term. We are not really psyches at all, there is no logic to it, and Buddhism does not exist. "Fundamentally there is just open space, the *basic ground*, what we really are. Our most fundamental state of mind, before the creation of ego, is such that there is basic openness, basic freedom, a spacious quality; and we have now and have always had this openness. . . . We *are* this space, we are *one* with it" (page 85).

These are words. Do they point to the truth? That is up to you, the reader, to decide. You lack nothing you need to make that determination.

Chögyam Trungpa Rinpoche is my teacher. I am able to write this foreword because I have the same mind as he. And you are able to read it because you also have that mind. It is the ground of sanity, from which all our miraculous, goofy, teeming world arises every moment.

My own path has in certain ways followed the outline I provide above. I have found meditation and psychotherapy to be powerfully linked practices of liberation, each necessary to the other. They engage the mind with indescribable precision, emancipating its activities from the inside out.

Some personal anecdotes may help illustrate this. For years whenever chaos struck, I'd transform into an investigative terrier, tearing through the flower beds to nab the culprit. But on both the meditation cushion and psychiatric couch I learned to rest in chaos itself. "She hates me because" returned to simple pain. "I hate her because" returned to simple anger, which returned to simple pain. In that pain there was no justification, reasoning, appropriate response, judicious assignment of blame, attempted forgiveness, in fact, nothing meaningful at all. Especially there was no cure. It was only pain. I found I could bear pain, it just hurt a lot. And then it didn't hurt quite so much.

That made it possible to adopt my emotions as my children—lively, adorable, impulsive, stubborn, convincing, and with unerring intuitions about their world. But as their loving parent, I got to choose what course of action we would take together.

I tried this out with other people as well, when they showed up in my mind. My father is in many ways a harsh, ambitious man. I remember sitting in my psychotherapist's office, suddenly envisioning myself as king. I was seated on a boulder atop a mountain, great green vistas opening far below. A dozen people were before me, including Dad. "I'm so glad you've come," I said. And silently I appointed him my lieutenant, seating him to my right just below the throne, facing outward. We had found the perfect role for his fierce discontent, one in which it would be acknowledged, ever-present, but expressed only in extremis.

Was that my father or myself? When I say, "I love you," whose energy is that? What is this "self"? My strong sense of being me, insistently individual and separate, gradually loosened. Inside and out became harder to distinguish. And basic goodness began seeping into things. Of course my wife and daughter didn't always experience me this way. But it was still evident there was enough love to go around, despite my habits of forgetfulness.

I also recall therapy sessions when nothing happened—I just looked into my therapist's eyes, and she into mine. And then I stopped going, at least for then. For though ego's patterns are endless in their complexity, there are times when we are sane enough. Then our psychology is not much different from the weather: we wear hat and coat in the rain, or we run naked through the rain, but it's difficult to take either one very personally. Or very earnestly. That frees huge energies for others. It also shows the whole of existence as a field of aimless, loving play.

Both psychology and meditation have a particular way of working with mind. Skillfully practiced, psychotherapy releases the elaborate disguises we have put upon our thoughts and feelings, revealing ancient gripes that seize them as their proxies. As these patterns come into sunlight, they become transparent—we can see through them, and treat them thus with a slightly distant courtesy.

Meditation introduces us to deeper and deeper registers of mind. At first it may be sufficient just to see we *have* a mind, that we *are* a mind. But gradually, and in a moment's flash, we realize that we are not exactly the thoughts and feelings that constantly occupy us, that had seemed to define us. There is space around them; better, we are this space, and thoughts and feelings occur here as our guests. Actually, though, that space is wisdom itself, and our thoughts and feelings its manifest intelligence. We can relax into this vibrant emptiness. That is the whole path, that relaxation, that falling apart into basic sanity.

My gratitude to all my teachers, parents, therapists, and friends, to all beings and nonbeings.

EDITOR'S INTRODUCTION

THE SANITY WE ARE BORN WITH: A Buddhist Approach to Psychology is a collection of writings by the Tibetan Buddhist meditation master Chögyam Trungpa Rinpoche. It presents insights into meditation, mind, and psychology that he shared with Western psychologists, psychotherapists, and students of Buddhist meditation in America in the 1970s and '80s. Fundamentally, this is a book about how any of us, all of us, can work with ourselves and others in a sane and gentle fashion. Beyond that, in the discussion of Buddhist psychology, the author also addresses the specific problems and needs of people in profound psychological distress. As well, he speaks to the concerns of psychotherapists and all health care professionals who work with their clients' states of mind as well as their physical well-being.

While the author acknowledges the need that many people have for professional psychological help and the importance of providing appropriate therapeutic environments and communities for some patients, the premise of this book is that all human beings have within them the resources to heal themselves at a deep level. Trungpa Rinpoche proclaims over and over again that all of us are born with basic sanity, which he also describes as basic goodness, healthiness, and wakefulness. Helping ourselves and others to contact this ground of sanity and health is both the path and the goal of Buddhist psychology as presented in this volume. As the author says in "Creating an Environment of Sanity":

> You should look into where the patient's *health* is coming from. . . . Someone might be acting paranoid and critical, but where is that accuracy coming from? They could be ex-

tremely neurotic and destructive, but where is the basic pinpoint of that energy? If you can look at people from that
point of view, from the point of view of basic goodness, then
there is definitely something you can do to help others. (page
150)

Chögyam Trungpa's entire life was dedicated to working with other
people and to helping them. The mahayana Buddhist tradition, which
was the foundation of his training, talks about the responsibility that
each one of us must ultimately assume to liberate all sentient beings—
starting with oneself, so that one can be of use to others. This is working
to benefit others on a very big scale!

Trungpa Rinpoche worked with people day in and day out. He introduced tens of thousands of people to the sitting practice of meditation and conducted thousands of individual and group interviews with
students. People came to him for advice about their meditation practice,
but also for advice about how to conduct their lives: whom to marry,
what job to take, whether to go into business or go back to school.
Rinpoche was with people when they were dying, when they were giving
birth, when they were meditating, when they were getting married, and
when they were ill. People came to him when they were depressed, when
their marriage broke up, when they felt suicidal—in just about every
circumstance and every state of mind. While one would not say that
being a teacher of Buddhism is the same as being a psychologist, nevertheless—and especially in the West—a Buddhist teacher is called upon
to respond to many of the same problems that are presented to clinical
psychologists. Of the similarity between the two enterprises, Chögyam
Trungpa said, "You shouldn't regard what you are doing as ordinary
medical work. As psychotherapists you should pay more attention to
your patients and share their lives. That kind of friendship is a long-
term commitment. It is almost like the student-teacher relationship on
the Buddhist path. You should be proud of that" (page 142).

For Chögyam Trungpa, spirituality, psychotherapy, and life altogether were about being the most fully human that we can be, rather
than trying to change ourselves into something we are not. He wrote,

"Mind cannot be altered or changed, only somewhat clarified. You have to come back to what you are, rather than reform yourself into something else" (page 177). It is this wisdom—the wisdom of who we are—that he passionately proclaimed and that is presented here as the basis for working with ourselves and others.

Meditation, Mind, and Psychology

This book is loosely divided into three parts: Meditation, Mind, and Psychology. (I say "loosely" because Chögyam Trungpa often addresses the nature of mind while discussing meditation; and in many of the discussions of mind and psychology, he refers to the practice of meditation.) The book opens with a Prelude, "The Meeting of Buddhist and Western Psychology," which presents the underlying logic that connects all of the material in this book. Here, Trungpa Rinpoche defines intrinsic health and explains the importance of meditation and the study of one's own mind as the ground for understanding and working with others. Then, Part One, "Meditation," introduces both the technique of meditation and its implications for understanding the nature of mind and self, as well as applying the insights gained in our relationships with others. Part Two, "Mind," presents material on the development of ego from a Buddhist perspective, as well as discussing aspects of human intelligence, perception, and cognition. In this section, the author also discusses the energy of emotions and the complex states of mind that we create. Part Three, "Psychology," looks specifically at working with others in a therapeutic context. The contemplative approach Trungpa Rinpoche advocates is based on the practice of meditation and the insights that arise from that practice. As the author says:

> One important question always seems to come up when Western psychologists begin to study Buddhism. Does one have to become a Buddhist in order to learn about Buddhism? The answer is that of course one does not, but it must be asked in return, what does one want to learn? What Buddhism really has to teach the Western psychologist is how

to relate more closely with his own experience, in its freshness, its fullness, and its immediacy. To do this, one does not
have to become a Buddhist, but one does have to practice
meditation. . . . A good taste of meditation is actually necessary in working with oneself and others. (page 5)

MEDITATION

Who am I? What am I? Why am I? Human beings have been asking
themselves these questions for many thousands of years. Over time our
species has articulated many answers, but still each person wrestles indi-
vidually with these concerns. Preformulated answers seem to leave us
unsatisfied—such is the centrality of these questions to the human predicament. Rather than offering articles of faith, the practice of meditation in the Buddhist tradition allows one to investigate these questions
in a firsthand, experiential fashion.

Meditation is an ancient technique, yet it is amazingly applicable
and appropriate to working with our contemporary situation. It reso-
nates with many of the discoveries of Western psychologists over the
past century. Buddhist meditation encourages us to start with our experience of our own minds and to use the experience gained through
meditation to investigate what we are, or seem to be. The Buddhist
teachings suggest that we need to examine more closely our habitual
patterns of thought and how they condition our experience. Investigat-
ing who we are through the practice of meditation can help us to free
ourselves from unnecessary mental baggage and to move forward in our
lives in a real way. It's not that we are necessarily going to be freed of
all our problems, but by beginning to look at *how* we are often uncomfortable, *how* we often suffer, *how* we are often dissatisfied and anxious,
we also begin to see *how* to step beyond or dissolve those predicaments.

There are many approaches to meditation, even within the Buddhist
tradition. There are significant variations in the techniques and how
they are applied, and these have an impact on one's experience of meditation and on the conclusions one may draw about the nature of mind
and reality. One might say these differences are akin to looking at the

world through different lenses. We can look with the naked eye; we can use glasses that correct farsightedness or nearsightedness; we can look through a microscope; we can use a telescope to gaze into outer space. Each of these will give us a distinct view. Some of these views support a commonsense interpretation of reality; some show us an aspect of the world that is radically different from what we might expect. Galileo was branded a heretic for describing what he saw when he turned his telescope to view the heavens. Meditation can offer us a view that might be equally revolutionary.

However, all tools, including meditation, can be used merely to confirm what we already believe, ignoring anything that doesn't conform to our views about reality; or we can use them to explore the territory with an open mind, which will lead us to fresh insights. Chögyam Trungpa's approach was that of the explorer. The technique he taught encourages us to suspend belief, proceed without a lot of preconceptions, and to continue without drawing too many conclusions. Just be. Just sit. See what happens. That is his prescription.

At the same time, as someone who has already made extensive explorations and who has consulted the work of other explorers, he shares with us the signposts one might find along the way. Also, rather than just setting us loose to hack our way through the wilderness, he gives us a way to start and a way to continue; he provides us with the tools we need to make our journey. These are, very simply, our body and our posture as a way of orienting ourselves and expressing basic wakefulness and human dignity; our breath, as a means to focus bare attention, as a reminder of our livelihood, or aliveness, and more profoundly as a means to mix our mind with space; and the techniques of labeling our thoughts—acknowledging that we are thinking—and applying a light-handed sense of effort, so that we can stay in the present and connect with the nowness of experience. He encourages us to bring all that we are and all that we experience to the meditation cushion. Bring the chaos; bring the confusion; bring the baggage. Don't leave anything out; don't push anything away. Bring it all. Don't hang on to it, but let it be. See what happens.

Chögyam Trungpa's approach to meditation—an approach that is free from goal orientation—is quite a radical prescription for how to live one's life. The technique he taught is based on developing an appreciation for nowness by focusing on an open-ended sense of being. This approach is not based on developing concentration, although it encourages awareness. It is not a relaxation technique, although it leads to the development of a sense of peace through the acceptance of who we are. Nor is it primarily a way to overcome problems or a means to change things about ourselves that we do not like. Rather, this approach embraces the richness and complexity—even the chaos—of our experience. It is based on opening to yourself, rather than trying to suppress or change something. Many times, Chögyam Trungpa talked about meditation as making friends with yourself.

One might say that because nothing changes through the practice of meditation as he presented it, everything is transformed. When we stop beating ourselves up and stop thinking that something is wrong with us, that brings fundamental liberation and relieves suffering and anxiety. Rather than manufacturing a means to overcome confusion, meditation allows us to connect with the sanity and wakefulness that are inherent in our experience. Thus, while meditation may help us to see that many of our fixed concepts about ourselves and our world are questionable, at the same time, it is not a technique that should discourage, depress, or fundamentally undermine us. It is rather a way to *appreciate* our life, ourselves, and others.

Sometimes in our meditation practice, we may be looking at difficult things about ourselves. However, we should recognize that it is basic intelligence that allows us to look and examine our lives at all. Without it, we could not ask the questions. This insight might be our first real glimpse of basic sanity. As we come to an appreciation of our own wakefulness, we also begin to see that there is something powerful and sacred about human life altogether. This connection to a larger world is the basis for appreciating and therefore genuinely helping others.

Trungpa Rinpoche felt that Western practitioners of meditation, as well as Western therapists and therapies, were often affected by a subtle, or not so subtle, hangover from the belief in "original sin." He talked about this as a preoccupation with guilt and a feeling of being condemned, feeling that we did or are doing something bad or that something bad has been done to us, which is the source of our problems. In contrast to that guilty feeling, which he felt was quite foreign to Buddhism, he spoke of "basic goodness" as the foundation of experience and of meditation practice. Basic goodness is good without reference to bad, goodness as the ground of experience before the dualism of good and bad ever occurred. From this point of view, some sin or crime is not the *fundamental* root of our problems, although it may be a contributory factor. We don't have to fear that, if we open up, we will discover some terrible inadequacy or secret about ourselves. When we clear away the clouds of confusion, we find that there has simply been a misunderstanding, which turns out to be our mistaken belief in a solid self or ego. We discover that our nature is like the sun shining in the sky: brilliant and fundamentally unobstructed. The discovery of the "myth" of ego leads us to the second section of the book.

Mind

Part Two, "Mind," presents writings from a Buddhist perspective on the nature of mind and the development of ego. This section examines some of the insights that might arise when examining one's experience through the lens of meditation. Whereas Western clinical psychology often begins its inquiry at the level of fully formed thoughts, emotions, and states of mind, the Buddhist view starts at a more fundamental level, looking into the constituents and basic faculties of mind, intellect, and the self. In the view presented by Trungpa Rinpoche, one starts with basic space, an open space that is related to the intrinsic state of intelligence and wakefulness that underlies all our experience. The various components of what we generally think of as our self or our ego arise out of, or in the midst of, this basic ground. When we panic—in response to the unsettling aspect of openness—we try to freeze this open ground, and we create the world of duality, the world of ego. In the Buddhist teachings, ego is seen as an unnecessary and duplicitous invention, a dualistic self-consciousness that prevents us from a genuine appreciation of our life. It is seen as a patchwork that has no real solidity, no actual existence. It is full of holes like a Swiss cheese, and the cheese itself is made out of thin air. While this may seem alien to some Western views, it is very much in tune with psychotherapeutic approaches that stress the benefits of embracing change, flexibility, and vulnerability. The other side of acknowledging the myth of ego is reconnecting with the basic open ground, recognizing this state of egolessness as basic healthiness, as the intrinsic state of being that we all possess.

There is also material here on the different faculties of knowing and intelligence that the mind exhibits. In Tibetan these are called sems, rikpa, lodrö, and yi. They are tools or ways of knowing, aspects of our intelligence and how we apply it, in contrast to the aspects or the components, the skandhas, of ego. The skandhas are progressive layers (*skandha* literally means "heaps") of complication and confusion that we create to cover up the basic openness and spaciousness of existence.

In the section on mind, Chögyam Trungpa also presents the six realms of existence, describing them as preoccupations or hallucinations that we create—although we often experience them as created or imposed on us from the outside. Chögyam Trungpa sometimes refers to them as "styles of imprisonment." The six realms are traditionally associated with teachings on the wheel of life in the Buddhist tradition and are described as actual realms of heaven and hell, and everything in between—the realm of the jealous gods, the human realm, the animal realm, the realm of hungry ghosts. Chögyam Trungpa makes this material accessible and relevant by relating these realms to the emotional and psychological states that we all go through in our lives.

Finally, there is a chapter in Part Two on different styles of perception, which Chögyam Trungpa also applies to different personality types and emotions. This discussion is based on the teaching of the "five buddha families" in the tantric tradition of Tibetan Buddhism. This teaching is a categorization of different qualities or styles that characterize both confusion and wisdom. To put it another way, the buddha families describe energy, both neurotic energy and the enlightened energy that can be transmuted or revealed behind any neurotic upheaval. Chögyam Trungpa was, I believe, the first person to apply the teachings on the buddha families so directly to human psychology and personality. He introduced this material in both his work with art and artists and in his activities with psychologists and mental health. He saw the five buddha families as one of the teachings from the Buddhist tantric tradition that would resonate with Western culture and thought. It remains one of the most original areas of his accomplishments.

PSYCHOLOGY

Finally, Part Three of the book, "Psychology," presents writings on the application of Buddhist psychology and meditation to Western psychology, psychotherapy, and working with others in a healing relationship in general. A short history of Chögyam Trungpa's involvement with Western psychology may help to lay the ground for appreciating the teachings he gave on this topic.

From his early exposure to Western views of Buddhism, which he encountered in India and England in the 1960s, Trungpa Rinpoche recognized that many Westerners had been confused by thinking of Buddhism as a religion. They often misconstrued Buddhist meditation as a form of worship or as a means to attain an altered or higher state of consciousness. Many of the people he first encountered in the West did not understand meditation as a method to investigate the nature of one's own mind.

Of all the schools of Buddhist thought, Tibetan Buddhism was probably the most misunderstood because of its elaborate rituals and symbolism and its depiction of tantric "deities." To many Western observers, Tibetan Buddhism appeared to be a system based on worship or communion with the gods, an attempt to summon up divine powers, or possibly even black magic. Without an understanding of the symbolism employed in Tibetan Buddhism, it was difficult to see that the deities depicted were in fact representations of the many facets of the human mind and its myriad thoughts and emotions.

When he came to the West in the early 1960s to study at Oxford University, Chögyam Trungpa soon realized that the language of psychology would be a better tool for communicating the Buddhist teachings than the language of Western religion had proven to be. Early on, he adopted the Western psychological term *ego* to refer to the experience of self-consciousness and coined the term *egolessness* to refer to the insight gained from meditation into the emptiness or illusoriness of self and of our habitual patterns. This will probably be noted as one of his most important contributions to the understanding of Buddhism in the West. Indeed, the *Oxford English Dictionary* noted his use of the term *egolessness* in the second edition of the dictionary, under the entry for the word "ego." He also used the term *neurosis,* but not primarily as a diagnosis of mental illness. Rather, neurotic mind was the distortion that arises from the common human experience of habitually clinging to a belief in self as a solid and separate entity. From the 1970s on, he chose to employ words and phrases such as anxiety, depression, guilt, neurotic patterns of mind, and unconscious tendencies to describe confused and painful experiences that are common to all of us and can be addressed through the practice of meditation. To use this psychological vocabulary in relationship to Buddhist practice may seem commonplace now, but it was a major departure in the 1970s.

In England in the 1960s, Chögyam Trungpa made the acquaintance of the English psychoanalyst R. D. Laing, who exposed him to some of the more radical views of Western psychology. In the early 1970s in America, he and the Zen Buddhist master Shunryu Suzuki Roshi talked about establishing a therapeutic community to work with mentally disturbed individuals. Suzuki Roshi unfortunately died of cancer in late 1971. However, Chögyam Trungpa persevered with their plans, and in 1972 he and a group of students who had been studying his ideas on psychology, as well as those of some Western psychologists, started the Maitri therapeutic community in upstate New York as a treatment facility for clients with severe psychological problems. Chögyam Trungpa had developed an experimental approach called Maitri Space Awareness that used a series of specially designed rooms and postures to accentuate neurosis, so that it could be clearly identified and worked with directly. He developed Maitri Space Awareness in accordance with his psychological understanding of the five buddha families, which is described in Part Two. His early thinking about Space Awareness is presented in Part

Three of this book, in the chapter "Maitri Space Awareness in a Buddhist Therapeutic Community."

After finding that they were inadequately trained to treat serious mental illness, the students who made up the staff of the Maitri program began to use the techniques developed by Chögyam Trungpa to further their own training and to make a study of their own psychology. This approach to working with Maitri Space Awareness has continued up to the present day.

In 1974 Chögyam Trungpa founded the Naropa Institute (now Naropa University) in Boulder, Colorado. From its inception, this Buddhist-inspired institution of higher learning included the study of contemplative psychology. Many of Chögyam Trungpa's views and insights into psychology were built into the program. Today, Maitri Space Awareness remains part of the training in contemplative psychology at Naropa.

Trungpa Rinpoche worked closely with the faculty and students at Naropa, and a number of the articles on psychology that are included in this volume were based on his discussions with students and faculty in the department. (Today there are several different psychology programs offered by different departments at Naropa. Originally, however, there was only one department.) Drawn by Chögyam Trungpa's reputation, therapists and psychologists flocked to Naropa in the 1970s and '80s to study and to teach classes. Many of them stayed and helped to build Naropa's psychology program. It would not be an exaggeration to say that there are hundreds if not thousands of clinical psychologists, psychotherapists, and psychiatrists who, through their association with Naropa, have been influenced by Chögyam Trungpa's insights into psychotherapy and the nature of mind.

Trungpa Rinpoche had a close relationship with Dr. Edward Podvoll, the director of the Naropa psychology department from 1977 until 1990. Ed worked with Chögyam Trungpa on editing several of the articles that appear in *The Sanity We Are Born With.* One of the important developments that came out of Naropa and the fertile interactions among Dr. Podvoll, his students, and Chögyam Trungpa was the establishment of Windhorse Community Services, which involves an intensive approach to working with people with severe mental problems. A Windhorse team sets up a therapeutic household for the client and lives with him or her during the treatment. In this situation, the team applies many of the principles of Buddhist psychology that Chögyam Trungpa helped to formulate. Windhorse began in Boulder, Colorado, with one or two such households in the 1980s. There are now forty treatment households in the Boulder area, as well as others in Northampton, Massachusetts; Vienna; and Zurich. As well, a number of groups in North America and Europe are studying the Windhorse approach.

Chögyam Trungpa also had many contacts with the transpersonal psychology community in Northern California. One of the chapters in this book, "Intrinsic Health: A Conversation with Health Professionals," was first published in the *Journal of Transpersonal Psychology*. As early as 1971, Trungpa Rinpoche gave a presentation on the practice of meditation at the national conference of the Association for Humanistic Psychology in Washington, D.C. This lecture was also edited for inclusion in the *Journal of Transpersonal Psychology*, where it appeared in 1973. It is reproduced in Part One of the present book as "An Approach to Meditation: A Talk to Psychologists."

The "Psychology" section of this book presents a number of the lectures Chögyam Trungpa gave to psychologists, students of psychology, and his own Buddhist students about the application of meditation to therapy and Western psychology in general. Many of these appeared originally as journal articles and have circulated for years as photocopies among those interested in Chögyam Trungpa's work.*

Throughout his writings on psychology, Chögyam Trungpa presents an approach based on insights that arise from the practice of meditation, the understanding of one's own mind, and the application of meditation in action to one's life as a whole. The link between formal practice and life situations was one that he drew early on in presenting the Buddhist

---

*All of them also appear in the hardcover series *The Collected Works of Chögyam Trungpa* (eight volumes published so far, in 2003 and 2004). The inspiration for *The Sanity We Are Born With* arose in part during the process of compiling material for this comprehensive compendium of Chögyam Trungpa's work. It occurred to me when I was reviewing material for that project that it would be very valuable to make the material on psychology available in a concise paperback volume dedicated to this topic.

teachings in the West. Indeed, his first book on meditation, published in England in 1968, is entitled *Meditation in Action*. Given this emphasis throughout his work, it is not surprising that he applied insights from the Buddhist tradition to the conduct of psychotherapy and clinical psychology, as well as to many other "secular" disciplines in the West.

Although Trungpa Rinpoche offers quite specific advice on how to work with others using a sane and compassionate approach, his prescription is at the same time broad and far-reaching. In the article "Becoming a Full Human Being," for example, he begins the discussion by telling the reader: "The basic work of health professionals in general, and of psychotherapists in particular, is to become full human beings and to inspire full human-beingness in other people who feel starved about their lives" (page 137).

The importance of basic sanity and healthiness as the ground for working with self and others is a major topic throughout this section. Chögyam Trungpa stresses that "we are in touch with basic health all the time" and that it is intrinsic rather than something we contrive. He writes:

> Health comes first: sickness is secondary. Health *is*. So being healthy is being fundamentally wholesome, with body and mind synchronized in a state of being which is indestructible and good. This attitude is not recommended exclusively for the patients but also for the helpers or doctors. It can be adopted mutually because this intrinsic, basic goodness is always present in any interaction of one human being with another. (page 137)

The author also stresses the importance of creating an uplifted environment for others, one that generates, for both caregiver and client, an appreciation of each other and of life as sacred. He discusses loss and impermanence as basic human experiences and how acknowledging them can positively influence healing.

Trungpa Rinpoche emphasizes that resentment and aggression are the root of deep psychological problems: "Whenever there is aggression and disliking in any aspect of the environment as you are growing up, that is the ground of insanity, from the Buddhist point of view" (page 144). The development of a balanced and nonaggressive psychological environment can help to cultivate maitri, a genuinely friendly and compassionate attitude that can overcome fear and aggression, both in oneself and in others. "The key point in overcoming aggression is to develop natural trust in yourself and in your environment, your world. In Buddhism, this trust in yourself is called maitri" (page 146).

The relationship of these writings on therapeutic practice to the practice of meditation is an important one to emphasize. As Chögyam Trungpa writes in "The Meeting of Buddhist and Western Psychology":

> Some Western psychologists have asked me whether the direct experience of meditation practice is really necessary. They have wanted to know whether the "interpersonal training" is not enough. To this I would answer that the interpersonal training is not adequate in itself. First, it is necessary to study and experience one's own mind. Then one can study and experience accurately the mind in the interpersonal situation. (page 7)

The earlier articles on meditation and mind allow the reader to understand the method that leads to this view of the human mind. These discoveries about oneself and the basic nature of mind then lead to certain suggestions or prescriptions for how to work with others. This again is the link between meditation as a practice and the application of meditation in action in every aspect of one's life—including working with others as a health professional.

By going through this progression, one is able to see that what Chögyam Trungpa proposes we offer to others is exactly the way that he suggests we work with ourselves. His unwavering message is that if you simplify and open to yourself, you will connect with sanity. Then, if you open yourself to others, *they* will connect with sanity. Practice, meditate, be without agenda, and you will find basic healthiness. Be with others, be with them without agenda, and they will find the same. From Trungpa

Rinpoche's point of view, there is no other way to work with people. If we don't appreciate the continuity that joins our own minds and experience with those of others, we have nothing of much value to offer.

One of the hallmarks of Chögyam Trungpa's approach is that it is more interested in asking questions than in supplying answers. The book ends, in fact, with a question: his provocative talk entitled "Is Meditation Therapy?" Trungpa Rinpoche suggested that we question our assumptions and ourselves, not only as the method for how to begin, but as a means to proceed in working both with oneself and with others. We don't have to have the answers; in fact, he posits that it's better if we don't. Rather, we need to provide an open space of inquiry for ourselves and also a safe and open space for those we work with, so that all kinds of discoveries can arise.

In this light, one hopes that this book will prove to be thought-provoking reading, that it will raise as many questions as it answers. It is hoped that this volume will be a valuable resource to students of psychology and philosophy, to those working in the health and healing professions, and to other readers curious about the discipline of meditation and the nature of their own minds.

CAROLYN ROSE GIMIAN
March 12, 2004

PRELUDE

The Meeting of Buddhist and Western Psychology

Experience and Theory

TRADITIONAL BUDDHIST PSYCHOLOGY emphasizes the importance of direct experience in psychological work. If one relies upon theory alone, then something basic is lost. From the Buddhist viewpoint, the study of theory is only a first step and must be completed by training in the direct experience of mind itself, in oneself and in others.

In Buddhist tradition, this experiential aspect is developed through the practice of meditation, a firsthand observation of mind. Meditation in Buddhism is not a religious practice, but rather a way of clarifying the actual nature of mind and experience. Traditionally, meditation training is said to be threefold, including shila (discipline), samadhi (the actual practice of meditation), and prajna (insight).

Shila is the process of simplifying one's general life and eliminating unnecessary complications. In order to develop a genuine mental discipline, it is first necessary to see how we continually burden ourselves with extraneous activities and preoccupations. In Buddhist countries, shila might involve following a particular rule of life as a monk or a nun, or adopting the precepts appropriate to a Buddhist layperson. In the Western secular context, shila might just involve cultivating an attitude of simplicity toward one's life in general.

Second is samadhi, or meditation, which is the heart of Buddhist experiential training. This practice involves sitting with your attention resting lightly and mindfully on your breath. The further discipline of meditation practice is to note when your attention has wandered from the breath and to bring it back to breathing as your focus. An attitude of bare attention is taken toward the various phenomena, including thoughts, feelings, and sensations, that arise in your mind and body during practice. Meditation practice could be called a way of making friends with oneself, which points to the fact that it is an experience of nonaggression. In fact, meditation is traditionally called the practice of dwelling in peace. The practice of meditation is thus a way of experiencing one's basic being, beyond habitual patterns.

Shila is the ground of meditation and samadhi is the actual path of the practice. The fruition is prajna, or the insight that begins to develop through one's meditation. In the experience of prajna, one begins to see directly and concretely how the mind actually functions, its mechanics and reflexes, moment to moment. Prajna is traditionally called discriminating awareness, which does not mean discriminating in the sense of developing bias. Rather prajna is unbiased knowledge of one's world and one's mind. It is discriminating in the sense of sorting out confusion and neurosis.

Prajna is immediate and nonconceptual insight, but at the same time it provides the basic inspiration for intellectual study. Because one has seen the actuality of one's own mental functioning, there is a natural desire to clarify and articulate what one has experienced. And there is a spontaneous curiosity about how others have expressed the nature and operation of mind. But at the same time, while one's immediate insight leads to study, it is necessary to maintain an ongoing discipline of meditative training. In that way, concepts never become merely concepts, and one's psychological work remains alive, fresh, and well grounded.

In the Buddhist culture of Tibet, where I was born and educated, a balance was always maintained between experiential training and theory. In my own upbringing, time was allotted in our regular monastic schedule to both study and meditation practice. During the year, there would also be special times set aside for intensive study and also for meditation retreats. It was part of our Buddhist tradition that such a balance was necessary for genuine learning to occur.

When I came to the West, to England in 1963, I was quite surprised to find that in Western psychology, theory is emphasized so much more than experience. Of course this made Western psychology immediately accessible to someone from another culture such as myself. Western psychologists do not ask you to practice, but just tell you what they are about from the very beginning. I found this approach very straightforward and something of a relief. But at the same time, one wonders about the profundity of a tradition that relies so heavily on concepts and opens its doors so easily.

On the other hand, Western psychologists do seem intuitively to recognize the need for greater emphasis on the direct experience of mind. Perhaps this is what has led so many psychologists to take an interest in Buddhism. Especially in relation to Zen, they are attracted to the enigma of it. And they are tantalized by the flavor of immediate experience, the possibility of enlightenment, and the impression of profundity. Such people seem to be looking to Buddhism for something they find lacking in their own traditions. This interest strikes me as appropriate, and in this respect Buddhism has something important to offer.

One important question always seems to come up when Western psychologists begin to study Buddhism. Does one have to become a Buddhist in order to learn about Buddhism? The answer is that of course one does not, but it must be asked in return, what does one want to learn? What Buddhism really has to teach the Western psychologist is how to relate more closely with his own experience, in its freshness, its fullness, and its immediacy. To do this, one does not have to become a Buddhist, but one does have to practice meditation. It is certainly possible to study only the theory of Buddhist psychology. But in doing so, one would miss the point. Without experience to rely on, one would end up simply interpreting Buddhist notions through Western concepts. A good taste of meditation is actually necessary in working with oneself and others. It is a tremendous help, whatever interest one may take in Buddhism as such.

Sometimes it is very hard to communicate to Westerners the importance of the experiential dimension. After we had started Samye Ling, our meditation center in Scotland, soon after I came from India to England, we found that a great many people with psychological problems came to us for help. They had been in all sorts of different therapies, and many of them were quite neurotic. They looked on us as physicians carrying out medical practice and wanted us to cure them. In working with these people I found that there was a frequent obstacle. Such people often wanted to take a purely theoretical approach, rather than actually experiencing and working with their neuroses. They wanted to understand their neuroses intellectually: where they themselves went wrong, how their neuroses developed, and so on. They often were not willing to let go of that approach.

The Training of a Therapist

In the training of a psychotherapist, theoretical and experiential training should be properly balanced. We combine these two elements in our Naropa Institute* psychology program: one begins with a taste of meditation, then applies oneself to study, then experiences meditation more fully, then does more intensive study, and so forth. This kind of approach actually has an interesting effect: it enhances one's appreciation of what one is doing. The experience of one's own mind whets the appetite for further study. And the study increases one's interest in observing one's own mental process through meditation.

In addition, when study is combined with meditation practice, it has a different flavor. Where direct experience is lacking, study tends to be mainly memorizing terms and definitions and trying to convince oneself of their validity. When balanced with meditative discipline, study takes on much more life and reality. It develops clarity about how the mind works and how that knowledge can be expressed. In this way, study and practice help one another enormously, and each becomes more real and satisfying. It is like eating a sandwich—because of the bread, you appreciate the meat much more.

One question comes up when you try to balance the experiential and theoretical sides of training. How much time should be spent on each? Generally I would say it should be roughly equal. But at the same time the amount of hours put into practice, for example, is not as important

---

*Now Naropa University.—Ed.

as the attitude with which it is done. If the trainee is wholehearted enough, and if his practice is sufficiently intent, then his meditation will have its proper role and permeate his study and daily life.

All of this is not to say that there is no experiential training in Western psychology. But, from the Buddhist viewpoint, it is greatly underemphasized. And when it does occur, it seems to happen almost exclusively in the interpersonal situation of people talking to one another, such as the classical training in psychoanalysis. Some Western psychologists have asked me whether the direct experience of meditation practice is really necessary. They have wanted to know whether the "interpersonal training" is not enough. To this I would answer that the interpersonal training is not adequate in itself. First, it is necessary to study and experience one's own mind. Then one can study and experience accurately the mind in the interpersonal situation.

We can see this by looking at how the Buddhist tradition of abhidharma works. First, there is an exploration of how the mind evolves in itself and how it functions. The expression of this is the first half of the abhidharma. The second half is concerned with how that mind begins to respond to things from outside itself. This parallels how a child develops. In the beginning, he is mainly concerned with himself. Later, in adolescence, his world begins to grow bigger and bigger.

In order to understand the interpersonal situation correctly, you have to know yourself in the beginning. Once you know the style of the dynamics of your own mind, then you can begin to see how that style works in dealing with others. And, in fact, on the basis of knowing oneself, the interpersonal knowledge comes naturally. You discover that somebody has developed his own mind. Then you can experience how the two minds interact with each other. This leads to the discovery that there is no such thing as outside mind and inside mind at all. So "mind" is really two minds meeting together, which is the same mind in some sense.

Therefore, the more you learn about your own mind, the more you learn about other people's minds. You begin to appreciate other worlds, other people's life situations. You are learning to extend your vision beyond what is just there in your immediate situation, on the spot, so your mind is opened that much more.

And that reflects in your work with others. It makes you more skillful in deeds and also gives you more of a sense of warmth and compassion, so you become more accommodating of others.

The Viewpoint of Health

Buddhist psychology is based on the notion that human beings are fundamentally good. Their most basic qualities are positive ones: openness,
intelligence, and warmth. Of course this viewpoint has its philosophical
and psychological expressions in concepts such as bodhichitta (awakened mind), and tathagatagarbha (birthplace of enlightened ones). But
this idea is ultimately rooted in experience—the experience of goodness
and worthiness in oneself and others. This understanding is very fundamental and is the basic inspiration for Buddhist practice and Buddhist
psychology.

Coming from a tradition that stresses human goodness, it was
something of a shock for me to encounter the Western tradition of
original sin. When I was at Oxford University, I studied Western religious and philosophical traditions with interest and found the notion of
original sin quite pervasive. One of my early experiences in England was
attending a seminar with Archbishop Anthony Blum. The seminar was
on the notion of grace, and we got into a discussion of original sin. The
Buddhist tradition does not see such a notion as necessary at all, and
I expressed this viewpoint. I was surprised at how angry the Western
participants became. Even the orthodox, who might not emphasize original sin as much as the Western traditions, still held it as a cornerstone
of their theology.

In terms of our present discussion, it seems that this notion of original sin does not just pervade Western religious ideas; it actually seems
to run throughout Western thought as well, especially psychological
thought. Among patients, theoreticians, and therapists alike, there seems
to be great concern with the idea of some original mistake which causes
later suffering—a kind of punishment for that mistake. One finds that a
sense of guilt or being wounded is quite pervasive. Whether or not such
people actually believe in the idea of original sin, or in God for that

matter, they seem to feel that they have done something wrong in the past and are now being punished for it.

It seems that this feeling of basic guilt has been passed down from one generation to another and pervades many aspects of Western life. For example, teachers often think that if children do not feel guilty, then they won't study properly and consequently won't develop as they should. Therefore, many teachers feel that they have to do something to push the child, and guilt seems to be one of the chief techniques they use. This occurs even on the level of improving reading and writing. The teacher looks for errors: "Look, you made a mistake. What are you going to do about it?" From the child's point of view, learning is then based on trying not to make mistakes, on trying to prove you actually are not bad. It is entirely different when you approach the child more positively: "Look how much you have improved, therefore we can go further." In the latter case, learning becomes an expression of one's wholesomeness and innate intelligence.

The problem with this notion of original sin or mistake is that it acts very much as a hindrance to people. At some point, it is of course necessary to realize one's shortcomings. But if one goes too far with that, it kills any inspiration and can destroy one's vision as well. So in that way, it really is not helpful, and in fact it seems unnecessary. As I mentioned, in Buddhism we do not have any comparable ideas of sin and guilt. Obviously there is the idea that one should avoid mistakes. But there is not anything comparable to the heaviness and inescapability of original sin.

According to the Buddhist perspective, there are problems, but they are temporary and superficial defilements that cover over one's basic goodness (tathagatagarbha). This viewpoint is a positive and optimistic one. But, again, we should emphasize that this viewpoint is not purely conceptual. It is rooted in the experience of meditation and in the healthiness it encourages. There are temporary habitual neurotic patterns that develop based on past experience, but these can be seen through. It is just this that is studied in the abhidharma: how one thing succeeds another, how volitional action originates and perpetuates itself, how things snowball. And, most important, abhidharma studies how, through meditation practice, this process can be cut through.

The attitude that results from the Buddhist orientation and practice is quite different from the "mistake mentality." One actually experiences mind as fundamentally pure, that is, healthy and positive, and "problems" as temporary and superficial defilements. Such a viewpoint does not quite mean "getting rid" of problems, but rather shifting one's focus. Problems are seen in a much broader context of health: one begins to let go of clinging to one's neuroses and to step beyond obsession and identification with them. The emphasis is no longer on the problems themselves but rather on the ground of experience through realizing the nature of mind itself. When problems are seen in this way, then there is less panic and everything seems more workable. When problems arise, instead of being seen as purely threats, they become learning situations, opportunities to find out more about one's own mind, and to continue on one's journey.

Through practice, which is confirmed by study, the inherent healthiness of your mind and others' minds is experienced over and over. You see that your problems are not all that deeply rooted. You see that you can make literal progress. You find yourself becoming more mindful and more aware, developing a greater sense of healthiness and clarity as you go on, and this is tremendously encouraging.

Ultimately, this orientation of goodness and healthiness comes out of the experience of egolessness, a notion that has created a certain amount of difficulty for Western psychologists. "Egolessness" does not mean that nothing exists, as some have thought, a kind of nihilism. Instead, it means that you can let go of your habitual patterns and then when you let go, you genuinely let go. You do not re-create or rebuild another shell immediately afterward. Once you let go, you do not just start all over again. Egolessness is having the trust to not rebuild again at all and experiencing the psychological healthiness and freshness that goes with not rebuilding. The truth of egolessness can only be experienced fully through meditation practice.

The experience of egolessness encourages a real and genuine sympathy toward others. You cannot have genuine sympathy with ego because then that would mean that your sympathy would be accompanied by some kind of defense mechanisms. For example, you might try to refer everything back to your own territory when you work with someone, if your own ego is at stake. Ego interferes with direct communication, which is obviously essential in the therapeutic process. Egolessness, on the other hand, lets the whole process of working with others be genuine and generous and free-form. That is why, in the Buddhist tradition, it is said that without egolessness, it is impossible to develop real compassion.

The Practice of Therapy

The task of the therapist is to help his or her patients connect back with their own fundamental healthiness and goodness. Prospective patients come to us feeling starved and alienated. More important than giving them a set of techniques for battling their problems, we need to point them toward the experience of the fundamental ground of health which exists in them. It might be thought that this is asking a great deal, particularly when we are working with confronting someone who has a history of problems. But the sanity of basic mind is actually close at hand and can be readily experienced and encouraged.

Of course, it goes without saying that the therapist must experience his own mind in this way to begin with. Through meditation practice, his clarity and warmth toward himself is given room to develop and then can be expanded outward. Thus his meditation and study provide the ground for working with disturbed people, with other therapists, and with himself in the same framework all the time. Obviously, this is not so much a question of theoretical or conceptual perspective, but of how we personally experience our own lives. Our existence can be felt fully and thoroughly so that we appreciate that we are genuine, true human beings. This is what we can communicate to others and encourage in them.

One of the biggest obstacles to helping our patients in this way is, again, the notion of a "mistake," and the preoccupation with the past that results from this. Many of our patients will want to unravel their past. But this can be a dangerous approach if it goes too far. If you follow this thread, you have to look back to your conception, then to your family's experiences before that, to your great-grandfathers, and on and on. It could go a long way back and get very complicated.

The Buddhist viewpoint emphasizes the impermanence and the transitoriness of things. The past is gone, and the future has not yet happened, so we work with what is here: the present situation. This actually helps us not to categorize or to theorize. A fresh, living situation is actually taking place all the time, on the spot. This noncategorizing approach comes from being fully here rather than trying to follow up some past event. We do not have to look back to the past in order to see what we ourselves or other people are made out of. Things speak for themselves, right here and now.

In my days at Oxford and since then, I have been impressed by some of the genuine strengths of Western psychology. It is open to new viewpoints and discoveries. It maintains a critical attitude toward itself. And it is the most experiential of Western intellectual disciplines.

But at the same time, considered from the viewpoint of Buddhist psychological tradition, there is definitely something missing in the Western approach. This missing element, as we have suggested throughout this introduction, is the acknowledgment of the primacy of immediate experience. It is here that Buddhism presents a fundamental challenge to Western therapeutics and offers a viewpoint and method that could revolutionize Western psychology.

Part One MEDITATION

ONE

Taming the Horse,
Riding the Mind

LEARNING, FROM A NON-EGO point of view, is based on opening one's heart and discovering a natural sense of discipline. Discipline in this case means attuning ourselves to our inherent purity. We don't have to borrow anything from outside ourselves or mimic anybody. We are naturally pure and intelligent. We may already have some idea or experience of that, but we also need to go further in opening ourselves.

When we begin to open, learning isn't a struggle anymore. It becomes like a thirsty person drinking cool water. It is refreshing and natural. And the more we learn, the more we appreciate. It is quite different from a military academy approach or learning based on struggle of any kind.

Our path is sometimes rough and sometimes smooth; nonetheless, life is a constant journey. Whether we sleep, eat, dress, study, meditate, attend class . . . whatever we do is regarded as our journey, our path. That path consists of opening oneself to the road, opening oneself to the steps we are about to take. The energy which allows us to go on such a journey is known as discipline. It is the discipline of educating oneself without ego, and it is also known as training one's mind.

Educating oneself is said to be like taming a wild horse, a horse which has never been touched by anyone. First you try putting a saddle on its back. The horse kicks, bites, bucks; you try again and again. Finally you succeed. And then you manage to put the rein over its head and the bit into its mouth. Maybe you have difficulty making the horse open its mouth, but at last the bit goes in.

That is a great success. You feel good; you feel that you have accomplished something. Nonetheless, you still have to ride the horse. And that is another process, another struggle. It is quite possible that the horse will throw you off. If you are able to hold on to the reins, that might help you to control the horse; but it is still questionable. Maybe that would give you 40 percent control. For the rest, you are taking a chance.

Our state of mind is like a wild horse. It contains memories of the past, dreams of the future, and the fickleness of the present. We find that to be a problematic situation, and so we practice what is known as meditation.

The word *meditation* has various meanings, as it is referred to in different traditions. According to *The Oxford English Dictionary*, meditation means that you meditate *on* something. For example, when you are in love, you meditate on your lover. Your lover is so beautiful. He or she is extraordinary in lovemaking—moves beautifully, kisses beautifully, and quite possibly smells fantastic! Meditating on those kinds of perceptions just means that you are dwelling on something, occupying yourself with something.

In the fundamental sense, Buddhist meditation does not involve meditating on anything. You simply arouse your sense of wakefulness and hold an excellent posture. You hold up your head and shoulders and sit cross-legged. Then very simply, you relate to the basic notion of body, speech, and mind, and you focus your awareness in some way, usually using the breath. You are breathing out and in, and you just experience that breathing very naturally. Your breath is not considered either holy or evil; it is just breath.

When thoughts arise, you just look at them and you notice "thought." It's not "good thought" or "bad thought." Whether you have a thought of wisdom or a thought of evil, you just look at it and say, "thought." And then you come back to the breath. By doing that, you begin to develop the notion of putting the saddle on the horse. Your mind begins to be trained. It becomes less crazy, less drowsy, and more workable at that point.

This particular practice of meditation is known as *shamatha*, which literally means "dwelling in peace." In this case, peace is not a euphoric or blissful state but simply a basic and down-to-earth situation that results from cutting out hassle and turmoil. We aren't trying to achieve any goal or attain any particular state of being, in either the religious or secular sense.

When we practice in this way, we find that thoughts which perpetuate neurosis melt or evaporate. Ordinarily we don't pay any attention to our thoughts. We unknowingly cultivate them by acting according to whatever they command. But when we sit down quietly and look at them, without judgment or goal—just look at them—they dissolve by themselves.

In shamatha meditation, one's attention span is naturally extended, and one's open-mindedness is developed. You become more steady and also more cheerful—free from turmoil. That is why it is called "shamatha," dwelling in peace.

So that is the first stage in learning: learning how to learn. That is the first step. First you cut through the basic notion of ego, of holding on to neurosis. Beyond that, there is what is known as *vipashyana*, which literally means "insight," practice. In this case, insight is seeing things as they are—not adding passion or aggression to them. Now we are beginning to step outside the meditation compound and examine how we relate to our world.

The world that we live in is fabulous. It is utterly workable. We see motorcars going by in the street, buildings standing as they are, trees growing, flowers blooming, rain and snow falling, water flowing, and wind clearing the air, ventilating . . . whether there is pollution or not. The world we live in is all right, to say the least. We can't complain at all.

We should begin to learn how to appreciate this world, this planet on which we live. We should realize that there is no passion, aggression, or ignorance existing in what we see. We begin by developing mindfulness of our steps, as we walk. Then we begin to experience the sacredness of brushing our hair and putting on our clothes.

Activities such as shopping, answering the telephone, typing, working in a factory, studying in school, dealing with our parents or our children, going to a funeral, checking ourselves in at the maternity department of the hospital . . . whatever we do is sacred. The way we develop that attitude is by seeing things as they are, by paying attention to the energy of the situation, and by not expecting further entertainment from our world. It is a matter of simply being, being natural, and always being mindful of everything that takes place in our day-to-day life.

That develops naturally from shamatha meditation. Sitting meditation is like taking a shower. Vipashyana, or awareness practice, is like drying your body with a towel and then putting on your clothes.

So there are two aspects to our journey, to our learning process: there is learning by sitting meditation and learning by life experiences. And there is no problem in joining these two together. It is like having a pair of eyes and then putting on glasses. It is the same thing.

TWO

Discovering Basic Goodness

A GREAT DEAL OF CHAOS in the world occurs because people don't appreciate themselves. Having never developed sympathy or gentleness toward themselves, they cannot experience harmony or peace within themselves, and therefore, what they project to others is also inharmonious and confused. Instead of appreciating our lives, we often take our existence for granted or we find it depressing and burdensome. People threaten to commit suicide because they aren't getting what they think they deserve out of life. They blackmail others with the threat of suicide, saying that they will kill themselves if certain things don't change. Certainly we should take our lives seriously, but that doesn't mean driving ourselves to the brink of disaster by complaining about our problems or holding a grudge against the world. We have to accept personal responsibility for uplifting our lives.

When you don't punish or condemn yourself, when you relax more and appreciate your body and mind, you begin to contact the fundamental notion of basic goodness in yourself. So it is extremely important to be willing to open yourself to yourself. Developing tenderness toward yourself allows you to see both your problems and your potential accurately. You don't feel that you have to ignore your problems or exaggerate your potential. That kind of gentleness toward yourself and appreciation of yourself is very necessary. It provides the ground for helping yourself and others.

As human beings, we have a working basis within ourselves that allows us to uplift our state of existence and cheer up fully. That working basis is always available to us. We have a mind and a body, which are very precious to us. Because we have a mind and body, we can comprehend this world. Existence is wonderful and precious. We don't know how long we will live, so while we have our life, why not make use of it? Before we even make use of it, why don't we appreciate it?

How do we discover this kind of appreciation? Wishful thinking or simply talking about it does not help. In the Shambhala tradition, the discipline for developing both gentleness toward ourselves and appreciation of our world is the sitting practice of meditation. The practice of meditation was taught by the Lord Buddha over twenty-five hundred years ago, and it has been part of the Shambhala tradition since that time. It is based on an oral tradition: From the time of the Buddha this practice has been transmitted from one human being to another. In this way, it has remained a living tradition, so that, although it is an ancient practice, it is still up to date. In this chapter we are going to discuss the technique of meditation in some detail, but it is important to remember that, if you want to fully understand this practice, you need direct, personal instruction.

By meditation here we mean something very basic and simple that is not tied to any one culture. We are talking about a very basic act: sitting on the ground, assuming a good posture, and developing a sense of our spot, our place on this earth. This is the means of rediscovering ourselves and our basic goodness, the means to tune ourselves in to genuine reality, without any expectations or preconceptions.

The word *meditation* is sometimes used to mean contemplating a particular theme or object: meditating *on* such and such a thing. By meditating on a question or problem, we can find the solution to it. Sometimes meditation also is connected with achieving a higher state of mind by entering into a trance or absorption state of some kind. But here we are talking about a completely different concept of meditation: unconditional meditation, without any object or idea in mind. In the Shambhala tradition meditation is simply training our state of being so that our mind and body can be synchronized. Through the practice of meditation, we can learn to be without deception, to be fully genuine and alive.

Our life is an endless journey; it is like a broad highway that extends infinitely into the distance. The practice of meditation provides a vehicle to travel on that road. Our journey consists of constant ups and downs, hope and fear, but it is a good journey. The practice of meditation allows us to experience all the textures of the roadway, which is what the journey is all about. Through the practice of meditation, we begin to find that within ourselves there is no fundamental complaint about anything or anyone at all.

Meditation practice begins by sitting down and assuming your seat cross-legged on the ground. You begin to feel that by simply being on the spot, your life can become workable and even wonderful. You realize that you are capable of sitting like a king or queen on a throne. The regalness of that situation shows you the dignity that comes from being still and simple.

In the practice of meditation, an upright posture is extremely important. Having an upright back is not an artificial posture. It is natural to the human body. When you slouch, that is unusual. You can't breathe properly when you slouch, and slouching also is a sign of giving in to neurosis. So when you sit erect, you are proclaiming to yourself and to the rest of the world that you are going to be a warrior, a fully human being.

To have a straight back you do not have to strain yourself by pulling up your shoulders; the uprightness comes naturally from sitting simply but proudly on the ground or on your meditation cushion. Then, because your back is upright, you feel no trace of shyness or embarrassment, so you do not hold your head down. You are not bending to anything. Because of that, your shoulders become straight automatically, so you develop a good sense of head and shoulders. Then you can allow your legs to rest naturally in a cross-legged position; your knees do not have to touch the ground. You complete your posture by placing your hands lightly, palms down, on your thighs. This provides a further sense of assuming your spot properly.

In that posture, you don't just gaze randomly around. You have a sense that you are *there* properly; therefore your eyes are open, but your gaze is directed slightly downward, maybe six feet in front of you. In that way, your vision does not wander here and there, but you have a further sense of deliberateness and definiteness. You can see this royal pose in some Egyptian and South American sculptures, as well as in Oriental statues. It is a universal posture, not limited to one culture or time.

In your daily life, you should also be aware of your posture, your head and shoulders, how you walk, and how you look at people. Even when you are not meditating, you can maintain a dignified state of existence. You can transcend your embarrassment and take pride in being a human being. Such pride is acceptable and good.

Then, in meditation practice, as you sit with a good posture, you pay attention to your breath. When you breathe, you are utterly there, properly there. You go out with the out-breath, your breath dissolves, and then the in-breath happens naturally. Then you go out again. So there is a constant going out with the out-breath. As you breathe out, you dissolve, you diffuse. Then your in-breath occurs naturally; you don't have to follow it in. You simply come back to your posture, and you are ready for another out-breath. Go out and dissolve: *tshoo;* then come back to your posture; then *tshoo,* and come back to your posture.

Then there will be an inevitable *bing!*—thought. At that point, you say, "thinking." You don't say it out loud; you say it mentally: "think-ing." Labeling your thoughts gives you tremendous leverage to come back to your breath. When one thought takes you away completely from what you are actually doing—when you do not even realize that you are on the cushion, but in your mind you are in San Francisco or New York City—you say "thinking," and you bring yourself back to the breath.

It doesn't really matter what thoughts you have. In the sitting prac-tice of meditation, whether you have monstrous thoughts or benevolent thoughts, all of them are regarded purely as thinking. They are neither virtuous nor sinful. You might have a thought of assassinating your father or you might want to make lemonade and eat cookies. Please don't be shocked by your thoughts: Any thought is just thinking. No thought deserves a gold medal or a reprimand. Just label your thoughts "thinking," then go back to your breath. "Thinking," back to the breath; "thinking," back to the breath.

The practice of meditation is very precise. It has to be on the dot, right on the dot. It is quite hard work, but if you remember the importance of your posture, that will allow you to synchronize your mind and body. If you don't have good posture, your practice will be like a lame horse trying to pull a cart. It will never work. So first you sit down and assume your posture, then you work with your breath; *tshoo,* go out, come back to your posture; *tshoo,* come back to your posture; *tshoo.* When thoughts arise, you label them "thinking" and come back to your posture, back to your breath. You have mind working with breath, but you always maintain body as a reference point. You are not working with your mind alone. You are working with your mind and your body, and when the two work together, you never leave reality.

The ideal state of tranquillity comes from experiencing body and mind being synchronized. If body and mind are unsynchronized, then your body will slump—and your mind will be somewhere else. It is like a badly made drum: The skin doesn't fit the frame of the drum; so either the frame breaks or the skin breaks, and there is no constant tautness. When mind and body are synchronized, then, because of your good posture, your breathing happens naturally; and because your breathing and your posture work together, your mind has a reference point to check back to. Therefore your mind will go out naturally with the breath.

This method of synchronizing your mind and body is training you to be very simple and to feel that you are not special, but ordinary, extraordinary. You sit simply, as a warrior, and out of that, a sense of individual dignity arises. You are sitting on the earth and you realize that this earth deserves you and you deserve this earth. You are there—fully, personally, genuinely. So meditation practice in the Shambhala tradition is designed to educate people to be honest and genuine, true to themselves.

In some sense, we should regard ourselves as being burdened: We have the burden of helping this world. We cannot forget this responsibility to others. But if we take our burden as a delight, we can actually liberate this world. The way to begin is with ourselves. From being open and honest with ourselves, we can also learn to be open with others. So we can work with the rest of the world, on the basis of the goodness we discover in ourselves. Therefore, meditation practice is regarded as a good and in fact excellent way to overcome warfare in the world: our own warfare as well as greater warfare.

THREE

The Four Foundations of Mindfulness

THE METHOD FOR BEGINNING to relate directly with mind, which was taught by Lord Buddha and which has been in use for the past twenty-five hundred years, is the practice of mindfulness. There are four aspects to this practice, traditionally known as the four foundations of mindfulness.

Mindfulness of Body

Mindfulness of body, the first foundation of mindfulness, is connected with the need for a sense of being, a sense of groundedness.

To begin with, there is some problem about what we understand by *body*. We sit on chairs or on the ground; we eat; we sleep; we wear clothes. But the body we relate with in going through these activities is questionable. According to the tradition, the body we think we have is what is known as psychosomatic body. It is largely based on projections and concepts of body. This psychosomatic body contrasts with the enlightened person's sense of body, which might be called "body-body." This sense of body is free from conceptualizations. It is just simple and straightforward. There is a direct relationship with the earth. As for us, we do not actually have a relationship with the earth. We have some relationship with body, but it is very uncertain and erratic. We flicker

24

back and forth between body and something else—fantasies, ideas. That seems to be our basic situation.

Even though the psychosomatic body is constituted by projections of body, it can be quite solid in terms of those projections. We have expectations concerning the existence of this body, therefore we have to refuel it, entertain it, wash it. Through this psychosomatic body we are able to experience a sense of being. For instance, as you listen to this talk, you feel that you are sitting on the ground. Your buttocks are resting on the earth; therefore you can extend your legs and lean back a little so you have less strain on your body. All of this affects your sense of being. You have some sense of relaxation as opposed to how it would be if you were standing—standing on your feet, standing on your toes, or standing on your palms. The posture that you are adopting at the moment seems to be an agreeable one; in fact it is one of the most congenial postures that one could ever think of. So being in this posture, you can relax and listen—you can listen to something other than the demands of your body.

Sitting down now, you feel somewhat settled. On the other hand, if the ground were very damp, you would not feel so settled. Then you would begin to perch on the ground, like a bird on a branch. This would be another matter altogether. If you are intensely concerned with some event about to happen or if you are worried about some encounter you are about to have—for example, if you are being interviewed for a job by some executive—you don't really sit on your chair, you perch on it. Perching happens when some demand is being made on you and you feel less of your body and more of your tension and nervousness. It involves a very different sense of body and of being than if you are just sitting, as you are doing now.

Right now you are sitting on the ground, and you are so completely sitting down that you have been able to shift gears and turn on your tape recorders, or even start taking notes, and you do not regard that as doing two things at once. You sit there, you have totally flopped, so to speak, and, having done that, you can turn to your other perceptions— listening, looking, and so on.

But your sitting here at this point is not actually very much a matter of your body per se sitting on the ground; it is far more a matter of your psychosomatic body sitting on the ground. Sitting on the ground as you are—all facing in one direction, toward the speaker; being underneath the roof of the tent; being attracted to the light that is focused on the stage—all gives you a particular idea; it creates a certain style of participation, which is the condition of your psychosomatic body. You are somewhat involved in sitting per se, but at the same time you are not. Mind is doing it; concept is doing it. Your mind is shaping the situation in accordance with your body. Your mind is sitting on the ground. Your mind is taking notes. Your mind is wearing glasses. Your mind has such-and-such a hairdo; your mind is wearing such-and-such clothes. Everyone is creating a world according to the body situation, but largely out of contact with it. That is the psychosomatic process.

Mindfulness of body brings this all-pervasive mind-imitating-body activity into the practice of meditation. The practice of meditation has to take into account that mind continually shapes itself into body*like* attitudes. Consequently, since the time of Buddha, sitting meditation has been recommended and practiced, and it has proved to be the best way of dealing with this situation. The basic technique that goes with sitting meditation is working with the breath. You identify with the breath, particularly with the out-breath. The in-breath is just a gap, a space. During the in-breath you just wait. So you breathe out and then you dissolve and then there is a gap. Breathe out . . . dissolve . . . gap. An openness, an expansion, can take place constantly that way.

Mindfulness plays a very important role in this technique. In this case, mindfulness means that when you sit and meditate, you actually do sit. You actually do sit as far as the psychosomatic body is concerned. You feel the ground, body, breath, temperature. You don't try specifically to watch and keep track of what is going on. You don't try to formalize the sitting situation and make it into some special activity that you are performing. You just sit. And then you begin to feel that there is some sense of groundedness. This is not particularly a product of being deliberate, but it is more the force of the actual fact of being there. So you sit. And you sit. And you breathe. And you sit and you breathe.

Sometimes you think, but still you are thinking sitting thoughts. The psychosomatic body is sitting, so your thoughts have a flat bottom.

Mindfulness of body is connected with the earth. It is an openness that has a base, a foundation. A quality of expansive awareness develops through mindfulness of body—a sense of being settled and of therefore being able to afford to open out.

Going along with this mindfulness requires a great deal of trust. Probably the beginning meditator will not be able simply to rest there, but will feel the need for a change. I remember someone who had just finished a retreat telling me how she had sat and felt her body and felt grounded. But then she had thought immediately how she should be doing something else. And she went on to tell me how the right book had "just jumped" into her lap, and she had started to read. At that point one doesn't have a solid base anymore. One's mind is beginning to grow little wings. Mindfulness of body has to do with trying to remain human, rather than becoming an animal or fly or etheric being. It means just trying to remain a human being, an ordinary human being.

The basic starting point for this is solidness, groundedness. When you sit, you actually sit. Even your floating thoughts begin to sit on their own bottoms. There are no particular problems. You have a sense of solidness and groundedness, and, at the same time, a sense of being.

Without this particular foundation of mindfulness, the rest of your meditation practice could be very airy-fairy—vacillating back and forth, trying this and trying that. You could be constantly tiptoeing on the surface of the universe, not actually getting a foothold anywhere. You could become an eternal hitchhiker. So with this first technique you develop some basic solidness. In mindfulness of body, there is a sense of finding some home ground.

Mindfulness of Life

The application of mindfulness has to be precise. If we cling to our practice, we create stagnation. Therefore, in our application of the techniques of mindfulness, we must be aware of the fundamental tendency to cling, to survive. We come to this in the second foundation of mindfulness, which is mindfulness of life, or survival. Since we are dealing with the context of meditation, we encounter this tendency in the form of clinging to the meditative state. We experience the meditative state and it is momentarily tangible, but in that same moment it is also dissolving. Going along with this process means developing a sense of letting go of awareness as well as of contacting it. This basic technique of the second foundation of mindfulness could be described as touch-and-go: you are there—present, mindful—and then you let go.

A common misunderstanding is that the meditative state of mind has to be captured and then nursed and cherished. That is definitely the wrong approach. If you try to domesticate your mind through meditation—try to possess it by holding on to the meditative state—the clear result will be regression on the path, with a loss of freshness and spontaneity. If you try to hold on without lapse all the time, then maintaining your awareness will begin to become a domestic hassle. It will become like painfully going through housework. There will be an underlying sense of resentment, and the practice of meditation will become confusing. You will begin to develop a love-hate relationship toward your practice, in which your concept of it seems good, but, at the same time, the demand this rigid concept makes on you is too painful.

So the technique of the mindfulness of life is based on touch-and-go. You focus your attention on the object of awareness, but then, in the same moment, you disown that awareness and go on. What is needed here is some sense of confidence—confidence that you do not have to securely own your mind, but that you can tune into its process spontaneously.

Mindfulness of life relates to the clinging tendency not only in connection with the meditative state, but, even more importantly, in connection with the level of raw anxiety about survival that manifests in us constantly, second by second, minute by minute. You breathe for survival; you lead your life for survival. The feeling is constantly present that you are trying to protect yourself from death. For the practical purposes of the second foundation, instead of regarding this survival mentality as something negative, instead of relating to it as ego-clinging as is done in the abstract philosophical overview of Buddhism, this particular practice switches logic around. In the second foundation, the survival struggle is regarded as a stepping-stone in the practice of meditation. Whenever you have the sense of the survival instinct functioning, that can be transmuted into a sense of being, a sense of having already survived. Mindfulness becomes a basic acknowledgment of existing. This does not have the flavor of "Thank God, I have survived." Instead, it is more objective, impartial: "I am alive, I am here, so be it."

We may undertake the practice of meditation with a sense of purity or austerity. We somehow feel that by meditating we are doing the right thing, and we feel like good boys or good girls. Not only are we doing the right thing, but we are also getting away from the ugly world. We are becoming pure; we are renouncing the world and becoming like the yogis of the past. We don't actually live and meditate in a cave, but we can regard the corner of the room that we have arranged for meditation as a cave. We can close our eyes and feel that we are meditating in a cave in the mountains. That kind of imagination makes us feel rather good. It feels fitting; it feels clean and secure.

This strong tendency is an attempt to isolate the practice of meditation from one's actual living situation. We build up all kinds of extraneous concepts and images about it. It is satisfying to regard meditation as austere and above life. But mindfulness of life steers us in just the opposite direction. The approach of mindfulness of life is that if you are meditating in a room, you are meditating in a room. You don't regard the room as a cave. If you are breathing, you are breathing, rather than convincing yourself you are a motionless rock. You keep your eyes open and simply let yourself be where you are. There are no imaginations involved with this approach. You just go through with your situation as it is. If your meditation place is in a rich setting, just be in the midst of it. If it is in a simple setting, just be in the midst of that. You are not trying to get away from here to somewhere else. You are tuning in simply and directly to your process of life. This practice is the essence of here and now.

In this way, meditation becomes an actual part of life, rather than just a practice or exercise. It becomes inseparable from the instinct to live that accompanies all one's existence. That instinct to live can be seen as containing awareness, meditation, mindfulness. It constantly tunes us in to what is happening. So the life force that keeps us alive and that manifests itself continually in our stream of consciousness itself becomes the practice of mindfulness. Such mindfulness brings clarity, skill, and intelligence. Experience is brought from the framework of intense psychosomatic confusion into that of the real body, because we are simply tuning into what is *already* happening, instead of projecting anything further.

Since mindfulness is part of one's stream of consciousness, the practice of meditation cannot be regarded as something alien, as an emulation of some picturesque yogi who has a fixation on meditating all the time. Seen from the point of view of mindfulness of life, meditation is the total experience of any living being who has the instinct to survive. Therefore meditating—developing mindfulness—should not be regarded as a minority-group activity or as some specialized, eccentric pursuit. It is a worldwide approach that relates to all experience: it is tuning in to life.

We do not tune in as part of trying to live further. We do not approach mindfulness as a further elaboration of the survival instinct. Rather we just see the sense of survival as it is taking place in us already. You are here; you are living; let it be that way—that is mindfulness. Your heart pulsates and you breathe. All kinds of things are happening in you at once. Let mindfulness work with that, let that be mindfulness, let every beat of your heart, every breath, be mindfulness itself. You do not have to breathe specially; your breath *is* an expression of mindfulness. If you approach meditation in this way, it becomes very personal and very direct.

Having such an outlook and such a relationship with the practice of meditation brings enormous strength, enormous energy and power. But this only comes if one's relationship to the present situation is accurate. Otherwise there is no strength because we are apart from the energy of that situation. The accuracy of mindfulness, on the other hand, brings not only strength, but a sense of dignity and delight. This is simply because we are doing something that is applicable that very moment.

And we are doing it without any implications or motives. It is direct and right on the point.

But again it is necessary to say, once you have that experience of the presence of life, don't hang onto it. Just touch and go. Touch that presence of life being lived, then go. You do not have to ignore it. "Go" does not mean that we have to turn our backs on the experience and shut ourselves off from it; it means just being in it without further analysis and without further reinforcement. Holding on to life, or trying to reassure oneself that it is so, has the sense of death rather than life. It is only because we have that sense of death that we want to make sure that we are alive. We would like to have an insurance policy. But if we feel that we *are* alive, that is good enough. We do not have to make sure that we actually do breathe, that we actually can be seen. We do not have to check to be sure we have a shadow. Just living is enough. If we don't stop to reassure ourselves, living becomes very clear-cut, very alive, and very precise.

So mindfulness here does not mean pushing oneself toward something or hanging on to something. It means allowing oneself to be there in the very moment of what is happening in one's living process and then letting go.

Mindfulness of Effort

The next foundation of mindfulness is mindfulness of effort. The idea of *effort* is apparently problematical. Effort would seem to be at odds with the sense of being that arises from mindfulness of body. Also, pushing of any kind does not have an obvious place in the touch-and-go technique of the mindfulness of life. In either case, deliberate, heavy-handed effort would seem to endanger the open precision of the process of mindfulness. Still we cannot expect proper mindfulness to develop without some kind of exertion on our part. Effort is necessary. But the Buddhist notion of right effort is quite different from conventional definitions of effort.

One kind of conventional effort is oriented purely toward the achievement of a result: there is a sense of struggle and pushing, which is egged on by the sense of a goal. Such effort picks up momentum and begins to thrive on its own speed, like the run of a roadrunner. Another approach to effort is fraught with a sense of tremendous meaningfulness: there is no sense of upliftedness or inspiration in the work. Instead there is a strong feeling of being dutiful. One just slogs along, slowly and surely, trying to chew through obligations in the manner of a worm in a tree. A worm just chews through whatever comes in front of its mouth; the channel that its belly passes through is its total space.

Neither of these kinds of effort has a sense of openness or precision. The traditional Buddhist analogy for right effort is the walk of an elephant or tortoise. The elephant moves along surely, unstoppably, with great dignity. Like the worm, it is not excitable, but unlike the worm, it has a panoramic view of the ground it is treading on. Though it is serious and slow, because of the elephant's ability to survey the ground there is a sense of playfulness and intelligence in its movement.

In the case of meditation, trying to develop an inspiration that is based on wanting to forget one's pain and on trying to make one's practice thrive on a sense of continual accomplishment is quite immature. On the other hand, too much solemnity and dutifulness creates a lifeless and narrow outlook and a stale psychological environment. The style of right effort, as taught by the Buddha, is serious but not *too* serious. It takes advantage of the natural flow of instinct to bring the wandering mind constantly back to the mindfulness of breathing.

The crucial point in the bringing-back process is that it is not necessary to go through deliberate stages: first preparing to do it, then getting a hold on one's attention, then finally dragging it back to the breathing as if we were trying to drag a naughty child back from doing something terrible. It is not a question of forcing the mind back to some particular object, but of bringing it back down from the dream world into reality. We are breathing, we are sitting. That is what we are doing, and we should be doing it completely, fully, wholeheartedly.

There is a kind of technique, or trick, here that is extremely effective and useful, not only for sitting meditation, but also in daily life, or meditation-in-action. The way of coming back is through what we might call the *abstract watcher*. This watcher is just simple self-consciousness, without aim 'or goal. When we encounter anything, the first flash that takes place is the bare sense of duality, of separateness. On that basis, we begin to evaluate, pick and choose, make decisions, execute our will. The abstract watcher is just the basic sense of separateness—the plain cognition of being there before any of the rest develops. Instead of condemning this self-consciousness as dualistic, we take advantage of this tendency in our psychological system and use it as the basis of the mindfulness of effort. The experience is just a sudden flash of the watcher's being there. At that point we don't think, "I must get back to the breath" or "I must try and get away from these thoughts." We don't have to entertain a deliberate and logical movement of mind that repeats to itself the purpose of sitting practice. There is just suddenly a general sense that something is happening here and now, and we are brought back. Abruptly, immediately, without a name, without the application of any kind of concept, we have a quick glimpse of changing the tone. That is the core of the mindfulness of effort practice.

One of the reasons that ordinary effort becomes so dreary and stagnant is that our intention always develops a verbalization. Subconsciously, we actually verbalize: "I must go and help so-and-so because it is half-past one" or "This is a good thing for me to do; it is good for me to perform this duty." Any kind of sense of duty we might have is always verbalized, though the speed of conceptual mind is so great that we may not even notice the verbalization. Still, the contents of the verbalization are clearly felt. This verbalization pins the effort to a fixed frame of reference, which makes it extremely tiresome. In contrast, the abstract effort we are talking about flashes in a fraction of a second, without any name or any idea with it. It is just a jerk, a sudden change of course which does not define its destination. The rest of the effort is just like an elephant's walk—going slowly, step by step, observing the situation around us.

You could call this abstract self-consciousness *leap* if you like, or *jerk,* or *sudden reminder;* or you could call it *amazement.* Sometimes it could also be felt as panic, unconditioned panic, because of the change of course—something comes to us and changes our whole course. If we work with this sudden jerk, and do so with no effort in the effort, then effort becomes self-existing. It stands on its own two feet, so to speak, rather than needing another effort to trigger it off. If the latter were the case, effort would have to be deliberately manufactured, which would run counter to the whole sense of meditation. Once you have had that sudden instant of mindfulness, the idea is not to try to maintain it. You should not hold on to it or try to cultivate it. Don't entertain the messenger. Don't nurse the reminder. Get back to meditation. Get into the message.

This kind of effort is extremely important. The sudden flash is a key to all Buddhist meditation, from the level of basic mindfulness to the highest levels of tantra. Such mindfulness of effort could definitely be considered the most important aspect of mindfulness practice. Mindfulness of body creates the general setting; it brings meditation into the psychosomatic setup of one's life. Mindfulness of life makes meditation practice personal and intimate. Mindfulness of effort makes meditation workable: it connects the foundations of mindfulness to the path, to the spiritual journey. It is like the wheel of a chariot, which makes the connection between the chariot and the road, or like the oar of a boat. Mindfulness of effort actualizes the practice; it makes it move, proceed.

But we have a problem here. Mindfulness of effort cannot be deliberately manufactured; on the other hand, it is not enough just to hope that a flash will come to us and we will be reminded. We cannot just leave it up to "that thing" to happen to us. We have to set some kind of general alarm system, so to speak, or prepare a general atmosphere. There must be a background of discipline which sets the tone of the sitting practice. Effort is important on this level also; it is the sense of not having the faintest indulgence toward any form of entertainment. We have to give something up. Unless we give up our reservations about taking the practice seriously, it is virtually impossible to have that kind of instantaneous effort dawn on us. So it is extremely important to have respect for the practice, a sense of appreciation, and a willingness to work hard.

Once we do have a sense of commitment to relating with things as they actually are, we have opened the way to the flash that reminds us: *that, that, that.* "That what?" does not apply any more. Just *that*, which triggers an entirely new state of consciousness and brings us back auto-matically to mindfulness of breathing or a general sense of being.

We work hard at not being diverted into entertainment. Still, in some sense, we can enjoy the very boring situation of the practice of sitting meditation. We can actually appreciate not having lavish re-sources of entertainment available. Because of having already included our boredom and ennui, we have nothing to run away from and we feel completely secure and grounded.

This basic sense of appreciation is another aspect of the background that makes it possible for the spontaneous flash of the reminder to occur more easily. This is said to be like falling in love. When we are in love with someone, because our whole attitude is open toward that person somehow or other we get a sudden flash of that person—not as a name or as a concept of what the person looks like; those are afterthoughts. We get an abstract flash of our lover as *that*. A flash of *that* comes into our mind first. Then we might ponder on that flash, elaborate on it, enjoy our daydreams about it. But all this happens afterward. The flash is primal.

Openness always brings that kind of result. A traditional analogy is that of the hunter. The hunter does not have to think of a stag or a mountain goat or a bear or any specific animal; he is looking for *that*. When he walks and hears some sound, or senses some subtle possibility, he does not think of what animal he is going to find; just a feeling of *that* comes up. Anybody in any kind of complete involvement—on the level of the hunter, the lover, or the meditator—has the kind of open-ness that brings about sudden flashes. It is an almost magical sensation of thatness, without a name, without concept, without idea. This is the instant of effort, concentrated effort, and awareness follows after that. Having disowned that sudden experience, awareness very slowly comes and settles back to the earthy reality of just being there.

Mindfulness of Mind

Often mindfulness is referred to as watchfulness. But that should not give the impression that mindfulness means watching something happening. Mindfulness means *being* watchful, rather than watching some *thing*. This implies a process of intelligent alertness, rather than the mechanical business of simply observing what happens. Particularly the fourth foundation—mindfulness of mind—has qualities of an aroused intelligence operating. The intelligence of the fourth foundation is a sense of light-handedness. If you open the windows and doors of a room the right amount, you can maintain the interior feeling of roomness and, at the same time, have freshness from outside. Mindfulness of mind brings that same kind of intelligent balance.

Without mind and its conflicts, we could not meditate or develop balance, or develop anything at all for that matter. Therefore, conflicts that arise from mind are regarded as a necessary part of the process of mindfulness. But at the same time, those conflicts have to be controlled enough so that we can come back to our mindfulness of breathing. A balance has to be maintained. There has to be a certain discipline so that we are neither totally lost in daydream nor missing the freshness and openness that come from not holding our attention too tightly. This balance is a state of wakefulness, mindfulness.

People with different temperaments bring different approaches to the practice of meditation. Some people are extremely orthodox, in fact dictatorial, with themselves. Others are extraordinarily loose; they just hang out, so to speak, in the meditation posture and let everything happen. Other people struggle back and forth between those two extremes, not knowing exactly what to do. How one approaches the sitting situation will depend on one's moods and the type of person one is, obviously. But always a certain sense of accuracy is required, and a certain sense of freedom is required.

Mindfulness of mind means being with one's mind. When you sit and meditate, you are there: you are being with your body, with your sense of life or survival, with your sense of effort, and at the same time, you are being with your mind. You are being there. Mindfulness of mind suggests a sense of presence and a sense of accuracy in terms of being there. You are there, therefore you can't miss yourself. If you are not there, then you might miss yourself. But that also would be a double take: if you realize you are not there, that means you are there. That brings you back to where you are—back to square one.

The whole process is very simple, actually. Unfortunately, explaining the simplicity takes a lot of vocabulary, a lot of grammar. However, it is a very simple matter. And that matter concerns you and your world. Nothing else. It does not particularly concern enlightenment, and it does not particularly concern metaphysical comprehension. In fact, this simple matter does not particularly concern the next minute, or the minute before this one. It only concerns the very small area where we are now.

Really we operate on a very small basis. We think we are great, broadly significant, and that we cover a whole large area. We see ourselves as having a history and a future, and here we are in our big-deal present. But if we look at ourselves clearly in this very moment, we see we are just grains of sand—just little people concerned only with this little dot which is called *nowness.*

We can only operate on one dot at a time, and mindfulness of mind approaches our experience in that way. We are there, and we approach ourselves on the very simple basis of *that. That* does not particularly have many dimensions, many perspectives; it is just a simple thing. Relating directly to this little dot of nowness is the right understanding of austerity. And if we work on this basis, it is possible to begin to see the truth of the matter, so to speak—to begin to see what nowness really means.

This experience is very revealing in that it is very personal. It is not personal in the sense of petty and mean. The idea is that this experience is *your* experience. You might be tempted to share it with somebody else, but then it becomes their experience, rather than what you wished for: your/their experience, jumbled together. You can never achieve that. People have different experiences of reality, which cannot be jumbled together. Invaders and dictators of all kinds have tried to make others have their experience, to make a big concoction of minds controlled by one person. But that is impossible. Everyone who has tried to make that kind of spiritual pizza has failed. So you have to accept that your experience is personal. The personal experience of nowness is very much there and very obviously there. You cannot even throw it away!

In sitting practice, or in the awareness practice of everyday life, for that matter, you are not trying to solve a wide array of problems. You are looking at one situation that is very limited. It is so limited that there is not even room to be claustrophobic. If it is not there, it is not there. You missed it. If it is there, it is there. That is the pinpoint of mindfulness of mind, that simplicity of total up-to-dateness, total directness. Mind functions singly. Once. And once. One thing at a time. The practice of mindfulness of mind is to be there with that one-shot perception, constantly. You get a complete picture from which nothing is missing: that is happening, now that is happening, now that is happening. There is no escape. Even if you focus yourself on escaping, that is also a one-shot movement of which you could be mindful. You can be mindful of your escape—of your sexual fantasy or your aggression fantasy.

Things always happen one at a time, in a direct, simple movement of mind. Therefore, in the technique of mindfulness of mind, it is traditionally recommended that you be aware of each single-shot perception of mind as thinking: "I am thinking I hear a sound." "I am thinking I smell a scent." "I am thinking I feel hot." "I am thinking I feel cold." Each one of these is a total approach to experience—very precise, very direct, one single movement of mind. Things always happen in that direct way.

Often we tend to think that we are very clever and we can get away from that direct nature of things. We feel we can get around that choiceless simplicity by approaching something from the back door—or from above, from the loft. We feel that we can prove ourselves to be extremely intelligent and resourceful that way. We are cunning and shifty. But somehow it does not work. When we think we are approaching something from the back door, we do not understand that it is an illusion that there is *something else* to approach. At that moment there is only the back-doorness. That one-shot back-doorness is the totality of what is. We *are* the back door. If we are approaching from the loft, you, me, everybody, all of us are up there. The whole thing is up there, rather than there being something else for us to go down and invade and control. There isn't anything else at all. It is a one-shot deal. That one-shot reality is all there is. Obviously we can make up an illusion. We can imagine that we are conquering the universe by multiplying ourselves into hundreds of aspects and personalities: the conquering and the conquered. But that is like the dream state of someone who is actually asleep. There is only the one shot; everything happens only once. There is just *that*. Therefore mindfulness of mind is applicable.

So meditation practice has to be approached in a very simple and very basic way. That seems to be the only way that it will apply to our experience of what we actually are. That way, we do not get into the illusion that we can function as a hundred people at once. When we lose the simplicity we begin to be concerned about ourselves: "While I'm doing this, such-and-such is going to happen. What shall I do?" Thinking that more than *that* is happening, we get involved in hope and fear in relation to all kinds of things that are not actually happening. Really it does not work that way. While we are doing *that*, we are doing that. If something else happens, we are doing something else. But two things cannot happen at once; it is impossible. It is easy to *imagine* that two things are happening at once, because our journey back and forth between the two may be very speedy. But even then we are doing only one thing at a time.

The idea of mindfulness of mind is to slow down the fickleness of jumping back and forth. We have to realize that we are not extraordinary mental acrobats. We are not all that well trained. And even an extraordinarily well-trained mind could not manage that many things at once—not even two. But because things are very simple and direct, we can focus on, be aware and mindful of, one thing at a time. That one-pointedness, that bare attention, seems to be the basic point.

It is necessary to take that logic all the way and realize that even to apply bare attention to what we are doing is impossible. If we try, we have two personalities: one personality is the bare attention; the other personality is doing things. Real bare attention is being there all at once. We do not apply bare attention *to* what we are doing; we are not mindful *of* what we are doing. That is impossible. Mindfulness is the act as well as the experience, happening at the same time. Obviously, we could have a somewhat dualistic attitude at the beginning, before we get into real mindfulness, that we are willing to be mindful, willing to surrender,

willing to discipline ourselves. But then we do the thing; we just do it.
It is like the famous Zen saying "When I eat, I eat; when I sleep, I sleep."
You just do it, with absolutely no implication behind what you are
doing, not even of mindfulness.

When we begin to feel implications of mindfulness, we are beginning to split ourselves. Then we are faced with our resistance, and hundreds of other things seemingly begin to attack us, to bother us. Trying
to be mindful by deliberately looking at oneself involves too much
watcher. Then we have lost the one-shot simplicity.

QUESTION: I was wondering if you could speak a little more about
how mind, or "minding," creates the world. Are you talking about creating in the sense that if we are not mindful of the world the world does
not exist? I feel you're saying something else besides that.

CHÖGYAM TRUNGPA RINPOCHE: Well, mind is very simple perception: it can only survive on "other." Otherwise it starves to death.

Q: You mean the mind can only exist on things outside of itself?

CTR: That is right. But there is also the possibility that mind can
go too far in that direction. Mind cannot exist without the projection of
a relative reference point; on the other hand, mind also cannot exist if
it is too crowded with projections. That way it also loses its reference
point. So mind has to maintain a certain balance. To begin with, mind
looks for a way to secure its survival. It looks for a mate, a friend; it
creates the world. But when it begins to get too crowded—too many
connections, too much world—it rejects its projections; it creates a little
niche somewhere and fights tooth and nail to maintain it in order to
survive. Sometimes mind loses the game. It becomes psychotic, completely mad. You "lose your mind," as we say: you cannot even function
on an ordinary logical level. Such psychosis results from either of the
two extremes: you are completely overcrowded by the whole projection
of the world or, on the other hand, you lack anything for mind to work
with. So mind can only exist in the neurosis of relative reference, not in
psychosis. When it reaches the psychotic level, mind ceases to function
as mind. It becomes something else, something poisonous.

Q: According to that model, how would meditation practice affect the relationship between mind and the world it's doing battle with?

CTR: The purpose of meditation practice is to try to save oneself from psychosis.

Q: But you still maintain the world? You still maintain the neurotic state, basically?

CTR: Not that necessarily, either. There is an alternative mind that does not need the neurotic world. This is where the idea of enlightenment comes in. Enlightened mind can go further and further, beyond questions of relative reference. It does not have to keep up with this world. It reaches a point where it does not have to sharpen itself on this neurotic world any more. There is another level of experience which still has a reference point, but it is a reference point without demand, a reference point that does not need further reference points. That is called nonduality. This does not mean to say that you dissolve into the world or the world becomes you. It's not a question of oneness but rather a question of zeroness.

Q: Rinpoche, how does the notion of mind that you've talked about relate to the notion of ego and the strategies of maintaining ego?

CTR: Mind as we have been talking about it *is* ego. Ego can survive only in relation to a reference point, not by itself. But I am trying to make the whole thing quite simple and relate it directly to the practice of meditation. If we think practicing meditation is concerned with working with ego, that sounds like too big a deal. Whereas if we just work with mind, that is an actual, real thing to us. In order to wake up in the morning you have to know it is morning—there is light outside and you have awakened. Those simple things are a perfect example of basic ego. Ego survives and thrives on reference point.

Q: Before, you were saying that when we are sitting here and taking notes, or focusing on the speaker and relaxing, we have a psychosomatic notion of body. And *psychosomatic*, the way I understand it, is sort of an imagined thing, or something that has to do with one's mind, with how the mind is affecting the body. Like when we say someone has a psychosomatic disease, it means their mind is having some effect on their body. How is that related to the fact that we're sitting here relaxing and listening to a speaker? How is that a psychosomatic sense of body?

CTR: The point is that whatever we do in our lives, we don't actually just do it; we are affected by mind. Maybe the body, the true body, is being pressured by the psychosomatic speed of the mind. You might say that there is a possibility that you are sitting here now properly, in a nonpsychosomatic way. But still, the whole situation of sitting here was brought together, the whole incident was moved into place, by a psychosomatic driving force. So your sitting here was set up by the psychosomatic system, basically. If you have some kind of psychosomatic convulsion and you throw up—you actually do throw up stuff, which is not psychosomatic stuff but body stuff—it is nevertheless manifested in psychosomatic style. Its being thrown up was instigated by a psychosomatic process. That is the kind of situation we are in. Fundamentally our whole world is psychosomatic from that point of view. The whole process of living is composed of psychosomatic hang-ups. The desire to listen to the teachings comes from beginning to be aware of one's hang-ups. Since we have begun to be aware of our hang-ups we would like to create this further hang-up to clear up the existing hang-ups.

Q: Instead of relating directly?

CTR: Well, one never does that until one has some kind of flash of something on the level of enlightenment. Until that point everything one does is always by innuendo.

Q: So any kind of disease or anything that's affecting you is psychosomatic?

CTR: It is not only disease that is psychosomatic. Your process of health is psychosomatic, already. Actually, disease is sort of an extra thing, like yeast growing on top of your back.

FOUR

An Approach to Meditation

A TALK TO PSYCHOLOGISTS

MEDITATION SEEMS to be the basic theme of spiritual practice. It is a vast subject and one that is very loosely defined, so there is a tremendous possibility of distorting it, adding our own version to it. Therefore, it seems quite important to take a look at meditation scientifically in the way it applies to our spiritual practice.

There are all sorts of concepts about meditation. One involves trying to establish communication with a divine power and using exotic techniques to tune in to this power. This particular style of meditation could be defined as a religious practice. Another way of approaching meditation is as a spiritual practice rather than a religious one, working with the perceiver rather than focusing on external divine forces of any kind.

Do such things as divine forces exist or not? Does a God exist or not? The answer is that it is not certain until we work with the perceiver of that particular energy. In the Buddhist form of meditation we try to look at the perceiver of the universe, the perceiver which is self, ego, me, mine. In order to receive guests, we have to have a place to receive them. It is possible, however, that we may not find it necessary to invite any guests at all. Once we have created the place where guests are welcome, we may find they are there already.

The practice of meditation is based, not on how we would like things to be, but on what is. We often do not have a proper understanding of what we are, of what we are actually doing. Instead our attention is focused on the possible end product of the processes we are involved in. Spirituality should be taken very seriously, very honestly. This means it should not partake of that exotic quality which is filled with promises. From the beginning, it should be concerned with the actuality of who is involved in the practice.

In the tradition of Buddhism, each person in the lineage of teachers develops a self-understanding which adds to the tradition. The process is like handing down a recipe for bread. In each generation the bread is exactly like the original bread, but possibly more flavorful because of the added experience of the bakers involved in the handing down. In each generation the bread is fresh, delicious, and healthy.

One might say, "How can I know that these experiences are valid for me?" I can't say that they are particularly valid for particular individuals unless I have a personal relationship and understanding with them. But certainly the process of working on one's psychological states from a fresh point of view is valid. What I have to say about these psychological states is that they are purely one's own experience. Studying and learning about them is more of a confirmation than new information.

There is a great need to be realistic and critical about what we are. We must not be spiritually gullible. Often we find that what we are is not attractive; we find looking at ourselves discouraging. But looking at ourselves is not finally discouraging; rather it develops the ability to be more realistic. We always ask a question when there is uncertainty. Questions would not arise at all if we did not have the creative ground of uncertainty within us. The questions we ask already contain the answers in embryonic form. In other words, they are expressions of the answers. The answer may turn out to be negative and disappointing, causing us to hate ourselves, but nevertheless, we will have discovered something real.

This self-disillusionment seems to be the starting point of meditation practice. The starting point is dissatisfaction, the absence of a dream, or wishful thinking. It is something realistic, down-to-earth, and direct.

Ego starts from bewilderment; bewilderment or dissatisfaction or not knowing how to step to the next solution. Finding a solution, we haven't actually found it, because we're not exactly certain to whom the solution applies. There is, therefore, a basic suspicion of the nonexistence of ourselves, a basic confusion. Somehow that basic bewilderment or confusion is the working base. From that confusion, basic bewilderment, or basic paranoia, whatever we call it, arises the attempt to communicate further in order to establish our ego.

Each time we try to establish our so-called reality, the basic paranoia becomes larger and larger; for establishing relationships with the apparent phenomenal world makes demands, requires energy, and the facing of overwhelming situations. When the phenomenal world becomes greater and more powerful than us, there is automatically a feeling of bewilderment. As we continually feel bewildered, we do our best to establish our pattern. In a materialistic sense, we try and become a rich, respectable, or powerful person. In a spiritual sense, we try and adapt to a basic discipline. Finding a basic discipline could be a process which enriches the ego or the self. Even if we follow a spiritual rather than a worldly life, if we don't have the basic understanding of why we are trying to accumulate, we are still materialistic in outlook. This is what is known as psychological or spiritual materialism.

What we do, what we collect doesn't matter. The style of the collection is based on the notion of developing a fundamental health which should be seen as basic ego trying to relate to things as sedatives. Any kind of spiritual practice based on that attitude could be extremely dangerous. One can attain a state that could be called spiritual egohood.

We have a problem there. The question is, how can we approach spirituality otherwise? Is there any possibility of approaching it in another way at all? You might say, "Please don't say no, please tell us some more." Well, that's it in a sense. Once we realize that there is no way out from this end, we want to break through something; we want to step out more, to jump. Jumping or leaping is a very dignified thing to do. It is being willing to be an explorer on the biggest scale, willing to be a samurai in the widest sense, willing to break through, to be a warrior. It seems that the question begins from that point when we actually want to break through something. That leap consists, of course, of giving up goal, aim, and object at the same time. What we are doing in this case is stepping out of even the basic bewilderment; not trying to creep around from underneath or by the back door, but stepping out completely.

We find that in spite of the willingness to explore, we still have the basic bewilderment within us and we have to work with that. This involves accepting the basic bewilderment or paranoia as it is. That is the working base. That basic psychological state consists of layers of psychological facades of all kinds. The basic bewilderment is overwhelmingly stupid and yet intelligent in that it plays its game of deaf and dumb cunningly. Beyond the bewilderment, ego develops certain patterns of emotions and sensations. When emotions are insufficient to fortify the ego, we apply concept, the conceptual process of labeling and naming things. Things having names and concepts attached to them help us domesticate the bewilderment or confusion. Beyond that, ego collects neurotic thoughts, neurotic not in the sense of mad, but in the sense of irregular. Thoughts in this case change direction all the time and are on very shaky ground. A single thought pattern never develops. Rather, one thought overlaps another—thoughts on spirituality, sexual fantasies, money matters, domestic matters, etc., overlapping all the time. That is the last stage of ego development. In a sense, ego is systematically well fortified.

Bewilderment, as we have said, is reinforced by processes developing at the emotional level. Emotion in this case is the basic magnetizing quality, which is passion, or the basic repelling quality, which is aggression. The next level comes in when the emotions cease to function as impulsive processes. At this point, we need an analytical mind to reinforce them, to put them in their proper place, to confirm their right to be there. The analytical process creates concepts. Concepts are scientifically, mathematically, philosophically, or spiritually worked out.

Concepts and emotions are very crude spokes of the wheel. There is a gap between the two, an area of not knowing where we are, a fear of being nothing. These gaps could be filled with thoughts of all kinds. Discursive thoughts, grasshopperlike thoughts, drunken-elephant-type thoughts all fill the gaps of not knowing what we are, where we're at. If we want to work on that particular base, the idea is to not collect any new things, new subjects.

Further collecting would be inviting invasion from the outside. Since the whole structure of ego is so well fortified against attack, an external invasion is not going to destroy the ego at all. In fact, it is going to reinforce the whole structure because the ego is being given more material with which to work. Meditation practice is based on an undoing, unlearning process. It is an infiltration into this well-fortified structure of the ego.

Beginning meditation practice works purely on dealing with thought processes. It begins there because these thought processes are the last fringes of ego's development. Working on them makes use of certain very simple techniques. The techniques are very important and must be very simple. Presenting exotic techniques tends to emphasize the foreign quality rather than the familiar, "homey" quality that is most desirable. The technique most often used in the Buddhist tradition is awareness of breathing or walking. These techniques are not ways of developing concentration, tranquillity, or peacefulness, for these qualities cannot be forcibly developed. All of these things are beyond achievement if they are sought after.

The other way of approaching the practice is the gamelike approach. The game is that the path and the goal are the same. You are not trying to achieve anything, but are trying to relate to the path which is the goal. We try to become completely one with the techniques (breathing, walking, etc.). We do not try to do anything with the technique but identify and become one with it. The beginning level of any of the traditions of meditation could be said to be a game, a trip of its own. It's purely imagination; we imagine ourselves meditating. It's another type of dreaming. One has to accept that dreamlike quality and work along with it. We can't start perfectly and beautifully, but if we are willing to start by accepting our neuroses and basic chaos, we have a stepping-stone. Don't be afraid of being a fool; start as a fool.

The techniques of meditation practice are not designed to reduce active thoughts at all. They provide a way of coming to terms with everything that goes on inside. Once we have accepted what goes on in

our mind as neither good nor bad, but just flashes of thoughts, we have
come to terms with it. So long as we regard the mind's activity as a
foreign invasion, we are introducing another new element to the chaos
and are feeding it more. If we accept it as part of our ego development,
ego structure, and don't evaluate it or put any labels on it, we come
much closer to seeing the interior.

After the thought processes, the next barrier is the pattern of concepts. We should not try to push away the concepts, but try to see them
realistically. Concepts are based on irrelevant evaluations. There is nothing which is absolutely good or bad. Once we cease to plant the seed of
evaluation, the conceptual processes become a neutral and open ground.

The next process is that of emotion: love, hate, etc. A problem arises
when we tend to become too ambitious in terms of dealing with emotions—particularly those involved with the spiritual practice. We've
been told to be kind, gentle, good people. Those are the conventional
ideas of spirituality. When we begin to find the spiky quality in ourselves, we see it as antispirituality and try to push it away. That is the
biggest mistake of all in working with our basic psychological patterns.
Once we try to push the biggest problems away and look for a dramatic
cure for them, we are constantly pushed back, defeated all the time. The
idea is not to seduce ourselves into trying to create a Utopian spirituality, but to try and look into the details of the peak emotions, the dramatic qualities of the emotions. We don't have to wait for situations
which are regarded as big and meaningful to us; we should make use of
even the small situations in which these emotions occur. We should
work on the small or minor irritations and their particular emotional
qualities. Do not suppress or let go of irritations, but become part of
them; feel their abstract qualities. The irritations then have no one to
irritate. They might fade away or become creative energy. If we are able
to work brick by brick with those smaller, seemingly insignificant emotions, at some point we will find that removing each brick has taken
away the whole wall.

We tend to be involved with ambition in spiritual practice. There's
no hope if we become too ambitious in any way. Once this occurs and
we try to achieve something very quickly, we are forced to remove the

awareness of knowing the situation as it is now. Ambition seduces us into thinking of something that we want to achieve in the future. We become too future-oriented, missing the point of a given situation. Our greatest opportunity is in the present moment and we begin to lose it. However, feeling that the future is an open situation is what meditation practice actually is. Relating with the present situation removes the basic bewilderment that we have discussed, the fundamental heart of the whole ego structure. If we are able to relate with the actual situation as it is, without referring to the past or future, then there are flashes of gaps, possibilities of approaching the present situation. That freshness or sharpness, the penetrating quality of knowing the present situation, brings in a way of looking at the bewilderment with clarity and precision. If we're trying to achieve something in terms of spiritual ambition, that ambition itself becomes a hang-up.

The only way to relate to the present situation of spirituality or the neurotic state of the moment is by meditation. I don't mean sitting meditation only, but relating with the emotional situations of daily life in a meditative way, by working with them, being aware of them as they come up. Every situation then becomes a learning process. These situations are the books; they are the scriptures. You don't need more than that. Books and sacred writings become purely a source of inspiration. We have to realize that we already have within us the potential of developing spirituality before we read the books or regard them as part of our collection.

By undoing the successive layers of facades, we begin to discover that the precision and sharpness we spoke of is there already. We don't have to develop it or nurse it. It's just a question of acknowledging it. That is what is known as faith and devotion. The fundamental meaning of faith is recognizing that precision, clarity, and health are already there. That is the psychologically wealthy way of looking at situations. You see that you are already rich, that you don't have to search for something else or introduce a new element.

We say that the sun is behind the clouds, but actually it is not the sun but the city from which we view it that is behind the clouds. If we realized that the sun is never behind the clouds we might have a different attitude toward the whole thing.

QUESTION: For me you made it very clear—the neutral ground of our concepts. But when you talked about emotions, you introduced another word—working on the "small irritations," which is somewhat different. . . . I would like to hear you elaborate on the small emotions.

CHÖGYAM TRUNGPA RINPOCHE: Well, the seemingly smaller irritations are not really small but "small" is a way of viewing them. We view them as being insignificant things—such as the little bug crawling up your leg or a drafty window blowing at your face. Little details like that are seemingly insignificant because they have less concepts from your point of view. But they still do have the irritating quality in full flesh. So the way to deal with it is that you have a tremendous opportunity there, because you don't have that heavy concept, so you have a very good open approach toward working with that irritation.

When I say "working with" irritation, I don't mean to say suppress irritation or let go of irritation. But trying to become part of the irritation, trying to feel the abstract quality. You see, generally what happens when we have irritation is that we feel we are being undermined by irritation, and we begin to lose our own basic dignity; something else overwhelms us. That kind of power game goes on always. That is the source of the problem. When we are able to become completely one with irritations or feel the abstract quality of the irritation as it is, then irritation has no one to irritate. So it becomes a sort of judo practice, the using of the irritation's energy as part of your basic development.

Q: Could you please relate what you have just discussed with this leap into the void, or this great adventure you mentioned earlier? How do they tie in?

CTR: Well, you see, generally there is a basic bewilderment of not knowing anything. One is uncertain how to approach, how to relate with the situation. Then there is an occasional gap within the basic bewilderment, that something is happening. It's not an overcrowded situation but it's more like a dark corner. Basic bewilderment is a crowded situation under light—you see so many things crowded, the situation is happening in front of your eyes. But then you begin to realize there is also a quiet corner which is still dark but you don't know what is behind that. In such areas there is no bewilderment, only suspicion, of course. Naturally. The whole thing is based on trying to enrich our ego all the time. So the shunyata principle, or the empti-ness—leaping into the emptiness—is, one can almost say, leaping into those dark corners. And by the time you leap into dark corners they seem to be brilliant corners, not dark. Darkness, as opposed to what you see purely in front of your eyes, relating with the overcrowded situation, is dark because it is not overcrowding. That is why we begin to regard it as an insignificant or mysterious corner. It is very tricky to talk about leaps because we immediately begin to think where we are leaping from. It's actually more a question of accepting mysterious corners, open space, which doesn't bring any psychological comfort or security for the ego. That is why they are frightening and mysterious, because there is no security of anything at all. So once you acknowledge that complete ultimate freedom of absence of security, then suddenly the carpet is pulled out from under your feet. That is the leap, rather than leaping somewhere deliberately.

Q: Am I reading you right when you say the effect of meditation begins when one empties oneself from preconceived ideas and notions, and one must empty oneself before one can be filled?

CTR: Well, I wouldn't say that is the aim of meditation particularly, but that is the by-product of meditation. In actual practice you don't have to achieve anything, but you try to be with the technique.

Q: We have a pattern of becoming one with whatever it is that concerns one and going with it; and in the process it is no longer a problem. I understand Buddhism also contains this thinking.

CTR: I think so, yes. But the whole point is not trying to solve the problem. It's having a friendly, welcoming attitude to the problem.

Q: I'm amazed that so many of our so-called modern concepts—breathing, etc.—Buddhism has used for thousands of years. I had the pleasure of being with a Buddhist monk in Bali and found that all my "original" thinking was already contained within Buddhism.

CTR: Well, it's something basic, the voice of basic sanity. I mean, you can find it anywhere, in any tradition if it faces reality. It doesn't necessarily have to be Buddhist.

Q: Is meditation a continuous process of dynamic living?

CTR: Definitely. Without ambition, of course.

Q: When one is liberated, when one has practiced meditation in the proper way, without ambition, and one reaches the goal, how does one live? What is the nature of his being?

CTR: Well, the actual nature of that being is quite dangerous to talk about.

Q: Why is it dangerous?

CTR: Well, that could be a temptation.

Q: An attempt to go there artificially?

CTR: Or unwise.

Q: Can't we discuss it?

CTR: I would say the continual process of living becomes more real. You are actually in touch with more real reality, the nakedness of reality where there is natural confidence without a framework of relativity. So I would imagine that that state of being, from a personal psychological point of view, is extremely free. But not being free about anything, but just being free, being true.

Q: Is there ecstasy and rapture?

CTR: I don't think so, because then you have to maintain that ecstasy. It is a state which doesn't involve any maintenance.

Q: What are the prerequisites before one begins to meditate?

CTR: That you are willing to meditate, willing to go into discipline or practice—a conviction which could be a false conviction at that time, but it doesn't matter.

Q: How does one go about escaping from the belief in the analytical mind in order to begin?

CTR: Well, it seems that in terms of meditation the literal quality of the technique automatically brings you down, because there is no room for any sidetracks at all. It is quite an absurd, repetitive, ordinary technique, quite boring often; yet somehow you are put into a framework where an instinctive understanding of relating with the technique, rather than an intellectual one, begins to develop.

You see, the problem is that analytical mind cannot be freed by another aspect of analytical mind until the questions of analytical mind are dissolved. This is the same as the method of "Who am I?" in Ramana Maharshi's teaching. If you regard "Who am I?" as a question, then you are still analyzing yourself, but when you begin to realize that "Who am I?" is a statement, the analytical mind becomes confused. One realizes there is something personal about it. Something instinctive which is freed by the actual living situation. The disciplined technique of practicing meditation amounts to putting yourself into an inconceivable situation in which the analytical mind doesn't function anymore. So I would say that the disciplines of the Buddhist teachings are largely a way of freeing oneself from analytical mind. Which has a dream quality. Analytical mind is close to the clouds, while the instinctual level is much closer to the earth. So in order to come down to earth, you have to use the earth as a means of bringing you down.

Q: What is the relationship between being a vegetarian and the Buddhist practice?

CTR: Well, I think there again we've got a problem. If we regard the whole thing as introducing a foreign element into our system, then we get involved in a particular style of living and we have to maintain that style. And if we don't maintain that style, we feel threatened by it;

whereas the natural living situation might present being a vegetarian as a relevant subject for the individual. In other words, the first is dogma and the latter more of a direct situation.

You see, the problem is if you give up something, that automatically means that you take on something. Naturally. And you have to maintain that. And each time there is a congratulatory quality of viewing yourself that develops as well: I'm doing good today, I feel grateful and I'm going to be good tomorrow, and so on. That becomes a further self-deception. Unfortunately, no one can remove your self-deception by his magical powers. You have to work on yourself.

Q: Could you give us some examples of the meditation practices?

CTR: Generally in the Buddhist tradition the first step is working on the breathing—not concentrating, not contemplating, but identifying with the breath. You are the technique; there is no difference between you and the technique at all. By doing that, at a certain stage the technique just falls away, becomes irrelevant. At that point, your practice of meditation is much more open to meditation in action, everyday life situations.

But that doesn't mean that the person should become absorbed in the state of meditation in the vague sense at all. You see, the basic meditation is being, I suppose we could say. But at the same time it is not being dazed by being. You can describe being in all sorts of ways. You could say being is a cow on a sunny afternoon in a meadow, dazed in its comfort. You could think in terms of an effort of being, trying to bring some effort to yourself to be being. That is to say, being with the watcher watching yourself doing. Then there is actual being—we could call it "actual"—which I suppose is just being right there with precision and openness. I call it panoramic awareness, aerial view. You see a very wide view of the whole area because you see the details of each area. You see the wide view, each area, each detail. Black is black and white is white; everything is being observed. And that kind of openness and being is the source of daily practice. Whether the person is a housewife or secretary or politician or lawyer, whatever it may be, his life could be viewed that way. In fact, his work could become an application of skillful means in seeing the panoramic view. Fundamentally, the idea of enlightenment—the notion or term *enlightenment* or *buddha* or *awakened one*—implies tremendous sharpness and precision along with a sense of spaciousness.

We can experience this; it is not myth at all. We experience a glimpse of it, and the point is to start from that glimpse and gradually as you become more familiar with that glimpse and the possibilities of reigniting it, it happens naturally. Faith is realizing that there is some open space and sharpness in our everyday life. There occurs a flash, maybe a fraction of a second. These flashes happen constantly, all the time.

Q: If being is being in everyday life as present in the moment, then what is the tradition of monasteries in Buddhism? Are monasteries just for people who can't cope with very much stress so they have to withdraw to what can be handled? What is the role?

CTR: Well, I would say that monasteries are the training ground. It is the same as putting yourself in a certain discipline when you sit and meditate. You are a monk for that whole time, if you like to put it that way.

Q: But the goal and object would be finally to leave the monastery and—

CTR: Teach people, work with them. Obviously, yes. That's one of the differences, I would say, between Catholic contemporary enclosure orders and Buddhist ones, that monasteries are training grounds for potential teachers.

Q: I have a question about one's actual needs in meditation. From books that I've read on meditation and the spiritual way, it seems that the people begin to leave their sexual lives, heterosexual or homosexual, in a way. I'd like your feeling on this—sex, meditation, the spiritual way.

CTR: Well, there again it's entirely relative to the situation where the person is. The brahmacharya idea—which prohibits sex—sees it as something which destroys your completeness. On the other hand, in some traditions of Buddhism, sexuality is regarded as the highest way of living in the world, as the last answer and development. But I don't think the two are contradictory to each other at all. Sex can be a destruction of completion if the person's style of living is demanding, in other words, if there is no space in the relationship at all. Then it is purely a battlefield. But if the relationship becomes dance, the essence of exchange or communication, then the whole pattern of how to perceive that develops. I would say that the situation is very much dependent on the individual person, and sex generally is supposed to be the essence of communication. Communication can be demanding, which could be destructive and even a way of dissociating oneself from people. Or communication could be inviting people.

Q: Do you feel it is necessary to have a guru?

CTR: I think so, yes, but at the same time, there are all sorts of dangers involved with shopping for a guru.

Q: Can the willingness to meditate be differentiated from the awareness of the advantages to be gained from meditating?

CTR: That seems to be an evolutionary pattern. You begin to see the need for it and you put your effort into it. It's like taking medicine.

Q: What is your opinion about dealing with the chakra system?

CTR: The chakra system is part of the teachings of India, both Hindu and Buddhist. However, it fits differently into the pattern of spiritual evolution of the two traditions. In Hinduism, working with the chakras is familiarizing yourself with spirituality. In Buddhism, having familiarized yourself already, it becomes dancing with spiritual knowledge. And it seems in the latter case that chakra and all those concepts come from that dancing quality which is a using of the energy you have already developed. You have prepared your ground already and you are using the energy around it. I will say that for beginners it is extremely dangerous to play with energy, but for advanced students such work becomes relevant naturally.

Q: It is said that when one is ready one recognizes his guru. Is it true also that the guru recognizes his disciple?

CTR: I think so, yes. Otherwise he wouldn't be guru.

Q: Does this recognition take form on the physical plane or only on the subtle?

CTR: Well, the physical plane is also a psychological state. So it's the same thing.

FIVE

Natural Dharma

To BEGIN WITH, the main point of meditation is that we need to get to know ourselves: our minds, our behavior, our being. You see, we think we know ourselves, but actually we don't. There are all sorts of undiscovered areas of our thoughts and actions. What we find in ourselves might be quite astounding.

Meditation often means "to meditate on" something, but in this case I am referring to a state of meditation without any contents. In order to experience this state of being, it is necessary to practice what is known as "mindfulness." You simply pay attention to your breath, as you breathe in and out, and to every detail in your mind, whether it is a thought pattern of aggression, passion, or ignorance, or just insignificant mental chatter. Mindfulness also means paying attention to the details of every action, for example, to the way you extend your hand to reach for a glass. You see yourself lifting it, touching it to your lips, and then drinking the water. [*Rinpoche takes a sip from his glass.*] So every detail is looked at precisely—which doesn't make you self-conscious, particularly, but it may give you quite a shock; it may be quite real. When mindfulness begins to grow and expand, you become more aware of the environment around you, of something more than just body and mind alone. And then, at some point, mindfulness and awareness are joined together, which becomes one open eye, one big precision. At that point, a person becomes much less crude. Because you have been paying attention to your thoughts and actions, you become more refined.

Out of that precision and refinement comes gentleness. You are not just paying attention, but you are also aware of your own pain and pleasure, and you develop sympathy and friendship for yourself. From that you are able to understand, or at least see, the pain and suffering of others, and you begin to develop a tremendous sense of sympathy for others. At the same time, such sympathy also helps the mindfulness-awareness process develop further. Basically, you become a gentle person. You begin to realize that you are good: totally good and totally wholesome. You have a sense of trust in yourself and in the world. There is something to grip on to, and the quality of path or journey emerges out of that. You feel you want to do something for others and something for yourself. There is a sense of universal kindness, goodness, and genuineness.

When you experience precision and gentleness, the phenomenal world is no longer seen as an obstacle—or as being particularly helpful, for that matter. It is seen and appreciated as it is. At this point, you are able to transmute the various defilements of passion, aggression, and ignorance into a state of wisdom. For example, when aggression occurs, you simply look at the aggression, rather than being carried away by it or acting it out. When you look at the aggression itself, it becomes a mirror reflecting back to your face. You realize that the aggression has no object; there is nothing to be aggressive toward. At that point, the aggression itself subsides, but its strength or energy is kept as a positive thing. It becomes wisdom. Here wisdom does not mean the usual notion of being wise. Wisdom is egolessness, or a state of being, simply being. The whole process requires a certain amount of mindfulness and awareness throughout, obviously. But you naturally develop a habit of seeing whatever defilement occurs just as it is, even if it is just for a glimpse. Then you begin to be freed from anxiety, and you begin to achieve a state of mind that need not be cultivated and which cannot be lost. You experience a natural state of delight. It is not that you are always beaming and happy, or that you just stay in a state of mystical ecstasy. You feel other people's suffering. It has been said in the texts that the Buddha's sensitivity to others' pain and suffering, compared to the sensitivity of an ordinary person, is like the difference between having a hair on your eyeball and having a hair on the palm of your hand.

So delight in this case means total joy, having a total sense of "isness." Then you are able to help others, you are able to help yourself, and you are able to influence the universe with an all-pervasive sense of isness which neither comes nor goes.

We follow these stages of meditation methodically, with tremendous diligence and the help of a teacher. When one reaches a state of no-question [*Startled laughter erupts among the audience, as a loud thunderclap occurs nearby*] the natural dharma is proclaimed. [*Rinpoche indicates environment with his fan.*] Therefore one begins to feel, without egotism, that one is the king of the universe. Because you have achieved an understanding of impersonality, you can become a person. It takes a journey. First you have to become nothing, and then you can become somebody. One begins to develop tremendous conviction and doubtlessness, without pretense. This stage is called enlightenment, or wakefulness in the ultimate sense. From the beginning, wakefulness has been cultivated through mindfulness, awareness, and sympathy toward oneself and others. Finally one reaches the state where there is no question whatsoever. One becomes part of the universe. [*More loud thunder, accompanied by tumultuous rain.*]

I think that is probably enough at this point. There are various details and technicalities regarding the types and stages of meditation, but since time is short, and also since it would be futile to talk about this and that too much, I would like to stop here. Thank you.

Part Two MIND

SIX

Mind

THE OPEN SECRET

FOR THE FOLLOWER of the buddhadharma, the teachings of Buddhism, there is a need for great emphasis on the practice of meditation. One must see the straightforward logic that mind is the cause of confusion and that by transcending confusion one attains the enlightened state. This can only take place through the practice of meditation. The Buddha himself experienced this, by working on his own mind; and what he learned has been handed down to us.

Mindfulness is a basic approach to the spiritual journey that is common to all traditions of Buddhism. But before we begin to look closely at that approach, we should have some idea of what is meant by spirituality itself. Some say that spirituality is a way of attaining a better kind of happiness, transcendental happiness. Others see it as a benevolent way to develop power over others. Still others say the point of spirituality is to acquire magical powers so we can change our bad world into a good world or purify the world through miracles. It seems that all of these points of view are irrelevant to the Buddhist approach. According to the buddhadharma, spirituality means relating with the working basis of one's existence, which is one's state of mind.

There is a problem with one's basic life, one's basic being. This problem is that we are involved in a continual struggle to survive, to maintain our position. We are continually trying to grasp onto some solid image of ourselves. And then we have to defend that particular fixed conception. So there is warfare, there is confusion, and there is passion and aggression; there are all kinds of conflicts. From the Buddhist point of view, the development of true spirituality is cutting through our basic fixation, that clinging, that stronghold of something-or-other, which is known as ego.

In order to do that we have to find out what ego is. What is this all about? Who are we? We have to look into our already existing state of mind. And we have to understand what practical step we can take to do that. We are not involved here in a metaphysical discussion about the purpose of life and the meaning of spirituality on an abstract level. We are looking at this question from the point of view of a working situation. We need to find some simple thing we can do in order to embark on the spiritual path.

People have difficulty beginning a spiritual practice because they put a lot of energy into looking for the best and easiest way to get into it. We might have to change our attitude and give up looking for the best or the easiest way. Actually, there is no choice. Whatever approach we take, we will have to deal with what we are already. We have to look at who we are. According to the Buddhist tradition, the working basis of the path and the energy involved in the path is the mind—one's own mind, which is working in us all the time.

Spirituality is based on mind. In Buddhism, mind is what distinguishes sentient beings from rocks or trees or bodies of water. That which possesses discriminating awareness, that which possesses a sense of duality—which grasps or rejects something external—that is mind. Fundamentally, it is that which can associate with an "other"—with any "something" that is perceived as different from the perceiver. That is the definition of mind. The traditional Tibetan phrase defining mind means precisely that: "That which can think of the other, the projection, is mind."

So by mind we mean something very specific. It is not just something very vague and creepy inside our heads or hearts, something that just happens as part of the way the wind blows and the grass grows. Rather, it is something very concrete. It contains perception—perception that is very uncomplicated, very basic, very precise. Mind develops its particular nature as that perception begins to linger on something other than oneself. Mind makes the fact of perceiving something else stand for the existence of oneself. That is the mental trick that constitutes mind. In fact, it should be the opposite. Since the perception starts from oneself, the logic should be: "I exist, therefore the other exists." But somehow the hypocrisy of mind is developed to such an extent that mind lingers on the other as a way of getting the feedback that it itself exists, which is a fundamentally erroneous belief. It is the fact that the existence of self is questionable that motivates the trick of duality.

This mind is our working basis for the practice of meditation and the development of awareness. But mind is something more than the process of confirming self by the dualistic lingering on the other. Mind also includes what are known as *emotions*, which are the highlights of mental states. Mind cannot exist without emotions. Daydreaming and discursive thoughts are not enough. Those alone would be too boring. The dualistic trick would wear too thin. So we tend to create waves of emotion which go up and down: passion, aggression, ignorance, pride— all kinds of emotions. In the beginning we create them deliberately, as a game of trying to prove to ourselves that we exist. But eventually the game becomes a hassle; it becomes more than a game and forces us to challenge ourselves more than we intended. It is like a hunter who, for the sport of practicing his shooting, decides to shoot one leg of a deer at a time. But the deer runs very fast, and it appears it might get away altogether. This becomes a total challenge to the hunter, who rushes after the deer, now trying to kill it completely, to shoot it in the heart. So the hunter has been challenged and feels defeated by his own game.

Emotions are like that. They are not a requirement for survival; they are a game we developed that went wrong at some point—it went sour. In the face of this predicament we feel terribly frustrated and absolutely helpless. Such frustration causes some people to fortify their relationship to the "other" by creating a god or other projections, such as saviors, gurus, and mahatmas. We create all kinds of projections as henchmen, hitmen, to enable us to redominate our territory. The implicit sense is that if we pay homage to such great beings, they will function as our helpers, as the guarantors of our ground.

So we have created a world that is bittersweet. Things are amusing but, at the same time, not so amusing. Sometimes things seem terribly funny but, on the other hand, terribly sad. Life has the quality of a game of ours that has trapped us. The setup of mind has created the whole thing. We might complain about the government or the economy of the country or the prime rate of interest, but those factors are secondary. The original process at the root of the problems is the competitiveness of seeing oneself only as a reflection of the other. Problematic situations arise automatically as expressions of that. They are our own production, our own neat work. And that is what is called mind.

According to the Buddhist tradition, there are eight types of consciousness and fifty-two types of conceptions and all kinds of other aspects of mind, about which we do not have to go into detail. All these aspects are based largely on the primeval dualistic approach. There are the spiritual aspects and the psychological aspects and all sorts of other aspects. All are bound up in the realm of duality, which is ego.

As far as meditation practice is concerned, in meditation we work on *this* thing, rather than on trying to sort out the problem from the outside. We work on the projector rather than the projection. We turn inward, instead of trying to sort out external problems of A, B, and C. We work on the creator of duality rather than the creation. That is beginning at the beginning.

According to the Buddhist tradition, there are three main aspects of mind, which in Tibetan are called sem, rikpa, and yi. The basic mind, the simple capacity for duality we have already described, is sem. Rikpa literally means "intelligence" or "brightness." In colloquial Tibetan, if you say that somebody has rikpa, it means he is a clever, sharp fellow. This sharpness of rikpa is a kind of side function that develops from the basic mind; it is a kind of lawyer's mentality that everybody develops. Rikpa looks at a problem from various angles and analyzes the possibilities of different ways of approaching it. It looks at a problem in every possible way—inside out and outside in.

The third aspect, yi, is traditionally classified as the sixth sense consciousness. The first five sense consciousnesses are sight, smell, taste, hearing, and touch, and the sixth is yi. Yi is mental sensitivity. It is associated with the heart and is a kind of balancing factor that acts as a switchboard in relation to the other five sense consciousnesses. When you see a sight and hear a sound at the same time, the sight and sound are synchronized by the sixth sense to constitute aspects of a single event. Yi does a kind of automatic synchronization, or automatic computerization, of the whole process of sense experience. You can see, smell, hear, taste, and feel all at the same time, and all of those inputs are coherently workable. They make sense to you because of yi.

So yi is a sort of central-headquarters switchboard which coordinates experience into a coherent whole. In some sense it is the most important of all the three aspects of mind. It is not as intelligent in the sense of manipulation as sem. Sem has something of a political attitude toward one's relationship with the world; it is somewhat strategy oriented. The sixth sense is more domestic in function. It just tries to maintain the coordination of experience so that all information comes through efficiently and there is no problem of being out of communication with anything that is going on. On the other hand, rikpa, which is the intelligence—the research worker, as it were—in this administration of mind, takes an overall view of one's whole situation. It surveys the relationship between mind and the sixth sense and tries to search out all the possibilities of where things are going wrong, where things might go wrong, where things have gone wrong, how things could be put right. This research worker does not have the power actually to take action on the level of external relations. It is more like an adviser to the State Department.

These three principles of sem, rikpa, and yi are the most important for us to be aware of at this point. Many other aspects of mind are described in the traditional literature, but these three will suffice for our present understanding.

We should consider this understanding not so much as something that we have been told and therefore we should believe in. The experience described here can actually be felt personally. It can be worked on, related to. A certain part of our experience is organized by basic mind, a certain part by the sixth sense, and a certain part by intelligence. In order to understand the basic functions of mindfulness-awareness practice, I think it is very important for us to understand and realize these complexities of mind.

A gigantic world of mind exists to which we are almost totally unexposed. This whole world—this tent and this microphone, this light, this grass, the very pair of spectacles that we are wearing—is made by mind. Minds made this up, put these things together. Every bolt and nut was put in by somebody-or-other's mind. This whole world is mind's world, the product of mind. This is needless to say; I am sure everybody knows this. But we might remind ourselves of it so that we realize that meditation is not an exclusive activity that involves forgetting this world and getting into something else. By meditating, we are dealing with the very mind that devised our eyeglasses and put the lenses in the rims, and the very mind that put up this tent. Our coming here is the product of our minds. Each of us has different mental manifestations, which permit others to identify us and say, "This guy is named so-and-so, this girl is named so-and-so." We can be identified as individuals because we have different mental approaches, which also shape the expressions of our physical features. Our physical characteristics are part of our mental activity as well. So this is a living world, mind's world. Realizing this, working with mind is no longer a remote or mysterious thing to do. It is no longer dealing with something that is hidden or somewhere else. Mind is right here. Mind is hanging out in the world. It is an open secret.

SEVEN

The Spiritual Battlefield

WHEN WE TALK ABOUT the word *mind,* we are talking about the different levels or states of consciousness. It does not have anything to do with higher levels of consciousness, whatever that might be. We are talking about mind and its different functions—the literal mind, or simple thought process that takes place in our everyday life: before you drive, you check that you have a key in your pocket; before you smoke cigarettes, you make sure that you have a match in your pocket; before you eat, you make sure the meal's been cooked, and little things like that. That kind of reasoning mind is intelligent, and it functions constantly.

Of course, depending on adulthood or adolescence or infanthood, that kind of logic begins to grow and become somewhat more sophisticated. As you become a grown-up person and after that, an old man or woman, your training as to how to work things out develops so that you don't run into unnecessary chaos. Our parents used to train us, and our elders used to criticize us, so that finally we think we've got our trip together, so to speak. If you are going to see somebody, you call them first and make sure they are at home or that it is convenient for you to visit. Simple little situations like that are the basic intelligence taking place.

In the business realm, domestic realm, and ordinary everyday life, whatever you do, there is a sense of priority. You know what you are going to do and everything is planned. Often people make lists of things in notebooks and put them in their pockets. You have your style of

69

making sure everything is okay and in order so that you don't run into any unexpected chaos and problems. The important thing is that things don't bounce back on you, that you don't lose control of them. So you make sure that everything is under control, that you have control over everything.

We do everything in a very meticulous way, very special, very careful. We would like to take care of ourselves as much as we can. Although we are abused and blamed by our elders or our parents saying, "You don't care for yourself. You should pull yourself together!" nevertheless we think that we are doing a pretty good job of ourselves, taking care of our food, housing, and clothes. Whatever way you would like to present yourself to the world, you just buy the appropriate clothes, appropriate haircut, appropriate way of speaking. All of that is a function of what is called mind. The Tibetan word for that [aspect of mind] is *sem*, which means "whatever can communicate to the object world."

Lodrö

Then we have another type of mind, which seems to be an entirely different angle—maybe not entirely, but relatively different—which is that we have whole avenues of unexplored areas of all kinds. We have memories of the past, we have expectations of the future, we might become somewhat proud of ourselves occasionally. We look for resources, maybe through the information that we learned in high school or at the first-grade level. We look back at our grammar, look back at our mathematics, look back at our science course. We look back and if we cannot find anything at those levels, we try to work our reasonable logic. Usually we can do a pretty good job of that. We can dig up some kind of intelligence or continuity.

We don't have to give up the whole thing as if we had a complete mental blockage. Sometimes we panic, thinking we might have a mental blockage. We are completely freaked out and thinking of dropping out of school. Maybe you have done so already or are about to do so. All kinds of things happen. The language of philosophy and metaphysics may be too complicated even to relate with. At the beginning, it turns out to be a mishmash of all kinds of jumbled-up large vocabulary which is almost incomprehensible. Particularly if you have an attitude against Greek and Latin, when you look back on our language, you are intimidated. You don't have any understanding about the languages we have used to understand philosophy, science, mathematics, or cosmology. But if you push yourselves hard enough and are diligent, you usually make a good job out of that. That's common knowledge. If you don't freak out and panic halfway through, if you push yourself hard enough and indulge yourself in the pride of becoming a scholar, one day you are going to make it. There is a strong possibility of doing that.

That particular stage is called *lodrö* in Tibetan, which means "intellect." The Sanskrit word is *mati. Lo* is "intelligence," *drö* is a sense of "warming up the intelligence." So there is a sense of warmth, or heat. You don't chicken out. When we talk about chickening out in this case, we are talking about when we feel cold, as when we say, "I'm getting cold feet about something or other." You don't get cold feet, but you get warm feet—warm head. Heat or warmth takes place. We feel we can exhaust ourselves and push ourselves to the limit, that we could pull ourselves up to understand and study. That is the lodrö level, which is intellect. We can *use* our mind from that point of view.

Rikpa

Then we have another layer of the definition of mind, which is beyond intellect. In Tibetan it is called *rikpa,* which means "a sense of fundamental intelligence." The Sanskrit word for rikpa is *vidya,* which means "the knowledge that can comprehend subtle scientific experiences and demonstrations." So rikpa is experience. It also could refer to particular disciplines, which could be regarded as rikpas of all kinds: the rikpa of scientific language or knowledge, or whatever.

Vidya, or rikpa, is intelligence, pointed intelligence. With this kind of intelligence, the mind becomes very sharp and so precise and completely proud of itself. It turns itself into a computer in some sense—not only in the sense of mathematics alone, but in the sense of self-respect. There is a sense of wholesomeness, of complete command of the discipline that you are studying. That sense of completely covering the whole area is rikpa. Rikpa, or vidya, can comprehend that fundamental sense of survival. What this particular computer is all about is appreciating that sense of survival, the sense of dualism, sense of behavior, sense of pattern—but fundamentally, it comprehends a sense of *being*.

Professor [Herbert] Guenther talks about analytical mind in his writings. That is a similar reference. There is a subtle sense of being which brings the actuality of a sense of being at the same time. Because you have subtle understanding, therefore you begin to relax more. You have less fear of your existence, your particular state of mind. Whatever goes on, everything is going to be okay. I can understand. I exist and you exist, so everything is going to be okay. There is nothing to panic about. Everything can be worked out mathematically and logically, or experientially. Things are workable. That fundamental, basic pride of ego is that there is something that is workable. That seems to be one of the basic points of mind.

The Five Skandhas

Then the mind is divided into another five types of process. I don't want to present you with a lot of figures, but I think this one is necessary for you to understand. There are five types of consciousness, which are called the five *skandhas*, or "heaps of collective things that happen in our mind." We don't exist from that point of view. Even our pride of self-existence, or sense of being, is by no means one entity. It is a collective entity of all kinds of things jumbled together. That is why the skandhas are called heaps. Maybe the closest to it, a free translation with a touch of humor, is "garbage." When we talk about disposing of the garbage we have collected, we don't usually talk about just one thing as garbage. We have collected lots of things to build such garbageness, that air of being garbage. Everything has been collected, and everything is related with each other—and it is decayed and smelly and unpleasant, and we want to get rid of that collective thing, or garbage. Skandhas are a similar situation.

The first skandha is called the skandha of *form*. It is a state of uncertainty. A sense of being is constantly operating in our state of mind, but we don't really want to commit ourselves to it. There is basic bewilderment and uncertainty as to who is this being. Who we are, what we are, is uncertain. We think we do exist, we think our name is so-and-so, we think we have an ego of some kind, but we actually have no idea how and why, what exactly is the case. We are completely uncertain experientially. Of course, logically we can explain it in complete detail, but that seems to be simply trying to reinforce ourselves constantly.

Actually, personally, experientially, when we look into our state of being, this me that seems to be the experiencer—*I* seem to be experiencing me-ness, and *I* seem to be experiencing thisness, *I* seem to be experiencing there is something happening here. As we say, something is cooking. But what is this? It could be all kinds of things. For one thing, I don't feel particularly good; therefore I feel very self-conscious myself. I feel my clumsiness and my uptightness—I did this and I did that and I don't feel so good—therefore maybe this is a product of sickness of some kind. Maybe I am freaking out. That is the popular answer that you get, that bad message—here was something, but it's gone rotten, therefore finally it's giving itself in. Of course not! That is the state of being *in any case,* all the time.

That self-existing Danish blue cheese is constantly fermenting itself, whether you pass store after store of it or customers bought it and put it in their refrigerators. That Danish blue cheese is still fermenting itself, growing fungus after fungus in it. It's taking place all the time. It is not because you behaved badly in a particular year, particular month, particular week, and therefore things have gone wrong. It has nothing to do with sudden chaos. It was the case all the time—or the basic reason that you don't really exist. And trying to make yourself exist is like the blue cheese trying to maintain itself by overgrowing its fungus and becoming dissolved into nothingness.

Ladies and gentlemen, that is the case. That is the perfect case. We don't exist as one whole being, one whole entity at all. We are collective. We are a collection of lots of things, and all of those entities are uncertain whether that entity exists or not. Every cell of this consciousness is defeating itself and uncertain of itself. So there is no sense of being, really, fundamentally. It's purely a dream we try to put together. That seems to be the basic point of the skandha of form.

Then we have the skandha of *feeling*. Having at least had some experience that if you have a bag of sand in your hand, the grains of sand are separate and perishable, still you try to hold on to the bag. That is the state of consciousness on the level of [feeling or] emotion. In this case, emotion is not a particularly highly developed state of emotion. It is emotion from the point of view of trying to feel out the textures of life. "If I get into this situation, will it be kind and harmonious? If I get into that situation, on the other hand, maybe it would be more friendly and harmonious to me." You are constantly looking further and further—for a strong and solid bag that you can put the grains of sand that you collected into, trying to hold them together. That chaos that exists, that no-entity that exists, is trying to create a bag or container, territory.

Out of that feeling comes *impulse*. In the same way that there is the desire to take an immediate leap, you could communicate with that, as if there is a message of your existence coming back to you: "This experience is very aggressive to you, trying to fight you; this experience is very yielding to you, you can include it in part of your system." We begin to celebrate that; we feel very good about it. We begin impulsively, very frivolously, to try to latch on to such information, such reinforcement coming to us. Whether it is aggressive or passive doesn't really matter. We are looking for some kind of reinforcement, some kind of response. That is the point of impulse.

Impulse leads us into what's known as *concept*. Concept is that we don't only try to name or conceptualize particular shades of impulse into that quality or this quality. Now we begin to realize that we have magnetized enough reinforcement as our friend, as our army of soldiers, and we begin to give them authority: "You be my secretary; you should be my general; you should be my lieutenant; you should be my colonel; you should be my soldier." You begin to label things so that you could protect *me, my existence*. Concepts of all kinds are being developed.

On the level of spirituality, a certain religious practice is very helpful, and that is going to reinforce my existence. A certain political move may be good to maintain myself. A certain domestic move might be good. Certain behavior and eating certain prescribed food might be good to maintain myself. Experiencing certain types of physical exercises might be good for me. Following particular disciplines would be good for me to experience. We can go haywire on that and collect so many things, from tuning in to cosmic consciousness and getting high and tripped out, to the point of being kind to your next-door neighbor. There is a long range of possibilities. Spiritually and domestically, there are all kinds of concept-oriented possibilities.

After that, there is what is known as *consciousness*. It is the state of consciousness that exists in the realm of past information and memories coming back to you and present thoughts coming to you all the time. In order to maintain ourselves, to at least hold on to our ego, we are trying to hold on to something that is there—which is subconscious gossip of all kinds, visual types of discursive thoughts, quotations coming back to you, past glimpses of experiences, and future expectations coming back to you. So the thought process acts as a kind of screening process for you: finally you have your castle, you have your soldiers, you have your army, and you have your subjects. You have become king of the ego realm. Everything is worked out from detail to detail. The emotions that exist in our state of being are related with the fifth skandha, the skandha of consciousness. Emotions of all kinds—such as anger, pride, passion, jealousy, and ignorance—are the highlights of the thought process. The less important thought process is the ordinary gossip that goes on through our mind. So finally we make ourselves a completely solid being out of nothingness.

The five-skandha process is by no means a personal experience we have already gone through. It is happening all the time. It is not that those experiences already happened and therefore all of that process is purely a myth at all, that once upon a time you had the first skandha and now you are at the level of the fifth skandha. What we are talking about here is a personal experience that happens constantly in our state of being. It becomes very real to us all the time. Every moment is a state of the first, second, third, fourth, and fifth skandha. That seems to be the basic point.

Meditation

The practice of meditation in relationship with that is to undo the skandhas step-by-step, constantly. Hold back the sense of frivolousness, but work with the inspiration. The first step of meditation practice is dealing with the fifth skandha of consciousness with the understanding that you have basic mistrust or confusion or bewilderment in your state of being—which is an understanding of the first skandha, the skandha of ignorance, bewilderment.

Understanding that and taking that as a basic standpoint, we then can work on the further skandha process, beginning with the fifth skandha.

It seems that there is no other way than the practice of meditation that you can deal with such an advanced subject, such a vast state of mind. There is no other way, absolutely no other way. That seems to be the only possibility. Otherwise, if you look into alternatives of all kinds, you may be able to find somebody who thought up some great idea in the corner of the universe, maybe a fantastic thing to try. However, its relationship to our state of being is uncertain. We are not quite certain.

This project is a huge project, an enormous project. It has been the battlefield between enlightenment and samsara for billions of years. It is the heart of spirituality. So it seems much better and more sensible at this point to get into that big project first, to try to deal with the greatest problem and difficulty that exists, rather than trying to pick up the crumbs first, saying to ourselves, "Well, let me try to pick the whole thing up before we get into this big thing"—because that means you are chickening out. You find all kinds of little things that you can tidy up to make sure that you don't have to get to the big project, which is a very big deal. So it seems to be necessary to take some kind of leap or jump. It takes a state of heroism. We are launching into the big project without discussing the little details.

Even asking how to do it, "What is the way?"—whenever we talk about how to do it and what is the way, we are talking in terms of saving problems and pain. We are trying to buy a pair of gloves, a pair of pliers, so that we don't have to strain our hands dealing with things. This particular approach is that we can use our naked hands to deal with our naked mind very directly, very precisely.

The attitude is not so much to destroy ego as a villain or evil force, but to work with that situation as a stepping-stone, as a process. At this point, the only material we have is ego. There is no other way to spirituality. Ego is the starting point. It is the only way, the only path we have in relating with spirituality and enlightenment. So in fact, from that point of view we should celebrate that we have ego. We have some hope of attaining enlightenment because we have ego, which is the starting point. That seems to be the attitude of the warrior.

EIGHT

The Birth of Ego

TRADITION IS NOT NECESSARILY a system developed by anybody, but tradition is the natural understanding of things as they are, which is based on why we see—and everybody agrees—that the sky is blue and the grass is green. Tradition is that way, rather than anybody's established law and order or personal opinion of any kind. Therefore tradition is common sense at its best.

Enlightenment is also the height of common sense. Therefore it is regarded as a tradition. It is also regarded as infallible, as true and powerful. It never can be contradicted. Nobody can say "the sky is green" or "the grass is red"—maybe some people, but basically speaking, nobody can say that [laughs]. That basic logic—that hot is hot, cold is cold, daytime is light, and nighttime is dark—is tradition. That is the truth and at the same time it is tradition.

There is no notion of ego at all at the beginning, but there is the notion of intelligence. That particular intelligence begins to look at others, at one's surroundings. Therefore one begins to develop awareness of other. Because others exist, therefore one begins to realize that one has to match up to them. It's like a matching fund: if you have $40,000, then you ask somebody else to match that $40,000, so we can raise $80,000 together. I hope my mathematics are right there. In turn, we might begin to raise $16,000 beyond that, because we have already raised the first matching fund. And then we go beyond, beyond, and beyond, raising lots of funds because of the original matching fund.

That's how it actually begins with the ego situation as well. You exist; therefore I exist, to begin with, very simply. And the reason we know you exist is because we have no idea at all! The first thing is that you don't exist; therefore others exist first. Ladies and gentlemen, I don't want to confuse you further, nonetheless it is quite a tempting discussion. When others exist, that is what you see first, before you realize you are there. Before you think you are there, you begin to see other very strongly. And then, since there is other, there are possibilities that the other should be conquered, subjugated, or seduced. So those two possibilities of aggression and passion begin to develop. And the third possibility is that, when others exist, and you think you can't match your fund with them, then you just ignore them completely, totally. Then ignorance begins to develop. "Couldn't care less" begins to develop. So those three possibilities—passion, aggression, and ignorance—begin to develop. We begin to feel that we have something substantial to hold on to. That is what's known as ego, so-called ego, which is based on a snowballing situation. There is nothing really such as ego, but there is a somewhat fictional idea of some kind based on reference point. Because of other, we begin to develop our selves. Therefore we begin to reject possibilities of gentleness and to develop one-upmanship, aggression, and what's known as "macho-ness," egohood. We begin to impose our possibilities of power over others: that when you see red, you should conquer the red; when you see blue, you should seduce the blue; and so forth. We begin to develop that particular system, which is completely unnecessary.

In turn, we begin to develop the notion that the sky, or heaven, is not vast enough. We begin to regard heaven as a pie, which we think we can cut up into pieces, eat it, chew it, swallow it, and taste it. In turn, we begin to shit it out, so to speak. So we cease to have greater vision of heaven altogether, sky altogether. Therefore we begin to fix our existence, based on either passion, aggression, or ignorance.

In order to overcome such egomaniac possibilities, we are talking in terms of developing greater vision. Nonetheless, in order to overcome ego, we have to undo our habitual patterns, which we have been developing for thousands of years, thousands of eons, up to this point. Such habitual patterns may not have any realistic ground, but nonetheless,

we have been accustomed to doing dirty work, so to speak. We are used
to our habitual patterns and neuroses at this point. We have been used
to them for such a long time that we end up believing they are the real
thing.

In order to overcome that, to begin with, we have to see our egolessness. That's quite a lengthy discussion we might have later on: seeing
the egolessness of oneself and the egolessness of other, and how we can
actually overcome our anxiety and pain, which in Buddhist terms is
known as freedom, liberation, freedom from anxiety. That is precisely
what nirvana means—relief. So as we will discuss other possibilities further, particularly the four types of obstacles, I would like to stop here.
Maybe we could have some discussion. Thank you very much.

QUESTION: Sir, you mentioned that first there's ego of other, and
then ego of self develops. But don't they arise simultaneously?

CHÖGYAM TRUNGPA RINPOCHE: Not necessarily. First there is
other. It is like when you wake up in the morning. The first thing you
are woken up by is the daylight. And if you fall in love with somebody,
you see your sweetheart first; after that you fall in love. You don't just
fall in love to begin with, because you don't have anyone to fall in love
with. So there is always *other* to begin with; then you have your things
going after that.

Q: Well, how is it then that to realize egolessness of other, you work
backward from the egolessness of oneself?

CTR: That's because you have done the whole thing already. Therefore you begin to realize you are the starter, not necessarily from the
point of view of logistics, particularly, but that you have a strong hold
on the whole thing. You fall in love with somebody, the other; therefore
you are as much in love with yourself. Therefore we start with *here*, to
overcome other. It's very basic and very ordinary. In other words, if you
are not supposed to take sugar, you see sugar first, but then *you* stop
taking it, which starts with you, right?

Q: I guess I just feel that there has to be some sort of echo, some sort of trace there, even to react to other.

CTR: Well, in any case, that's the point you perceive first: so first thought is other; second thought is this. Next the action is *that*, and then after that, *this*, which goes back and forth many times. But the first and only way to stop is to stop *this*.

Q: Rinpoche, I'd like to ask a question about last night's talk. When you spoke of basic goodness, fundamental goodness, and then went on to say that without white there's not black, without blue there's no red, and developed that dialectic; well, how about basic badness—the opposite of goodness? That brings to mind the Christian mystics' belief, Thomas Merton and others, of a basic sort of badness—original sin.

CTR: That's very interesting. When we talk about basic goodness, we are not talking about good as a goody-goody principle, but we are talking about the application and possibilities of fertility of any kind. Before even the notion of good or bad happens at all, there is basic goodness, which allows things to happen, allows things to manifest in their own right or at their own behest. The basic point of the Catholic tradition of original sin and punishment, I regard as purely a teaching technique, rather than a presentation of totality or an evolutionary principle, particularly. I could quite safely say that the notion of original sin came about at the beginning by people being told that "You are made out of the image of God himself." There are a lot of possibilities of going wrong with that, taking lots of pride and arrogance in that: "I'm made out of God." Nonetheless, even though you are made out of God, you do something wrong. So there is original sin, first sin, which comes from arrogance. That seems to be fine.

Q: Sir, when you were speaking of there being nothing—I think you said—the first thing was *other*, and then because of that, we have a sense of self. Is that still simple perception at that point, before you get into some kind of reverberation or echo back and forth? Is that the ego part or is it already ego at that point?

CTR: At the beginning? I don't think there is any ego at the beginning at all. When we first perceive the other, even then there is no ego. But then you begin to perceive *yourself* because of the other—that is the beginning of ego.

Q: Is it when you begin to perceive yourself, at that point?

CTR: Perceive oneself, yes. Linguistically, it goes: "am . . . I." "Am" is the other, "I" is me, which is a question, as we use the English language—"Am I?" That actually works quite fine with that principle. So first is "am." "Am what?" You may be able to liberate from that without saying "Am I?" Then you have just "am." After that we become "I." "Am *I* good?" "Am *I* bad?" It begins with a question, which is very interesting from the logic of philology, how the English language actually developed.

Q: Sir, I just wanted to ask when that happened, because there are all kinds of implications for children, for babies. Are you saying that that happened at some time in our development, or before we were born?

CTR: Well, we can't actually make sure children don't have ego. That's part of education. You have to have education and children have to have ego. We can't actually make sure that children are egoless. That goes along with a natural process. They have to learn to say, "I" and "no" and "yes." I think we can't do anything very much about that.

Q: But that state before recognizing *other,* is that something that we've ever had as people after we were born?

CTR: Well, as soon as the child sees *you,* that is *other.* Although you have been busy telling your child that there are other people so that children should be careful and not shit on them, not pee on them, that is something else, actually. That's used for the sake of convenience. But the others are always there. When children begin to open their eyes, they are aware of others, always there. So we can't really raise children in a very sneaky Buddhist style [laughter], so that they don't have any egos left.

Q: So we only really experience that egolessness through meditation practice . . .

CTR: That's right, that's the only way. First they have to know what not to have, to have what not to have, in order that they should have what they should have.

Q: It seems then very obvious that you can't get rid of ego, because you can't get rid of something that doesn't exist.

CTR: I beg your pardon?

Q: You can't really conquer something that doesn't exist.

CTR: Well, by realizing it doesn't exist, that *is* conquering, right?

Q: But in the sense of an aggressive act of conquering.

CTR: Well, you can't destroy it, particularly, but realizing it doesn't exist as such is at the level of conquering. Because there is so much myth in it, we are more or less destroying the myth, which is regarded as conquering.

Okay, ladies and gentlemen, we could stop this point. I would like to encourage you to take sitting practice more seriously. Since we are getting into much deeper subjects from now onward, it will be very important for you to sit and find out for yourselves what it is all about. Thank you very much.

NINE

The Development of Ego

I THINK IT WOULD BE best to start with something very concrete and realistic, the field we are going to cultivate. It would be foolish to study more advanced subjects before we are familiar with the starting point, the nature of ego. We have a saying in Tibet that, before the head has been cooked properly, grabbing the tongue is of no use. Any spiritual practice needs this basic understanding of the starting point, the material with which we are working.

If we do not know the material with which we are working, then our study is useless; speculations about the goal become mere fantasy. These speculations may take the form of advanced ideas and descriptions of spiritual experiences, but they only exploit the weaker aspects of human nature, our expectations and desires to see and hear something colorful, something extraordinary. If we begin our study with these dreams of extraordinary, "enlightening," and dramatic experiences, then we will build up our expectations and preconceptions so that later, when we are actually working on the path, our minds will be occupied largely with what *will be* rather than with what *is*. It is destructive and not fair to people to play on their weaknesses, their expectations and dreams, rather than to present the realistic starting point of what they are.

It is necessary, therefore, to start on what we are and why we are searching. Generally, all religious traditions deal with this material, speaking variously of alayavijnana or original sin or the fall of man or the basis of ego. Most religions refer to this material in a somewhat pejorative way, but I do not think it is such a shocking or terrible thing.

We do not have to be ashamed of what we are. As sentient beings we have wonderful backgrounds. These backgrounds may not be particularly enlightened or peaceful or intelligent. Nevertheless, we have soil good enough to cultivate; we can plant anything in it. Therefore, in dealing with this subject we are not condemning or attempting to eliminate our ego-psychology; we are purely acknowledging it, seeing it as it is. In fact, the understanding of ego is the foundation of Buddhism. So let us look at how ego develops.

Fundamentally there is just open space, the *basic ground,* what we really are. Our most fundamental state of mind, before the creation of ego, is such that there is basic openness, basic freedom, a spacious quality; and we have now and have always had this openness. Take, for example, our everyday lives and thought patterns. When we see an object, in the first instant there is a sudden perception which has no logic or conceptualization to it at all; we just perceive the thing in the open ground. Then immediately we panic and begin to rush about trying to add something to it, either trying to find a name for it or trying to find pigeonholes in which we could locate and categorize it. Gradually things develop from there.

This development does not take the shape of a solid entity. Rather, this development is illusory, the mistaken belief in a "self" or "ego." Confused mind is inclined to view itself as a solid, ongoing thing, but it is only a collection of tendencies, events. In Buddhist terminology this collection is referred to as the five skandhas or five heaps. So perhaps we could go through the whole development of the five skandhas.

The beginning point is that there is open space, belonging to no one. There is always primordial intelligence connected with the space and openness. *Vidya,* which means "intelligence" in Sanskrit—precision, sharpness, sharpness with space, sharpness with room in which to put things, exchange things. It is like a spacious hall where there is room to dance about, where there is no danger of knocking things over or tripping over things, for there is completely open space. We *are* this space, we are *one* with it, with vidya, intelligence, and openness.

But if we are this all the time, where did the confusion come from, where has the space gone, what has happened? Nothing has happened, as a matter of fact. We just became too active in that space. Because it is spacious, it brings inspiration to dance about; but our dance became a bit too active, we began to spin more than was necessary to express the space. At this point we became *self*-conscious, conscious that "I" am dancing in the space.

At such a point, space is no longer space as such. It becomes solid. Instead of being one with the space, we feel solid space as a separate entity, as tangible. This is the first experience of duality—space and I, I am dancing in this space, and this spaciousness is a solid, separate thing. Duality means "space and I," rather than being completely one with the space. This is the birth of "form," of "other."

Then a kind of blackout occurs, in the sense that we forget what we were doing. There is a sudden halt, a pause; and we turn around and "discover" solid space, as though we had never before done anything at all, as though we were not the creators of all that solidity. There is a gap. Having already created solidified space, then we are overwhelmed by it and begin to become lost in it. There is a blackout and then, suddenly, an awakening.

When we awaken, we refuse to see the space as openness, refuse to see its smooth and ventilating quality. We completely ignore it, which is called avidya. *A* means "negation," *vidya* means "intelligence," so it is "un-intelligence." Because this extreme intelligence has been transformed into the perception of solid space, because this intelligence with a sharp and precise and flowing luminous quality has become static, therefore it is called avidya, "ignorance." We deliberately ignore. We are not satisfied just to dance in the space but we want to have a partner, and so we choose the space as our partner. If you choose space as your partner in the dance, then of course you want it to dance with you. In order to possess it as a partner, you have to solidify it and ignore its flowing, open quality. This is avidya, ignorance, ignoring the intelligence. It is the culmination of the first skandha, the creation of ignorance-form.

In fact, this skandha, the skandha of ignorance-form, has three different aspects or stages which we could examine through the use of another metaphor. Suppose in the beginning there is an open plain without any mountains or trees, completely open land, a simple desert without any particular characteristics. That is how we are, what we are. We are very simple and basic. And yet there is a sun shining, a moon shining, and there will be lights and colors, the texture of the desert. There will be some feeling of the energy which plays between heaven and earth. This goes on and on.

Then, strangely, there is suddenly someone to notice all this. It is as if one of the grains of sand had stuck its neck out and begun to look around. We are that grain of sand, coming to the conclusion of our separateness. This is the "birth of ignorance" in its first stage, a kind of chemical reaction. Duality has begun.

The second stage of ignorance-form is called "the ignorance born within." Having noticed that one is separate, then there is the feeling that one has always been so. It is an awkwardness, the instinct toward self-consciousness. It is also one's excuse for remaining separate, an individual grain of sand. It is an aggressive type of ignorance, though not exactly aggressive in the sense of anger; it has not developed as far as that. Rather it is aggression in the sense that one feels awkward, unbalanced, and so one tries to secure one's ground, create a shelter for oneself. It is the attitude that one is a confused and separate individual, and that is all there is to it. One has identified oneself as separate from the basic landscape of space and openness.

The third type of ignorance is "self-observing ignorance," watching oneself. There is a sense of seeing oneself as an external object, which leads to the first notion of "other." One is beginning to have a relationship with a so-called "external" world. This is why these three stages of ignorance constitute the skandha of form-ignorance; one is beginning to create the world of forms.

When we speak of "ignorance" we do not mean stupidity at all. In a sense, ignorance is very intelligent, but it is a completely two-way intelligence. That is to say, one purely reacts to one's projections rather than just seeing what is. There is no situation of "letting be" at all, because one is ignoring what one is all the time. That is the basic definition of ignorance.

The next development is the setting up of a defense mechanism to protect our ignorance. This defense mechanism is feeling, the second skandha. Since we have already ignored open space, we would like next to feel the qualities of solid space in order to bring complete fulfillment to the grasping quality we are developing. Of course space does not mean just bare space, for it contains color and energy. There are tremendous, magnificent displays of color and energy, beautiful and picturesque. But we have ignored them altogether. Instead there is just a solidified version of that color; and the color becomes captured color, and the energy becomes captured energy, because we have solidified the whole space and turned it into "other." So we begin to reach out and feel the qualities of "other." By doing this we reassure ourselves that we exist. "If I can feel that out there, then I must be here."

Whenever anything happens, one reaches out to feel whether the situation is seductive or threatening or neutral. Whenever there is a sudden separation, a feeling of not knowing the relationship of "that" to "this," we tend to feel for our ground. This is the extremely efficient feeling mechanism that we begin to set up, the second skandha.

The next mechanism to further establish ego is the third skandha, perception-impulse. We begin to be fascinated by our own creation, the static colors and the static energies. We want to relate to them, and so we begin gradually to explore our creation.

In order to explore efficiently there must be a kind of switchboard system, a controller of the feeling mechanism. Feeling transmits its information to the central switchboard, which is the act of perception. According to that information, we make judgments, we react. Whether we should react for or against or indifferently is automatically determined by this bureaucracy of feeling and perception. If we feel the situation and find it threatening, then we will push it away from us. If we find it seductive, then we will draw it to us. If we find it neutral, we will be indifferent. These are the three types of impulse: hatred, desire, and stupidity. Thus perception refers to receiving information from the outside world and impulse refers to our response to that information.

The next development is the fourth skandha, concept. Perception-impulse is an automatic reaction to intuitive feeling. However, this kind of automatic reaction is not really enough of a defense to protect one's ignorance and guarantee one's security. In order to really protect and deceive oneself completely, properly, one needs intellect, the ability to name and categorize things. Thus we label things and events as being "good," "bad," "beautiful," "ugly," and so on, according to which impulse we find appropriate to them.

So the structure of ego is gradually becoming heavier and heavier, stronger and stronger. Up to this point, ego's development has been purely an action and reaction process; but from now on ego gradually develops beyond the ape instinct and become more sophisticated. We begin to experience intellectual speculation, confirming or interpreting ourselves, putting ourselves into certain logical, interpretive situations. The basic nature of intellect is quite logical. Obviously there will be the tendency to work for a positive condition: to confirm our experience, to interpret weakness into strength, to fabricate a logic of security, to confirm our ignorance.

In a sense, it might be said that the primordial intelligence is operating all the time, but it is being employed by the dualistic fixation, ignorance. In the beginning stages of the development of ego this intelligence operates as the intuitive sharpness of feeling. Later it operates in the form of intellect. Actually it seems that there is no such thing as the ego at all; there is no such thing as "I am." It is an accumulation of a lot of stuff. It is a "brilliant work of art," a product of the intellect which says, "Let's give it a name, let's call it something, let's call it 'I am'," which is very clever. "I" is the product of intellect, the label which unifies into one whole the disorganized and scattered development of ego.

The last stage of the development of ego is the fifth skandha, consciousness. At this level an amalgamation takes place: the intuitive intelligence of the second skandha, the energy of the third, and the intellectualization of the fourth combine to produce thoughts and emotions. Thus at the level of the fifth skandha we find the six realms* as well as the uncontrollable and illogical patterns of discursive thought.

This is the complete picture of ego. It is in this state that all of us have arrived at our study of Buddhist psychology and meditation.

---

*See chapter 12, "The Six Realms."

In Buddhist literature there is a metaphor commonly used to describe this whole process, the creation and development of ego. It speaks of a monkey locked in an empty house, a house with five windows representing the five senses. This monkey is inquisitive, poking its head out of each window and jumping up and down, up and down, restlessly. He is a captive monkey in an empty house. It is a solid house, rather than the jungle in which the monkey leapt and swung, rather than the trees in which he could hear the wind moving and the rustling of the leaves and branches. All these things have become completely solidified. In fact, the jungle itself has become his solid house, his prison. Instead of perching in a tree, this inquisitive monkey has been walled in by a solid world, as if a flowing thing, a dramatic and beautiful waterfall, had suddenly been frozen. This frozen house, made of frozen colors and energies, is completely still. This seems to be the point where time begins as past, future, and present. The flux of things becomes solid tangible time, a solid idea of time.

The inquisitive monkey awakens from his blackout, but he does not awaken completely. He awakens to find himself trapped inside of a solid, claustrophobic house with just five windows. He becomes bored, as though captured in a zoo behind iron bars, and he tries to explore the bars by climbing up and down. That he has been captured is not particularly important; but the idea of capture is magnified a thousand times because of his fascination with it. If one is fascinated, the sense of claustrophobia becomes more and more vivid, more and more acute, because one begins to explore one's imprisonment. In fact fascination is part of the reason he remains imprisoned. He is captured by his fascination. Of course at the beginning there was the sudden blackout which confirmed his belief in a solid world. But now having taken solidity for granted, he is trapped by his involvement with it.

Of course this inquisitive monkey does not explore all the time. He begins to become agitated, begins to feel that something is very repetitive and uninteresting, and he begins to become neurotic. Hungry for entertainment, he tries to feel and appreciate the texture of the wall, attempting to make sure that this seeming solidity is really solid. Then, assured that the space is solid, the monkey begins to relate to it by grasping it, repelling it, or ignoring it. If he attempts to grasp the space in order to possess it as his own experience, his own discovery, his own understanding, this is desire. Or, if the space seems a prison to him so that he tries to kick and batter his way out, fighting harder and harder, then this is hatred. Hatred is not just the mentality of destruction alone; but it is even more a feeling of defensiveness, defending oneself against claustrophobia. The monkey does not necessarily feel that there is an opponent or enemy approaching; he simply wants to escape his prison.

Finally the monkey might try to ignore that he is imprisoned or that there is something seductive in his environment. He plays deaf and dumb and so is indifferent and slothful in relation to what is happening around him. This is stupidity.

·To go back a bit, you might say that the monkey is born into his house as he awakens from the blackout. He does not know how he arrived in this prison, so he assumes he has always been there, forgetting that he himself solidified the space into walls. Then he feels the texture of the walls, which is the second skandha, feeling. After that, he relates to the house in terms of desire, hatred, and stupidity, the third skandha, perception-impulse. Then, having developed these three ways of relating to his house, the monkey begins to label and categorize it: "This is a window. This corner is pleasant. That wall frightens me and is bad." He develops a conceptual framework with which to label and categorize and evaluate his house, his world, according to whether he desires, hates, or feels indifferent to it. This is the fourth skandha, concept.

The monkey's development through the fourth skandha has been fairly logical and predictable. But the pattern of development begins to break down as he enters the fifth skandha, consciousness. The thought pattern becomes irregular and unpredictable and the monkey begins to hallucinate, to dream.

When we speak of "hallucination" or "dream," it means that we attach values to things and events which they do not necessarily have. We have definite opinions about the way things are and should be. This is projection: we project our version of things onto what is there. Thus we become completely immersed in a world of our own creation, a world of conflicting values and opinions. Hallucination, in this sense, is a misinterpretation of things and events, reading into the phenomenal world meanings which it does not have.

This is what the monkey begins to experience at the level of the fifth skandha. Having tried to get out and having failed, he feels dejected, helpless, and so he begins to go completely insane. Because he is so tired of struggling, it is very tempting for him to relax and let his mind wander and hallucinate. This is the creation of the six lokas or six realms. There is a great deal of discussion in the Buddhist tradition about hell beings, people in heaven, the human world, the animal realm, and other psychological states of being. These are the different kinds of projections, the dream worlds we create for ourselves.

Having struggled and failed to escape, having experienced claustrophobia and pain, this monkey begins to wish for something good, something beautiful and seductive. So the first realm he begins to hallucinate is the deva loka, the god realm, "heaven," a place filled with beautiful, splendid things. The monkey dreams of strolling out of his house, walking in luxuriant fields, eating ripe fruit, sitting and swinging in the trees, living a life of freedom and ease.

Then he also begins to hallucinate the asura realm, or the realm of the jealous gods. Having experienced the dream of heaven, the monkey wants to defend and maintain his great bliss and happiness. He suffers from paranoia, worrying that others may try to take his treasures from him, and so he begins to feel jealousy. He is proud of himself, has enjoyed his creation of the god realm, and this has led him into jealousy of the asura realm.

Then he also perceives the earthbound quality of these experiences. Instead of simply alternating between jealousy and pride, he begins to feel comfortable, at home in the "human world," the "earthy world." It is the world of just leading a regular life, doing things ordinarily, in a mundane fashion. This is the human realm.

But then the monkey also senses that something is a bit dull, something is not quite flowing. This is because, as he progresses from the realm of the gods to the realm of the jealous gods to the realm of human beings and his hallucinations become more and more solid, then this whole development begins to feel rather heavy and stupid. At this point he is born into the animal realm. He would rather crawl or moo or bark than enjoy the pleasure of pride or envy. This is the simplicity of the animals.

Then the process is intensified, and the monkey starts to experience a desperate feeling of starvation, because he really does not want to descend to any lower realms. He would like to return to the pleasure realms of the gods; so he begins to feel hunger and thirst, a tremendous feeling of nostalgia for what he remembers once having had. This is the realm of the hungry ghosts or *preta* realm.

Then there is a sudden losing of faith and the monkey begins to doubt himself and his world, begins to react violently. All this is a terrible nightmare. He realizes that such a nightmare could not be true and he begins to hate himself for creating all this horror. This is the dream of the hell realm, the last of the six realms.

Throughout the entire development of the six realms the monkey has experienced discursive thoughts, ideas, fantasies, and whole thought patterns. Up to the level of the fifth skandha his process of psychological evolution has been very regular and predictable. From the first skandha each successive development arose in a systematic pattern, like an overlay of tiles on a roof. But now the monkey's state of mind becomes very distorted and disturbed, as suddenly this mental jigsaw puzzle erupts and his thought patterns become irregular and unpredictable. This seems to be our state of mind as we come to the teachings and the practice of meditation. This is the place from which we must start our practice.

I think that it is very important to discuss the basis of the path—ego, our confusion—before we speak of liberation and freedom. If I were only to discuss the experience of liberation, that would be very dangerous. This is why we begin by considering the development of ego. It is a kind of psychological portrait of our mental states. I am afraid this has not been an especially beautiful talk, but we have to face the facts. That seems to be the process of working on the path.

TEN

The Basic Ground and the Eight Consciousnesses

WE COULD BEGIN by discussing the origin of all psychological problems, the origin of neurotic mind. This is a tendency to identify oneself with desires and conflicts related to a world outside. And the question is immediately there as to whether such conflicts actually exist externally or whether they are internal. This uncertainty solidifies the whole sense that a problem of some kind exists. What is real? What is not real? That is always our biggest problem. It is ego's problem.

The abhidharma, its whole contents with all the details, is based on the point of view of egolessness. When we talk about egolessness, that does not mean simply the absence of ego itself. It means also the absence of the projections of ego. Egolessness comes more or less as a by-product of seeing the transitory, transparent nature of the world outside. Once we have dealt with the projections of ego and seen their transitory and transparent nature, then ego has no reference point, nothing to relate to. So the notions of inside and outside are interdependent—ego began and its projections began. Ego managed to maintain its identity by means of its projections. When we are able to see the projections as nonsubstantial, ego becomes transparent correspondingly.

According to the abhidharma, ego consists, in one of its aspects, of eight kinds of consciousness. There are the six sense consciousnesses (thinking mind is regarded as a sixth sense). Then there is a seventh consciousness, which has the nature of ignorance, cloudiness, confusion.

This cloudy mind is an overall structure which runs right through the six sense consciousnesses. Each sense consciousness relates to this cloudy situation of not knowing exactly what you are doing. The seventh consciousness is an absence of precision. It is very blind.

The eighth consciousness is what you could call the common ground or the unconscious ground of all this. It is the ground that makes it possible for all the other seven to operate. This ground is different from the basic ground of which I have sometimes spoken, which is the background of all of existence and contains samsara and nirvana both. The eighth consciousness is not as basic as that ground. It is a kind of secondary basic level where confusion has already begun; and that confusion provides an accommodation for the other seven consciousnesses to operate.

There is an evolutionary process which starts from this unconscious ground, the eighth consciousness. The cloudy consciousness arises from that and then the six sense consciousnesses. Even the six senses evolve in a certain order according to the level of experiential intensity of each of them. The most intense level is attained with sight which develops last.

These eight types of consciousness can be looked at as being on the level of the first of the five skandhas, form. They are the form of ego, the tangible aspect of it. They constitute the ultimate grounding element of ego—as far as ego's grounding goes; which is not very far. Still, from a relative point of view, they do comprise something fixed, something definite.

I think to place this in perspective, it would be good to discuss briefly the basic ground—even though the abhidharma teaching does not talk very much about it—the all-prevading basic ground which we have just contrasted to the eighth consciousness. This basic ground does not depend on relative situations at all. It is natural being which just is. Energies appear out of this basic ground and those energies are the source of the development of relative situations. Sparks of duality, intensity, and sharpness, flashes of wisdom and knowledge—all sorts of things come out of the basic ground. So the basic ground is the source of confusion and also the source of liberation. Both liberation and confusion are that energy which happens constantly, which sparks out and then goes back to its basic nature, like clouds emerging from and disappearing back into the sky.

As for ego's type of ground, the eighth consciousness, that arises when the energy which flashes out of the basic ground brings about a sort of blinding effect, bewilderment. That bewilderment becomes the eighth consciousness, the basic ground for ego. Dr. Herbert Guenther* calls it "bewilderment-errancy." It is error that comes out of being bewildered—a kind of panic. If the energy were to go along with its own process of speed, there would be no panic. It is like driving a car fast; if you go along with the speed, you are able to maneuver accordingly. But if you suddenly panic with the thought that you have been going too fast without realizing it, you jam on the brakes and probably have an accident. Something suddenly freezes and brings the bewilderment of not knowing how to conduct the situation. Then actually the situation takes you over. Rather than just being completely one with the projection, the projection takes you over. Then the unexpected power of the projection comes back to you as your own doing, which creates extremely powerful and impressive bewilderment. That bewilderment acts as the basic ground, the secondary basic ground of ego, away from the primordial basic ground.

So ego is the ultimate relative, the source of all the relative concepts in the whole samsaric world. You cannot have criteria, notions of comparison, without ego. Things begin from ego's impression of relativity. Even nirvana begins that way. When ego began, nirvana, the other side of the same coin, began also. Without ego, there could be no such thing as nirvana or liberation, since a free state without relativity would be the case. So as ego develops, freedom and imprisonment begin to exist; and that relative situation contains the basic quality of ignorance.

The abhidharma does not talk very much about ignorance in the fundamental sense of ignoring oneself, but understanding this adds a further dimension to the teaching of the eight consciousnesses. Once there is bewilderment, then a sort of double take begins to happen of wanting to find out where you were, what you are, where you are at.

---

*A well-known translator of Buddhist texts.

But the nature of the bewilderment is that you do not want to go back and find out your original situation, you do not want to undo everything and go back. Since, with the bewilderment, you have created something to latch on to, you want to ignore the case history that led to that altogether. You want to make the best of the present moment and cling to it. That is the ignoring—refusing to go back because it is too painful, too frightening. As they say, "Ignorance is bliss." Ignoring of ignoring is bliss, at least from ego's point of view.

This understanding of ignorance comes from the mahamudra teaching of the vajrayana tradition. The difference between the abhidharma and basic sutra teachings on ignorance and the more direct and daring mahamudra teaching is that the sutra and abhidharma teaching relates to ignorance as a one-way process—bewilderment and grasping and the six sense consciousnesses develop and ignorance takes over. But in the vajrayana teaching, ignorance is seen not only from the angle of the development of ego, but also as containing the potential for wisdom. This is not mentioned at all in the lower teachings. But within the eight consciousnesses, including the six sense consciousnesses, there actually is the possibility of ignorance turning into wisdom. This is a key point because wisdom cannot be born from theory, it must be born from your actual state of mind which is the working basis for all spiritual practice.

The wisdom of dealing with situations as they are, and that is what wisdom is, contains tremendous precision that could not come from anywhere else but the physical situations of sight, smell, feelings, touchable objects, and sounds. The earthy situation of actual things as they are is the source of wisdom. You can become completely one with smell, with sight, with sound, and your knowledge *about* them ceases to exist; your knowledge becomes wisdom. There is nothing to know about things as an external educational process. You become completely one with them; complete absorption takes place with sounds, smells, sights, and so on. This approach is at the core of the mandala principle of the vajrayana teaching. At the same time, the great importance given to the six sense consciousnesses in the abhidharma has a similar concrete significance in its application to the practice of meditation and a person's way of relating to his experiences. Both levels of teaching put tremendous emphasis on direct relationship with the down-to-earth aspect of experience.

QUESTION: Can you say more about how the six senses connect up with meditation?

CHÖGYAM TRUNGPA RINPOCHE: The implication of the abhidharma teaching on the six senses for the practice of meditation is identifying yourself with sounds, touchable objects, feelings, breathing, and so on. The only way to develop sound meditative technique is to take something ordinary and use that. Unless you take something simple, the whole state of mind of your meditation will be based on the conflict of what is real and what is not and your relationship to that. This brings all kinds of complications and one begins to interpret these complications as psychological problems, neurotic problems, and to develop a sort of paranoid frame of mind in which what is going on represents to one much more than is actually there. So the whole idea is to start by relating to nonduality on a practical level, to step out of these paranoid conflicts of who in us is controlling whom. We should just get into actual things, sights and sounds as they are. A basic part of the tradition of meditation is using the sense perceptions as a way of relating with the earth. They are sort of middlemen for dealing with the earth. They contain neither good nor bad, are connected with neither spirituality nor samsara, nor anything at all. They are just neutral.

ELEVEN

Intellect

LOOKING AT THE GENERAL PICTURE of psychology as we get involved with more and more complex patterns of the skandhas, it becomes clear that it is a pattern of duality developing stronger and stronger. The general tendency of ego is uncertain at the beginning how to establish its link with the world, its identity, its individuality. As it gradually develops more certainty, it finds new ways of evolving; it becomes more and more brave and daring in stepping out and exploring new areas of possible territory or new ways of interpreting and appropriating the world available around it. So it is a pattern of a kind of stubborn bravery making itself more complicated patterns. The fourth skandha, samskara, is a continuation of this pattern. It could be called "intellect." Samskara is intellect in the sense of being the intelligence which enables the ego to gather further territory, further substance, more things.

Samskara does not seem to have any good exact literal translation or equivalent term. The basic literal meaning has the sense of a gathering or accumulation, meaning specifically a tendency to accumulate a collection of mental states as territory. These mental states are also physical; they are mind/body states. So samskara has quite a lot of varieties of different types of classifications of mental patterns. But this is not just a series of names in a list; the patterns are related to each other in an evolutionary pattern they form together as well. The various aspects of samskara are mind/body patterns that have different emotional qualities to them. There are fifty-one general types of these. I do not think we have to go to great lengths here to cover all the types in detail, but let me try to give you some rough idea of them.

There are certain samskaric patterns or attitudes associated with virtue or religion or goodness, which we could say are the expression of basic intelligence, buddha nature; but they also are appropriated by ego and so help constitute its natural tendency of spiritual materialism. There are eleven of these types of good attitudes or tendencies among which are surrendering or faith, awareness, discipline, equanimity, absence of passion, absence of anger, absence of ignorance, humbleness or shyness, a tendency of nonviolence, a tendency of energy or effort or bravery. An important point here is that nobody had to invent these religious or spiritual ideas, but they are a natural part of human psychology. There is a natural sort of gentleness, absence of aggression and passion, a hardworkingness and a nonviolence; and these tendencies develop as part of samskara.

Altogether the general nature of this particular group of samskaric tendencies is absence of aggression. They are a sort of dharma mind. By dharma we generally mean passionlessness in the sense of nongrasping or nonclinging. That which has a context of passion is nondharma. So these tendencies are characterized by an absence of speed or aggression. These thoughts are generally considerate thoughts. They contain a certain amount of conscience. They do not just exist arbitrarily, but they have some reason to be. For one thing there is the absence of aggression, openness, and for another thing this kind of mind/body pattern carries a high degree of awareness of the situations outside oneself. In other words, there is an absence of ego in the superficial sense; in the ordinary sense they are not egocentric. But this is not a question of the fundamental ego; such thoughts are not necessarily egoless. This depends on the user of the thoughts. However, the general quality of them reminds one of a good person, considerate and not egocentric in the ordinary, popular sense.

Then there are the six opposite types of thoughts, the egocentric thoughts. They are ignorance, passion, anger, pride, doubt, and dogmatism. These are considered to be the absence of the virtues of the kinds of thoughts we have just discussed.

Here again, the ignorance in question is quite different from the basic ignorance that constitutes the ego, that sort of fundamental ignoring of oneself. The ignorance we are referring to here is the source of all the other kinds of evil thoughts, those which are not considerate, those which are the absence of the spiritual type of thoughts. They are characterized by a sort of sudden boldness which acts without considering the situation. They just act out on impulse, without any sharpness and precision. They are wholly intoxicated by a sense of whatever one wants to accomplish, so they act brashly without seeing one's relationship to the situation.

And passion here is also actual passion rather than the fundamental passion of grasping. It is the actualized passion of desire. Whereas the fundamental passion is sort of an innate quality of grasping within ego, this is the actual active movement of grasping. On this level, passion, hatred, and pride are all directly active qualities rather than fundamental ones. Pride here is the sense of preservation of oneself in relationship with others. Doubt is the sense of not having enough security in oneself. Dogmatic belief is clinging to a particular discovery that we have made and not wanting to let go of that idea because we feel if we did there would be nothing left to cling to.

Dogmatic belief itself is divided into different types, for instance, the philosophical beliefs in eternalism and nihilism. Eternalism is the idea that everything in the worldly or spiritual spheres is continuous and permanent. Part of this is the notion that there is a permanent significance to our experience, that there could be an ultimate and permanent salvation within the realm of the experiencer. Nihilism is the opposite extreme. It is the fatalistic belief that everything has no value and is meaningless. Another of the dogmatic tendencies is the false belief in morality or a particular discipline that one follows, dogmatically clinging to it and trying to hold on to it as a philosophical view.

Then there are four types of neutral thoughts; sleep or slothfulness, intellectual speculation, remorse, and knowing. These are neutral in that they can fit in with different patterns, the virtuous or the evil ones. Theoretical intellectual speculation is obviously neutral in that it functions in the service of either kind of tendency. Remorse is, in a sense, a questioning process that further clarifies a situation: you have done something wrong and feel doubtful about it, which leads you on a kind of a process of rediscovery. That is neutral in that that process of discovery could function in relation to either the considerate or egocentric patterns. Knowing is a neutral state because when you learn something you have a sudden open attitude to it at that moment, before you get into the next double take, that is, before ego appropriates it as territory. There is that momentary open feeling of acceptance of whatever you heard, whatever you understood. Sleep or slothfulness is of course also neutral, since it also contains that kind of possibility of belonging to an open or egocentric context.

Now all these kinds of thoughts are further classified according to the instinctive behavior connected with them, how you project them to the world outside. That is done on the basis either of hatred or desire. Hatred in this case is a natural kind of aggression, and desire is a natural kind of longing. All these thoughts are motivated either by instinctive hatred or desire. Even apparently good thoughts—compassion, for instance—on the level of ego, would have an underlying sense of hatred or of passion. It depends on whether the thought process is originally based on speed or on a kind of starvation, which is the need to grasp something, to absorb oneself in something. In addition, some thought patterns have ignorance as underlying motivation.

The study of the samskara skandha can teach us that all the phenomena of human psychology, whatever types of thought patterns occur, all have these good and bad and indifferent qualities. Therefore we cannot really define one thought pattern as being the only right kind—there is no such thing as absolute aggression or absolute passion or absolute ignorance. All of them have the slight tendency of the other types. The whole idea is that therefore one cannot just condemn one type and totally accept another, even if it is the spiritual virtuous type of thoughts. They are questionable as all the other kinds of thoughts are questionable. That is a very important point—nothing is really to be condemned or accepted.

On a larger scale, the whole pattern of the five skandhas is also neutral, rather than belonging particularly to samsara or particularly to nirvana. But one thing is quite certain and constant about the five skandhas—they manufacture karmic chain reactions all the time. That is always, unquestionably the case. The karmic pattern cannot exist by itself, of course, since karma is not some other kind of entity that exists independently. Karma is a creative process which brings results, which in turn sow seeds of further results. It is like an echo process. You shout and your voice bounces back on you as well as being transmitted to the next wall, and it goes on and on. And the skandhas could be said to be the horse of karma. The speed of karma is based on the five skandhas. The natural, sort of chemical cause-and-effect pattern remains within karma, but the speed that the cause-and-effect process requires in order to function is the skandhas.

Perhaps we should have some discussion.

QUESTION: Did you say that samskara is associated with neither nirvana nor samsara, or does that apply to all the skandhas?

CHÖGYAM TRUNGPA RINPOCHE: To all the skandhas.

Q: I am puzzled. You said that the good thoughts were somehow related to buddha nature.

CTR: Well, that is easily possible if there is underlying non-ego intonation. That is why they are called "good," because they are not acts of egomania in the literal, ordinary sense.

Q: Is there more possibility of buddha nature in the states of mind classified as good?

CTR: Yes, there is a tendency to be closer to the awakened state; but at the same time, if this good is being used by the ego, then it is not necessarily absolute good, but just sort of pseudo.

Q: Then does it make any difference? That is, is it worthwhile trying to be a good boy?

CTR: I don't think so, necessarily. Although these are said to be the good or virtuous ones, at the same time such thoughts—patience or nonviolence or whatever—cannot happen by themselves. They have to have the tinges of passion or aggression, as I said, or also ignorance. They cannot constitute the basic energy that has to go along with them for them to occur. So there is no such thing as 100 percent good in any case. The tendencies are sort of lighter and heavier rather than good and bad.

Q: So they all come from ignorance, hatred, and passion.
CTR: They do, yes.

Q: Is the thread that connects them perception, feeling, or both?
CTR: Quite likely it is form, the basic continuity, ignorance which makes it all possible for the others to continue.

Q: I am confused about speed. There is a speed of the ego being driven, going faster and faster, and there is also a speed of universal energy, or something like that. There is an evil speed, but is there also another speed?
CTR: Well, I'm trying to use the word *speed* as a sort of driving aggression. But that is not purely pejorative. This has a positive aspect as well, because any kind of aggression, any kind of movement that there is, always has neutral energy that goes along with it. So speed is pure force, neutral force, which could be used for different purposes. The buddha wisdom of the accomplishment of all actions could also be called speed. But somehow that speed is not based on a target. Once you have a target, or criteria in terms of reaching somewhere from somewhere else, that makes the whole pattern of speed destructive. In the case of the energy without a target, without a relativity notion, that speed just happens and returns just by its own nature. It fulfills actions completely and comes back. Fulfilling action in this case follows no criterion or model at all. The speed or energy just goes out and gets into the natural situation spontaneously, tries to bring the natural situation to its fullest state, and then comes back. This kind of speed does not behave in a dictatorial way. In the case of ego speed, you have a blueprint of what should be happening and you put out speed accordingly. You try to control situations or remold them. That leads to disappointment and confusion.

Q: Wouldn't these dogmatic beliefs that you talked about be beliefs on the part of the "watcher"?

CTR: If there is any tendency to get yourself to believe in certain ideas, particularly philosophical views such as the nihilistic and eternalistic ones, automatically you are aware of the learning process as being separate. You watch yourself in the process of learning and you use particular tools of different intensity, either gentle or aggressive ones, to bring about a certain result. So all these beliefs are, in a sense, very deliberate. It is a natural mind process, but that mind process involves deliberate effort—deliberately trying to be good or deliberately trying to grasp something and so on. Except for those four types of neutral patterns, sleep and the others: they are not deliberate, which is why they are called neutral. They can be influenced by either kind of deliberate thought pattern. They do not contain a watcher, actually. That is why they can be used by either kind of deliberate pattern or by ego or non-ego. But the rest of them are fixed and definite.

Q: That watcher is the one that puts everything that happens into one of those categories, these samskaric types of good and bad?

CTR: Yes. That is actually a certain kind of common sense developed by the establishment of ego. By this time ego is so well established, it has developed its own regulations and rules. This becomes a kind of common sense. You see, as long as you are involved with the ego game, all these flashes of different types of thoughts and concepts are not independent ones at all. They are purely dependent on central headquarters. You always have to report back to yourself in order to define the ground. That is the watcher. And the watcher has a watcher as well.

Q: Would you say a little more about doubt? You have just spoken of doubt as one of the negative factors. Previously you spoke about it in a positive sense.

CTR: We have been speaking about two quite different kinds of doubt. One kind is one of the six types of egocentric thoughts. This is ego's tendency to have doubt in terms of the motivation of passion and anger and ignorance. It is a fear of losing ground, bewilderment rather than doubt in the intelligent sense. We fear we may not be able to survive to implement our ambition properly in the perspective of our egohood. It is more a fear of losing ground than doubt.

The intelligent doubt we were talking of earlier on is a general sense that there is something wrong all the way through, a sort of seed of doubt which runs right through the whole five-skandha process. It is the quality of inquisitiveness, questioning mind, which is the seed of the awakened state of mind. This is doubt or intelligence which is not protecting anything. It is purely questioning rather than trying to serve either the ego or non-ego state. It is purely a process of critical view which goes on all the time.

Q: I'm trying to relate this to inner experience. Associations present themselves and many other things, you know, when one is sitting quietly. And then a thought happens and there is belief in it, and then remembrances, and then an impulse arises that this that I am believing is not necessarily so. It may or may not be. I think what I'm trying to ask is—is this still within the pattern of attachment, or is this in the direction of something a little bit more free?

CTR: You see, it is very difficult to make a generalization. What you described in itself could have different implications. The implication could be based solely on a survival notion; it could be based on a sense of "maybe that one, maybe this one"—ego jockeying for better position. Or there is the possibility of something else—that it could be based on a kind of open mind. It depends on your own relation to that.

Q: You mentioned slothfulness as one of the neutral states. But I'm wondering in what way slothfulness can be converted. Can it be channeled in the same way that intellectual speculation could be clarified?

CTR: Slothfulness could be sort of infiltrated rather than changed or channeled into something else. This is because slothfulness does not contain any definite thing. It is a process, a mind process of not having made up your mind quite. You are just trundling along. So it has the possibility of being infiltrated from any side.

Q: Is slothfulness synonymous with laziness?

CTR: Well, the words are complicated in this case. Somehow, laziness could have the connotation of being a naughty boy. You know, you should be doing thus and such, but you do not want to do it. Sort of stubbornness. But sloth is a general heaviness or being sleepy rather than game playing. It is just quite honest and ordinary.

Q: So in that sense slothfulness may be more receptive, more passive?

CTR: Precisely, yes. It could be infiltrated.

Q: Insofar as you try to be something, wouldn't it be better to try to be honest instead of trying to be good? I mean honest in the sense of trying to abandon one's own pretensions. Isn't that the basic effort?

CTR: I think so, yes. The reason why all these different types of thoughts and ideas are being introduced, in fact, is so you can see your psychological picture in its fullest perspective; so that you do not try to regard one kind of thought pattern as good or another as bad; so that instead you regard everything directly and simply.

Q: I have an image going in my mind that the skandhas represent energy which has gone astray from the awakened state of mind and has taken on various forms. Lost from its origin, it has taken on various forms. And it seems that spiritual understanding would return this lost energy to its origin in some way. But also I have another image from when you pointed out that ignorance or form has the thread that holds all the skandhas together. Then I had the thought that it is simply a question of not operating ignorance—if you're just completely still and unconcerned, it will all just blow away. And the two images give me two different attitudes. Do you know what I mean?

CTR: Well, I don't see any difficulties there. Ignorance is the binding factor for all the skandhas in their minute detail, but ignorance cannot exist by itself without relative situations, and the relative situation of ignorance is the awakened state of mind, intelligence, which makes ignorance survive or die. In other words, we could say that the awakened state of mind is the thread also, in the same way as ignorance. It runs right through the skandhas.

Q: But it wouldn't be awakened if it were doing that.

CTR: It would. Ignorance feels the other, the awakened, aspect of the polarity; therefore it does what it does. There is some subtle relationship ignorance is making with the basic intelligence of buddha nature. So ignorance in this case is not stupid, it is intelligent. The term for ignorance in Tibetan, *marikpa,* means "not seeing, not perceiving." That means deciding to not perceive, deciding to not see, deciding to not look. Ignorance makes certain decisions and, having already made a certain decision, it tries to maintain it no matter what. Often it faces a hard time keeping to that decision constantly, because one act of ignorance cannot persist indefinitely, once and for all. Ignorance also is based on sparks or flashes of ignorance operating on some ground, and the space between two sparks of ignoring is the intelligence that this process of ignorance is operating on. It also happens occasionally that ignorance forgets to maintain its own quality, so that the awakened state comes through. So a meditative state of mind occurs spontaneously when, occasionally, the efficiency of ego's administration breaks down.

Q: Would you explain what you mean by "ego game"?

CTR: I think that is what we have been discussing all along in this seminar. The basic notion of ego is the notion of survival, trying to maintain oneself as "I am," as an individual. Now, as we just said, there is a tendency for the coherency of that occasionally to break down. Therefore one needs to find all sorts of means of confirmation, of confirming a coherent, consistent me, a solid me. Sometimes, quite knowingly, ego has to play a game as though nothing had gone wrong with it. It pretends seeing through ego never happened, even though secretly it knows better. So ego trying to maintain itself leaves one in the strange position of trying to indoctrinate oneself oneself. This is a false pursuit, of course. But even knowing it is false does not particularly help, because ego says, "That's not the point. We have to go on trying to learn to survive, playing this survival game of grasping, using any situation available in the present moment as part of the survival technique." This involves a power game as well, because at a certain stage the defense mechanisms you have set up become more powerful than you are. They become overwhelming. Then, when you become used to the over-whelming quality of the defense mechanisms, when, for a moment, they are absent, you feel very insecure. That game of polarities goes on and on. On the whole, ego's game is played in terms of ignoring what is really happening in a situation. You constantly, quite stubbornly want to see it from your point of view rather than seeing what really is hap-pening there.

Q: You spoke of an aerial view of the five skandhas. Do you mean that with the development of meditative awareness one can actually ex-perience the development of the skandhas in oneself?

CTR: Yes. In a sudden glimpse of awareness, or in the meditation state, one sees the ups and downs of the five skandhas taking place and dissolving and beginning to develop again. The whole idea of meditation is to develop what is called the "wisdom eye," prajnaparamita, transcen-dental knowledge. It is knowledge, information, at the beginning, when you are watching yourself and beginning to discover yourself, your psy-chological pattern. And suddenly, strangely, that watching process be-gins to become an experiencing process, and it is, in a sense, already under control. That does not mean to say that the development of the five skandhas would stop taking place. The skandhas happen continu-ously until they are transmuted into what are called the "five tathaga-thas," the five types of awakened being.*

You see, at the beginning, we have to develop a very sharp, precise mind to see what we are. There is no other way of sharpening our intelligence. Pure intellectual speculation would not sharpen it at all, because there you have to introduce so much stuff that blunts, that overclouds. The only way to do it is just to leave intelligence as it is with the help of some technique. Then the intelligence begins to learn how to relax and wait and allow what takes place to reflect in it. The learning

---

*See chapter 13, "The Five Buddha Families."

process becomes a reflection rather than creating things. So waiting and letting what arises reflect on the intelligence is the meditation practice. It is like letting a pond settle down so the true reflection can be seen. There are already so many mental activities going on constantly. Adding further mental activities does not sharpen the intelligence. The only way is just to let it develop, grow.

Q: One of the six virtues of a bodhisattva is energy, exertion, virya. It is hard to relate this virtue to the idea of a waiting intelligence.

CTR: Well, I don't see any problem, particularly. You see, hard-workingness or exertion does not necessarily mean doing a lot of things. Waiting in itself could be very hard work, being is very hard work, and there are so many temptations not to do it.

Q: Is there some kind of recognizable psychological event which particularly reinstigates the process of the five skandhas and of karma?

CTR: Yes, that is what is called "immediate cause." It is the immediate occasion of getting into a further series of events, a sort of stepping-stone. Each transition has to have that intermediary moment. Even in sleep, things function that way. It allows you to fall asleep from being awake and in dreams pushes you from one moment to the next and then makes it possible to wake up again. Karma is dependent on that state, that immediate cause. It cannot function without it. The whole idea of the practice of meditation is that in the meditative state you do not have that impulse. That suddenness or the restlessness is automatically freed; that sudden impulse has been transmuted into a flowing process through the use of a meditation technique. That is how the process of meditation can be a way of preventing planting the seed of karma.

Q: It seems from what you've been saying that meditation in action has something to do with going very much into detail. You know something and then something else comes along. And if you could just go along with the new detail—

CTR: Well, you see, awareness meditation, meditation in action, is a process of providing fundamental space. If you are talking or you are doing things, you are acting within that open space, so that no sudden jolt can happen, no sudden confusion or slothfulness. That abrupt click-ing-in of confusion can only take place if the ground, the basic space, has been solidified or frozen. The karmic process operates against that kind of solidified background. Whereas once that solidity has been transformed by acknowledging there is another aspect to it, which is open space, openness, then any kind of sudden, impulsive movement is accommodated. Still the same rhythm goes on, but that rhythm now becomes a creative movement. The rhythm of events goes on, but you appreciate that that rhythm can happen on space, on open ground, and this brings back the message of meditation happening.

So you do not have to force yourself to remember; you do not have to try to maintain your awareness all the time. Once you are open to the challenges of the moment, somehow, as you go along, the situation flashes back the awareness to you. So a perpetually creative process de-velops and a highly precise one as well.

Q: If the situation doesn't flash back that awareness, then you for-get it?

CTR: Well, you disown whatever comes up. If you try to keep up and maintain something, then it does not work. It becomes your prod-uct. You are solidifying space again.

Q: Getting back to that transitional moment in karma where it picks up impetus. Do I understand that as you advance in your meditation you notice this happening, and by noticing it you can prevent it from happening and control the situation? Once you notice what leads to the karma, do the steps become much easier to deal with?

CTR: Well, that is rather tricky. Theoretically you might know the whole thing, but once you have the idea in mind that what you are doing is trying to escape from karma, to step out of it, then you are already double-crossed. The probability then is that you are automati-cally not in the right state of mind. That is why is it important in medita-tion practice that at the time of practice everything is just based on a simple technique, but with no aim or object at all, none whatsoever. You give up everything and go along with the practice entirely and fully.

Q: Yes, but in daily situations I think it's helpful to deliberately notice things happening.

CTR: You see, in daily situations if you have a certain understanding of the continuous quality of the meditation experience happening all the time, then, without trying to meditate deliberately, you automatically know the daily situation, because the daily situation comes to you as a reminder, rather than your trying to go to it. It becomes a personal creative process.

Q: You have talked about creation at times as though it were an ego process and now as though it is more egoless. Could you clarify?

CTR: I suppose you could say there is ego creation and true creation. I think here again it is a question of whether or not the notion of competitive achievement, of an ideal or a goal, is present. With ego's notion of creation you have a concept that you want to achieve something, and you try to match your situation with your idea of the actual achievement. You compare the dream and the actual reality. That is not the ultimate creative process but a one-way creation which can wear out. You build a thing and it is finished; you have no further place to go. It is a very limited inspiration.

Whereas in the other approach without aim and object, without a goal in mind, each situation acts as an end in itself. You go along with that situation and that situation brings another, it opens another possibility. So you go along and along. That is like the experience of the bodhisattva developing through the bhumis, or stages of development. When one bhumi is accomplished, he goes on to the next. Without ambition, he goes on and on. He had no desire for enlightenment, but one situation leads to another until he finds himself enlightened one day. This is because he relates to things on their own merits rather than in terms of a goal of his own.

So the ambition type of a creation is that of ego. The alternative is to have natural appreciation of creation itself rather than being fascinated by what *you* are doing. If you tune in to the actual creativity itself, the delight of it, it becomes an inexhaustible source of creativity.

TWELVE

The Six Realms

Self-Absorption

THE SIX REALMS, the different styles of samsaric occupation, are referred to as realms, in the sense that we dwell within a particular version
of reality. We are fascinated with maintaining familiar surroundings,
familiar desires and longings, so as not to give in to a spacious state of
mind. We cling to our habitual patterns because confusion provides a
tremendously familiar ground to sink into as well as a way of occupying
ourselves. We are afraid to give up this security and entertainment,
afraid to step into open space, into a meditative state of mind. The
prospect of the awakened state is very irritating because we are uncertain
how to handle it, so we prefer to run back to our prison rather than
release ourselves from it. Confusion and suffering become an occupation, often quite secure and delightful.

The six realms are: the realm of the gods, the realm of the jealous
gods, the human realm, the animal realm, the realm of the hungry
ghosts, and the hell realm, The realms are predominantly emotional
attitudes toward ourselves and our surroundings, emotional attitudes
colored and reinforced by conceptual explanations and rationalizations.
As human beings we may, during the course of a day, experience the
emotions of all the realms, from the pride of the god realm to the hatred
and paranoia of the hell realm. Nonetheless, a person's psychology is
usually firmly rooted in one realm. This realm provides us with a style
of confusion, a way of entertaining and occupying ourselves so as not

to have to face our fundamental uncertainty, our ultimate fear that we may not exist.

The fundamental occupation of the god realm is mental fixation, a meditative absorption of sorts, which is based upon ego, upon the spiritually materialistic approach. In such meditation practice the meditator maintains himself by dwelling upon something. The particular topic of meditation, no matter how seemingly profound, is experienced as a solid body rather than as transparent. This practice of meditation begins with a tremendous amount of preparation or "self-development." Actually the aim of such practice is not so much to create the solidity of a place to dwell as it is to create the self-consciousness of the dweller. There is tremendous self-consciousness, which of course reaffirms the meditator's existence.

You do get dramatic results from such practice, if you are successful at it. One might experience inspiring visions or sounds, seemingly profound mental states, physical bliss and mental bliss. All sorts of "altered states of consciousness" could be experienced or manufactured through the efforts of self-conscious mind. But these experiences are imitations, plastic flowers, man-made, manufactured, prefabricated.

We could dwell on a technique as well—repetition of a mantra or visualization. One is not completely absorbed into the visualization or mantra, but instead *you* are visualizing, *you* are repeating the mantra. Such practice, based upon "me," that "I am doing this," is once again the development of self-consciousness.

The realm of the gods is realized through tremendous struggle, is manufactured out of hope and fear. The fear of failure and the hope of gain builds up and up and up to a crescendo. One moment you think you are going to make it and the next moment you think you are going to fail. Alternation between these extremes produces enormous tension. Success and failure mean so much to us—"This is the end of me," or "This is my achievement of ultimate pleasure."

Finally we become so excited that we begin to lose the reference points of our hope and fear. We lose track of where we are and what we were doing. And then there is a sudden flash in which pain and pleasure become completely one and the meditative state of dwelling on the ego dawns upon us. Such a breakthrough, such a tremendous achievement. And then pleasure begins to saturate our system, psychologically and physically. We no longer have to care about hope or fear. And quite possibly we might believe this to be the permanent achievement of enlightenment or union with God. At that moment everything we see appears to be beautiful, loving; even the most grotesque situations of life seem heavenly. Anything that is unpleasant or aggressive seems beautiful because we have achieved oneness with ego. In other words, ego lost track of its intelligence. This is the absolute, ultimate achievement of bewilderment, the depths of ignorance—extremely powerful. It is a kind of spiritual atomic bomb, self-destructive in terms of compassion, in terms of communication, in terms of stepping out of the bondage of ego. The whole approach in the realm of the gods is stepping in and in and in, churning out more and more chains with which to bind oneself. The more we develop our practice, the more bondage we create. The scriptures cite the analogy of the silkworm which binds itself with its own silk thread until it finally suffocates itself.

Actually we have only been discussing one of two aspects of the realm of the gods, the self-destructive perversion of spirituality into materialism. However, the god realm's version of materialism can also be applied to so-called worldly concerns in the search for extreme mental and physical pleasure, the attempt to dwell on seductive goals of all kinds: health, wealth, beauty, fame, virtue, whatever. The approach is always pleasure-oriented, in the sense of maintenance of ego. What characterizes the realm of the gods is the losing track of hope and fear. And this might be achieved in terms of sensual concerns as well as in terms of spirituality. In both cases, in order to achieve such extraordinary happiness, we must lose track of who is searching and what is the goal. If our ambition expresses itself in terms of worldly pursuits, at first we search for happiness, but then we begin to enjoy the struggle toward happiness as well and we begin to relax into our struggle. Halfway to achieving absolute pleasure and comfort we begin to give in and make the best of our situation. The struggle becomes an adventure and then a vacation or holiday. We are still on our adventurous journey to the actual ultimate goal, but at the same time we consider every step along the way a vacation, a holiday.

So the realm of the gods is not particularly painful, in itself. The pain comes from the eventual disillusionment. You think you have achieved a continually blissful state, spiritual or worldly; you are dwelling on that. But suddenly something shakes you and you realize that what you have achieved is not going to last forever. Your bliss becomes shaky and more irregular, and the thought of maintenance begins to reappear in your mind as you try to push yourself back into your blissful state. But the karmic situation brings you all kinds of irritations and at some stage you begin to lose faith in the continuity of the blissful state. A sudden violence arises, the feeling that you have been cheated, that you cannot stay in this realm of the gods forever. So when the karmic situation shakes you and provides extraordinary situations for you to relate with, the whole process becomes profoundly disappointing. You condemn yourself or the person who put you into the god realm or what brought you out of it. You develop anger and disappointment because you think you have been cheated. You switch into another style of relating to the world, another realm. This is what is called samsara, which literally means "continual circle," "whirlpool," the ocean of confusion which spins around again and again and again, without end.

Paranoia

The dominant characteristic of the next realm, the jealous god or asura realm, is paranoia. If you are trying to help someone who has an asura mentality, they interpret your action as an attempt to oppress them or infiltrate their territory. But if you decide not to help them, they interpret that as a selfish act: you are seeking comfort for yourself. If you present both alternatives to them, then they think you are playing games with them. The asura mentality is quite intelligent: it sees all the hidden corners. You think that you are communicating with an asura face-to-face, but in actual fact he is looking at you from behind your back. This intense paranoia is combined with an extreme efficiency and accuracy which inspires a defensive form of pride. The asura mentality is associated with wind, speeding about, trying to achieve everything on the spot, avoiding all possibilities of being attacked. It is trying constantly to attain something higher and greater. To do so one must watch out for every possible pitfall. There is no time to prepare, to get ready to put your action into practice. You just act without preparation. A false kind of spontaneity, a sense of freedom to act develops.

The asura mentality is preoccupied with comparison. In the constant struggle to maintain security and achieve greater things, you need points of reference, landmarks to plot your movement, to fix your opponent, to measure your progress. You regard life situations as games, in the sense of there being an opponent and yourself. You are constantly dealing with them and me, me and my friends, me and myself. All corners are regarded as being suspicious or threatening, therefore one must look into them and be careful of them. But one is not careful in the sense of hiding or camouflaging oneself. You are very direct and willing to come out in the open and fight if there is a problem or if there is a plot or a seeming plot against you. You just come out and fight face-to-face, trying to expose the plot. At the same time that one is going out in the open and facing the situation, one is distrustful of the messages that you receive from the situation, so you ignore them. You refuse to accept anything, refuse to learn anything that is presented by outsiders, because everyone is regarded as the enemy.

Passion

Passion is the major occupation in the human realm. Passion in this sense is an intelligent kind of grasping in which the logical reasoning mind is always geared toward the creation of happiness. There is an acute sense of the separateness of pleasurable objects from the experiencer resulting in a sense of loss, poverty, often accompanied by nostalgia. You feel that only pleasurable objects can bring you comfort and happiness, but you feel inadequate, not strong or magnetic enough for the objects of pleasure to be drawn naturally into your territory. Nevertheless, you try actively to draw them in. This often leads to a critical attitude toward other people. You want to magnetize the best qualities, the most pleasurable, most sophisticated, most civilized situations.

This kind of magnetizing is different from that of the asura realm, which is not as selective and intelligent. The human realm by comparison involves a high degree of selectivity and fussiness. There is an acute sense of having your own ideology and your own style, of rejecting things not your style. You must have the right balance in everything. You criticize and condemn people who do not meet your standards. Or else you might be impressed by someone who embodies your style or is superior to you at achieving it, someone who is very intelligent and has very refined taste, who leads a pleasurable life and has the things you would like to have. It might be a historical figure or a mythological figure or one of your contemporaries who has greatly impressed you. He is very accomplished and you would like to possess his qualities. It is not simply a matter of being jealous of another person; you want to draw that person into your territory. It is an ambitious kind of jealousy in that you want to equal the other person.

The essence of the human realm is the endeavor to achieve some high ideal. Often those who find themselves in this realm will have visions of Christ or Buddha or Krishna or Muhammad or other historical figures who have tremendous meaning for them because of their achievements. These great personages have magnetized everything that one could possibly think of—fame, power, wisdom. If they wanted to become rich they could do so because of their enormous influence over other people. You would like to be like them—not necessarily better than but at least equal to them. Often people have visions in which they identify themselves with great politicians, statesmen, poets, painters, musicians, scientists, and so forth. There is a heroic attitude, the attempt to create monuments, the biggest, greatest, historical monument. This heroic approach is based on fascination with what you lack. When you hear of someone who possesses remarkable qualities, you regard them as significant beings and yourself as insignificant. This continual comparing and selecting generates a never-ending procession of desires.

The human mentality places a strong emphasis on knowledge, learning, and education, on collecting all kinds of information and wisdom. The intellect is most active in the human realm. There is so much going on in your mind as a result of having collected so many things and having planned so many projects. The epitome of the human realm is to be stuck in a huge traffic jam of discursive thought. You are so busy thinking that you cannot learn anything at all. The constant churning out of ideas, plans, hallucinations, and dreams is a quite different mentality from that of the god realm. There you are completely absorbed in a blissful state, a kind of self-stuck sense of satisfaction. In the jealous god realm you are completely drunk on competitiveness; there is less possibility of thought happening because your experiences are so strong that they overpower you, hypnotize you. In the case of the human realm there are more thoughts happening. The intellectual or logical mind becomes much more powerful so that one is completely overwhelmed by the possibilities of magnetizing new situations. Thus one tries to grasp new ideas, new strategies, relevant case histories, quotations from books, significant incidents that have occurred in one's life, and so on, and one's mind becomes completely full of thought. The things that have been recorded in the subconscious play back continually, much more so than in the other realms.

So it is a very intellectual realm, very busy and very disturbing. The human mentality has less pride than the mentalities of the other realms. In the other realms you find some occupation to hang on to and derive satisfaction from, whereas in the human realm there is no such satisfaction. There is a constant searching, constant looking for new situations or attempts to improve given situations. It is the least enjoyable state of mind because suffering is not regarded as an occupation nor as a way of challenging oneself; rather it is a constant reminder of ambitions created out of suffering.

Stupidity

The descriptions of the different realms are related to subtle but distinct differences in the ways individuals handle themselves in daily life—how they walk, talk, write letters, the way they read, eat, sleep, and so on. Everyone tends to develop a style which is peculiar to them. If we hear a tape recording of our voice or see a videotape or movie of ourselves, we are often shocked to see our style as someone else sees it. It feels extremely alien. Usually we find other people's point of view irritating or embarrassing.

Blindness to our style, to how others see us, is most acute in the animal realm. I am not speaking of literally being reborn as an animal but of the animal quality of mind, a mentality which stubbornly pushes forward toward predetermined goals. The animal mentality is very serious. It even makes humor into a serious occupation. Self-consciously trying to create a friendly environment, a person will crack jokes or try to be funny, intimate, or clever, However, animals do not really smile or laugh; they just behave. They may play, but it is unusual for animals to actually laugh. They might make friendly noises or gestures, but the subtleties of a sense of humor are absent. The animal mentality looks directly ahead, as if wearing blinders. It never looks to the right or left but very sincerely goes straight ahead, trying to reach the next available situation, continually trying to adjust situations to make them conform to its expectations.

The animal realm is associated with stupidity: that is, preferring to play deaf and dumb, preferring to follow the rules of available games rather than redefine them. Of course, you might try to manipulate your perception of any given game, but you are really just following along, just following your instinct. You have some hidden or secret wish that you would like to put into effect, so when you come to obstacles, to irritations, you just push forward, regardless of whether or not you may hurt someone or destroy something of value. You just go out and pursue whatever is available and if something else comes up, you take advantage of that as well and pursue it.

The ignorance or stupidity of the animal realm comes from a deadly honest and serious mentality which is quite different from the bewilderment of the basic ignorance of the first skandha. In animal ignorance you have a certain style of relating to yourself and refuse to see that style from other points of view. You completely ignore such possibilities. If somebody attacks you or challenges your clumsiness, your unskilled way of handling a situation, you find a way of justifying yourself, find a rationale to keep your self-respect. You are not concerned with being truthful as long as your deception can be maintained in front of others. You are proud that you are clever enough to lie successfully. If you are attacked, challenged, criticized, you automatically find an answer. Such stupidity can be very clever. It is ignorance or stupidity in the sense that you do not see the environment around you, but you see only your goal and only the means to achieve that goal, and you invent all kinds of excuses to prove that you are doing the right thing.

The animal mentality is extremely stubborn, but this stubbornness can be sophisticated as well and quite skillful and ingenious, but without a sense of humor. The ultimate sense of humor is a free way of relating with life situations in their full absurdity. It is seeing things clearly, including self-deception, without blinders, without barriers, without excuses. It is being open and seeing with panoramic vision rather than trying to relieve tension. As long as humor is used as a way to relieve tension or self-consciousness or pressure, then it is the humor of the animal realm, which is actually extremely serious. It is a way of looking for a crutch. So the essence of the animal style is to try to fulfill your desires with extreme honesty, sincerity, and seriousness. Traditionally, this direct and mean way of relating with the world is symbolized by the pig. The pig does not look to the right or left but just sniffs along, consuming whatever comes in front of its nose; it goes on and on and on, without any sense of discrimination—a very sincere pig.

Whether we are dealing with simple domestic tasks or highly sophisticated intellectual projects, we can have an animal style. It does not matter whether the pig eats expensive sweets or garbage. What is important is *how* he eats. The extreme animal mentality is trapped in a continual, self-contained, self-justifying round of activity. You are not able to relate with the messages given to you by your environment. You do not see yourself mirrored by others. You may be dealing with very intellectual matters, but the style is animal since there is no sense of humor, no way of surrendering or opening. There is a constant demand to move on from one thing to the next, regardless of failures or obstacles. It is like being a tank that rolls along, crushing everything in its path. It does not matter if you run over people or crash through buildings—you just roll along.

Poverty

In the preta or hungry ghost realm one is preoccupied with the process of expanding, becoming rich, consuming. Fundamentally, you feel poor. You are unable to keep up the pretense of being what you would like to be. Whatever you have is used as proof of the validity of your pride, but it is never enough, there is always some sense of inadequacy.

The poverty mentality is traditionally symbolized by a hungry ghost who has a tiny mouth, the size of the eye of a needle, a thin neck and throat, skinny arms and legs, and a gigantic belly. His mouth and neck are too small to let enough food pass through them to fill his immense belly, so he is always hungry. And the struggle to satisfy his hunger is very painful since it is so hard to swallow what he eats. Food, of course, symbolizes anything you may want—friendship, wealth, clothes, sex, power, whatever.

Anything that appears in your life you regard as something to consume. If you see a beautiful autumn leaf falling, you regard it as your prey. You take it home or photograph it or paint a picture of it or write in your memoirs how beautiful it was. If you buy a bottle of Coke, it is exciting to hear the rattlings of the paper bag as you unpack it. The sound of the Coke spilling out of the bottle gives a delightful sense of thirst. Then you self-consciously taste it and swallow it. You have finally managed to consume it—such an achievement. It was fantastic; you brought the dream into reality. But after a while you become restless again and look for something else to consume.

You are constantly hungering for new entertainment—spiritual, intellectual, sensual, and so on. Intellectually you may feel inadequate and decide to pull up your socks by studying and listening to juicy, thoughtful answers, profound, mystical words. You consume one idea after another, trying to record them, trying to make them solid and real. Whenever you feel hunger, you open your notebook or scrapbook or a book of satisfying ideas. When you experience boredom or insomnia or depression, you open your books, read your notes and clippings and ponder over them, draw comfort from them. But this becomes repetitive at some point. You would like to re-meet your teachers or find new ones. And another journey to the restaurant or the supermarket or the delicatessen is not a bad idea. But sometimes you are prevented from taking the trip. You may not have enough money, your child gets sick, your parents are dying, you have business to attend to, and so on. You realize that when more obstacles come up, then that much more hunger arises in you. And the more you want, the more you realize what you cannot get, which is painful.

It is painful to be suspended in unfulfilled desire, continually searching for satisfaction. But even if you achieve your goal then there is the frustration of becoming stuffed, so full that one is insensitive to further stimuli. You try to hold on to your possession, to dwell on it, but after a while you become heavy and dumb, unable to appreciate anything. You wish you could be hungry again so you could fill yourself up again. Whether you satisfy a desire or suspend yourself in desire and continue to struggle, in either case you are inviting frustration.

Anger

The hell realm is pervaded by aggression. This aggression is based on such a perpetual condition of hatred that one begins to lose track of whom you are building your aggression toward as well as who is being aggressive toward you. There is a continual uncertainty and confusion. You have built up a whole environment of aggression to such a point that finally, even if you were to feel slightly cooler about your own anger and aggression, the environment around you would throw more aggression at you. It is like walking in hot weather; you might feel physically cooler for a while, but hot air is coming at you constantly so you cannot keep yourself cool for long.

The aggression of the hell realm does not seem to be your aggression, but it seems to permeate the whole space around you. There is a feeling of extreme stuffiness and claustrophobia. There is no space in which to breathe, no space in which to act, and life becomes overwhelming. The aggression is so intense that, if you were to kill someone to satisfy your aggression, you would achieve only a small degree of satisfaction. The aggression still lingers around you. Even if you were to try to kill yourself, you would find that the killer remains; so you would not have managed to murder yourself completely. There is a constant environment of aggression in which one never knows who is killing whom. It is like trying to eat yourself from the inside out. Having eaten yourself, the eater remains, and he must be eaten as well, and so on and so on. Each time the crocodile bites his own tail, he is nourished by it; the more he eats, the more he grows. There is no end to it.

You cannot really eliminate pain through aggression. The more you kill, the more you strengthen the killer who will create new things to be killed. The aggression grows until finally there is no space: the whole environment has been solidified. There are not even gaps in which to look back or do a double take. The whole space has become completely filled with aggression. It is outrageous. There is no opportunity to create a watcher to testify to your destruction, no one to give you a report. But at the same time the aggression grows. The more you destroy, the more you create.

Traditionally aggression is symbolized by the sky and earth radiating red fire. The earth turns into a red hot iron and space becomes an environment of flame and fire. There is no space to breathe any cool air or feel coldness. Whatever you see around you is hot, intense, extremely claustrophobic. The more you try to destroy your enemies or win over your opponents, the more you generate resistance, counteraggression bouncing back at you.

In the hell realm we throw out flames and radiations which are continually coming back to us. There is no room at all in which to experience any spaciousness or openness. Rather there is a constant effort, which can be very cunning, to close up all the space. The hell realm can only be created through your relationships with the outside world, whereas in the jealous god realm your own psychological hang-ups could be the material for creating the asura mentality. In the hell realm there is a constant situation of relationship; you are trying to play games with something and the attempt bounces back on you, constantly recreating extremely claustrophobic situations; so that finally there is no room in which to communicate at all.

At that point the only way to communicate is by trying to recreate your anger. You thought you had managed to win a war of one-upmanship, but finally you did not get a response from the other person; you one-upped him right out of existence. So you are faced only with your own aggression coming back at you and it manages to fill up all the space. One is left lonely once more, without excitement, so you seek another way of playing the game, again and again and again. You do not play for enjoyment, but because you do not feel protected nor secure enough. If you have no way to secure yourself, you feel bleak and cold, so you must rekindle the fire. In order to rekindle the fire you have to fight constantly to maintain yourself. One cannot help playing the game; one just finds oneself playing it, all the time.

THIRTEEN

The Five Buddha Families

THE TANTRIC DISCIPLINE of relating to life is based on what are known as the five buddha principles, or the five buddha families. These principles are traditionally known as families because they are an extension of ourselves in the same way that our blood relations are an extension of us: we have our daddy, we have our mommy, we have our sisters and brothers, and they are all part of our family. But we could also say that these relatives are principles: our motherness, our fatherness, our sisterness, our brotherness, and our me-ness are experienced as definite principles that have distinct characteristics. In the same way, the tantric tradition speaks of five families: five principles, categories, or possibilities.

Those five principles or buddha families are called vajra, ratna, padma, karma, and buddha. They are quite ordinary. There is nothing divine or extraordinary about them. The basic point is that at the tantric level people are divided into particular types: vajra, ratna, padma, karma, and buddha. We constantly come across members of every one of the five families—people who are partially or completely one of those five. We find such people all through life, and every one of them is a fertile person, a workable person who could be related with directly and personally. So, from the tantric point of view, by relating directly with all the different people we encounter, we are actually relating with different styles of enlightenment.

The buddha family, or families, associated with a person describes his or her fundamental style, that person's intrinsic perspective or stance in perceiving the world and working with it. Each family is associated with both a neurotic and an enlightened style. The neurotic expression of any buddha family can be transmuted into its wisdom or enlightened aspect. As well as describing people's styles, the buddha families are also associated with colors, elements, landscapes, directions, seasons—with any aspect of the phenomenal world.

The first buddha family is the vajra family, which literally means the family of sharpness, crystallization, and indestructibility. The term *vajra* is superficially translated as "diamond," but that is not quite accurate. Traditionally, vajra is a celestial precious stone that cuts through any other solid object. So it is more than a diamond; it is complete indestructibility. The vajra family is symbolized by the vajra scepter, or *dorje* in Tibetan. This vajra scepter or superdiamond has five prongs, which represent relating to the five emotions: aggression, pride, passion, jealousy, and ignorance. The sharp edges or prongs of the vajra represent cutting through any neurotic emotional tendencies; they also represent the sharp quality of being aware of many possible perspectives. The indestructible vajra is said to be like a heap of razor blades: if we naively try to hold it or touch it, there are all kinds of sharp edges that are both cutting and penetrating. The notion here is that vajra corrects or remedies any neurotic distortion in a precise and sharp way.

In the ordinary world, the experience of vajra is perhaps not as extreme as holding razor blades in our hand, but at the same time, it is penetrating and very personal. It is like a sharp, cutting, biting-cold winter. Each time we expose ourselves to the open air, we get frostbite instantly. Intellectually vajra is very sharp. All the intellectual traditions belong to this family. A person in the vajra family knows how to evaluate logically the arguments that are used to explain experience. He can tell whether the logic is true or false. Vajra family intellect also has a sense of constant openness and perspective. For instance, a vajra person could view a crystal ball from hundreds of perspectives, according to where it was placed, the way it was perceived, the distance from which he was looking at it, and so forth. The intellect of the vajra family is not just encyclopedic; it is sharpness, directness, and awareness of perspectives. Such indestructibility and sharpness are very personal and very real.

The neurotic expression of vajra is associated with anger and intellectual fixation. If we become fixated on a particular logic, the sharpness of vajra can become rigidity. We become possessive of our insight, rather than having a sense of open perspective. The anger of vajra neurosis could be pure aggression or also a sense of uptightness because we are so attached to our sharpness of mind. Vajra is also associated with the element of water. Cloudy, turbulent water symbolizes the defensive and aggressive nature of anger, while clear water suggests the sharp, precise, clear reflectiveness of vajra wisdom. In fact, vajra wisdom is traditionally called the mirrorlike wisdom, which evokes this image of a calm pond or reflecting pool.

Incidentally, the use of the term *vajra* in such words as *vajrayana*, *vajra master*, and *vajra pride* does not refer to this particular buddha family, but simply expresses basic indestructibility.

The next buddha family is ratna. Ratna is a personal and real sense of expanding ourselves and enriching our environment. It is expansion, enrichment, plentifulness. Such plentifulness could also have problems and weaknesses. In the neurotic sense, the richness of ratna manifests as being completely fat, or extraordinarily ostentatious, beyond the limits of our sanity. We expand constantly, open heedlessly, and indulge ourselves to the level of insanity. It is like swimming in a dense lake of honey and butter. When we coat ourselves in this mixture of butter and honey, it is very difficult to remove. We cannot just remove it by wiping it off, but we have to apply all kinds of cleaning agents, such as cleanser and soap, to loosen its grasp.

In the positive expression of the ratna family, the principle of richness is extraordinary. We feel very rich and plentiful, and we extend ourselves to our world personally, directly, emotionally, psychologically, even spiritually. We are extending constantly, expanding like a flood or an earthquake. There is a sense of spreading, shaking the earth, and creating more and more cracks in it. That is the powerful expansiveness of ratna.

The enlightened expression of ratna is called the wisdom of equanimity, because ratna can include everything in its expansive environment. Thus ratna is associated with the element of earth. It is like a rotting log that makes itself at home in the country. Such a log does not want to leave its home ground. It would like to stay, but at the same time, it grows all kinds of mushrooms and plants and allows animals to nest in it. That lazy settling down and making ourselves at home, and inviting other people to come in and rest as well, is ratna.

The next family is padma, which literally means "lotus flower." The symbol of the enlightened padma family is the lotus, which grows and blooms in the mud, yet still comes out pure and clean, virginal and clear. Padma neurosis is connected with passion, a grasping quality and a desire to possess. We are completely wrapped up in desire and want only to seduce the world, without concern for real communication. We could be a hustler or an advertiser, but basically, we are like a peacock. In fact, Amitabha Buddha, the buddha of the padma family, traditionally sits on a peacock, which represents subjugating padma neurosis. A person with padma neurosis speaks gently, fantastically gently, and he or she is seemingly very sexy, kind, magnificent, and completely accommodating: "If you hurt me, that's fine. That is part of our love affair. Come toward me." Such padma seduction sometimes becomes excessive and sometimes becomes compassionate, depending on how we work with it.

Padma is connected with the element of fire. In the confused state, fire does not distinguish among the things it grasps, burns, and destroys. But in the awakened state, the heat of passion is transmuted into the warmth of compassion. When padma neurosis is transmuted, it becomes fantastically precise and aware; it turns into tremendous interest and inquisitiveness. Everything is seen in its own distinct way, with its own particular qualities and characteristics. Thus the wisdom of padma is called discriminating-awareness wisdom.

The genuine character of padma seduction is real openness, a willingness to demonstrate what we have and what we are to the phenomenal world. What we bring to the world is a sense of pleasure, a sense of promise. In whatever we experience, we begin to feel that there is lots of promise. We constantly experience a sense of magnetization and spontaneous hospitality.

This quality of padma is like bathing in perfume or jasmine tea. Each time we bathe, we feel refreshed, fantastic. It feels good to be magnetized. The sweet air is fantastic and the hospitality of our host is magnificent. We eat the good food provided by our host, which is delicious, but not too filling. We live in a world of honey and milk, in a very delicate sense, unlike the rich but heavy experience of the ratna family. Fantastic! Even our bread is scented with all kinds of delicious smells. Our ice cream is colored by beautiful pink lotus-like colors. We cannot wait to eat. Sweet music is playing in the background constantly. When there is no music, we listen to the whistling of the wind around our padma environment, and it becomes beautiful music as well. Even though we are not musicians, we compose all kinds of music. We wish we were a poet or a fantastic lover.

The next family is the karma family, which is a different kettle of fish. In this case we are not talking about karmic debts, or karmic consequences; karma in this case simply means "action." The neurotic quality of action or activity is connected with jealousy, comparison, and envy. The enlightened aspect of karma is called the wisdom of all-accomplishing action. It is the transcendental sense of complete fulfillment of action without being hassled or pushed into neurosis. It is natural fulfillment in how we relate with our world. In either case, whether we relate to karma family on the transcendental level or the neurotic level, karma is the energy of efficiency.

If we have a karma family neurosis, we feel highly irritated if we see a hair on our teacup. First we think that our cup is broken and that the hair is a crack in the cup. Then there is some relief. Our cup is not broken; it just has a piece of hair on the side. But then, when we begin to look at the hair on our cup of tea, we become angry all over again. We would like to make everything very efficient, pure, and absolutely clean. However, if we do achieve cleanliness, then that cleanliness itself becomes a further problem: We feel insecure because there is nothing to administer, nothing to work on. We constantly try to check every loose end. Being very keen on efficiency, we get hung up on it.

If we meet a person who is not efficient, who does not have his life together, we regard him as a terrible person. We would like to get rid of such inefficient people, and certainly we do not respect them, even if they are talented musicians or scientists or whatever they may be. On the other hand, if someone has immaculate efficiency, we begin to feel that he is a good person to be with. We would like to associate ourselves exclusively with people who are both responsible and clean-cut. However, we find that we are envious and jealous of such efficient people. We want others to be efficient, but not more efficient than we are.

The epitome of karma family neurosis is wanting to create a uniform world. Even though we might have very little philosophy, very little meditation, very little consciousness in terms of developing ourselves, we feel that we can handle our world properly. We have composure, and we relate properly with the whole world, and we are resentful that everybody else does not see things in the same way that we do. Karma is connected with the element of wind. The wind never blows in all directions but it blows in one direction at a time. This is the one-way view of resentment and envy, which picks on one little fault or virtue and blows it out of proportion. With karma wisdom, the quality of resentment falls away but the qualities of energy, fulfillment of action, and openness remain. In other words, the active aspect of wind is retained so that our energetic activity touches everything in its path. We see the possibilities inherent in situations and automatically take the appropriate course. Action fulfills its purpose.

The fifth family is called the buddha family. It is associated with the element of space. Buddha energy is the foundation or the basic space. It is the environment or oxygen that makes it possible for the other principles to function. It has a sedate, solid quality. Persons in this family have a strong sense of contemplative experience, and they are highly meditative. Buddha neurosis is the quality of being spaced-out rather than spacious. It is often associated with an unwillingness to express ourselves. For example, we might see that our neighbors are destroying our picket fence with a sledgehammer. We can hear them and see them; in fact, we have been watching our neighbors at work all day, continuously smashing our picket fence. But instead of reacting, we just observe them and then we return to our snug little home. We eat our breakfast, lunch, and dinner and ignore what they are doing. We are paralyzed, unable to talk to outsiders.

Another quality of buddha neurosis is that we couldn't be bothered.

Our dirty laundry is piled up in a corner of our room. Sometimes we use our dirty laundry to wipe up spills on the floor or table and then we put it back on the same pile. As time goes on, our dirty socks become unbearable, but we just sit there.

If we are embarking on a political career, our colleagues may suggest that we develop a certain project and expand our organization. If we have a buddha neurosis, we will choose to develop the area that needs the least effort. We do not want to deal directly with the details of handling reality. Entertaining friends is also a hassle. We prefer to take our friends to a restaurant rather than cook in our home. And if we want to have a love affair, instead of seducing a partner, talking to him or her and making friends, we just look for somebody who is already keen on us. We cannot be bothered with talking somebody into something.

Sometimes we feel we are sinking into the earth, the solid mud and earth. Sometimes we feel good because we think we are the most stable person in the universe. We slowly begin to grin to ourselves, smile at ourselves, because we are the best person of all. We are the only person who manages to stay stable. But sometimes we feel that we are the loneliest person in the whole universe. We do not particularly like to dance, and when we are asked to dance with somebody, we feel embarrassed and uncomfortable. We want to stay in our own little corner.

When the ignoring quality of buddha neurosis is transmuted into wisdom, it becomes an environment of all-pervasive spaciousness. This enlightened aspect is called the wisdom of all-encompassing space. In itself it might still have a somewhat desolate and empty quality, but at the same time, it is a quality of completely open potential. It can accommodate anything. It is spacious and vast like the sky.

In tantric iconography, the five buddha families are arrayed in the center and the four cardinal points of a mandala. The mandala of the five buddha families of course represents their wisdom or enlightened aspect. Traditionally, the buddha family is in the center. That is to say, in the center there is the basic coordination and basic wisdom of buddha, which is symbolized by a wheel and the color white. Vajra is in the east, because vajra is connected with the dawn. It is also connected with the color blue and is symbolized by the vajra scepter. It is the sharpness of experience, as in the morning when we wake up. We begin to see the dawn, when light is first reflected on the world, as a symbol of awakening reality.

Ratna is in the south. It is connected with richness and is symbolized by a jewel and the color yellow. Ratna is connected with the midday, when we begin to need refreshment, nourishment. Padma is in the west and is symbolized by the lotus and the color red. As our day gets older, we also have to relate with recruiting a lover. It is time to socialize, to make a date with our lover. Or, if we have fallen in love with an antique or if we have fallen in love with some clothing, it is time to go out and buy it. The last family is karma, in the north. It is symbolized by a sword and the color green. Finally we have captured the whole situation: We have everything we need, and there is nothing more to get. We have brought our merchandise back home or our lover back home, and we say, "Let's close the door; let's lock it." So the mandala of the five buddha families represents the progress of a whole day or a whole course of action.

Without understanding the five buddha families, we have no working basis to relate with tantra, and we begin to find ourselves alienated from tantra. Tantra is seen as such an outrageous thing, which seems to have no bearing on us as individuals. We may feel the vajrayana is purely a distant aim, a distant goal. So it is necessary to study the five buddha principles. They provide a bridge between tantric experience and everyday life.

It is necessary to understand and relate with the five buddha principles *before* we begin tantric discipline, so that we can begin to understand what tantra is all about. If tantra is a mystical experience, how can we relate it to our ordinary everyday life at home? There could be a big gap between tantric experience and day-to-day life. But it is possible, by understanding the five buddha families, to close the gap. Working with the buddha families we discover that we already have certain qualities. According to the tantric perspective, we cannot ignore them and we cannot reject them and try to be something else. We have our aggression and our passion and our jealousy and our resentment and our ignorance—or whatever we have. We belong to certain buddha families already, and we cannot reject them. We should work with our neuroses, relate with them, and experience them properly. They are the only potential we have, and when we begin to work with them, we see that we can use them as stepping-stones.

Part Three PSYCHOLOGY

FOURTEEN

Becoming a Full Human Being

THE BASIC WORK of health professionals in general, and of psychotherapists in particular, is to become full human beings and to inspire full
human-beingness in other people who feel starved about their lives.
When we say a "full human being" here, we mean a person who not
only eats, sleeps, walks, and talks, but someone who also experiences a
basic state of wakefulness. It might seem to be very demanding to define
health in terms of wakefulness, but wakefulness is actually very close to
us. We can experience it. In fact, we are touching it all the time.

We are in touch with basic health all the time. Although the usual
dictionary definition of *health* is, roughly speaking, "free from sickness,"
we should look at health as something more than that. According to the
Buddhist tradition, people inherently possess buddha nature; that is,
they are basically and intrinsically good. From this point of view, health
is intrinsic. That is, health comes first: sickness is secondary. Health *is*.
So being healthy is being fundamentally wholesome, with body and
mind synchronized in a state of being which is indestructible and good.
This attitude is not recommended exclusively for the patients but also
for the helpers or doctors. It can be adopted mutually because this intrinsic, basic goodness is always present in any interaction of one human
being with another.

There are many approaches to psychology and some of them are
problematic. From the Buddhist point of view, there is a problem with

any attempt to pinpoint, categorize, and pigeonhole mind and its contents very neatly. This method could be called psychological materalism. The problem with this approach is that it does not leave enough room for spontaneity or openness. It overlooks basic healthiness.

The approach to working with others that I would like to advocate is one in which spontaneity and humanness are extended to others, so that we can open to others and not compartmentalize our understanding of them. This means working first of all with our natural capacity for warmth. To begin with, we can develop warmth toward ourselves, which then expands to others. This provides the ground for relating with disturbed people, with one another, and with ourselves, all within the same framework. This approach does not rely so much on a theoretical or conceptual perspective, but it relies on how we personally experience our own existence. Our lives can be felt fully and thoroughly so that we appreciate that we are genuine and truly wakeful human beings.

When you work in this way with others, it is very powerful. When someone begins to feel that he is not being pigeonholed and that there is some genuine connection taking place between the two of you, then he begins to let go. He begins to explore you and you begin to explore him. Some kind of unspoken friendship begins to develop.

Although I am speaking as a Buddhist teacher, I do not believe that therapy should be divided into categories. We don't have to say, "Now I'm doing therapy in the Buddhist style," or "Now I'm doing it in the Western style." There is not much difference, really. If you work in the Buddhist style, it is just common sense. If you work in the Western style, that is common sense, too. Working with others is a question of being genuine and projecting that genuineness to others. The work you do doesn't have to have a title or a name particularly. It is just being ultimately decent. Take the example of the Buddha himself—he wasn't a Buddhist! If you have confidence in yourself and you develop some way of overcoming ego, then true compassion can be radiated to others. So the main point in working with people is to appreciate and manifest simplicity rather than trying to create new theories or categories of behavior. The more you appreciate simplicity, the more profound your understanding becomes. Simplicity begins to make much more sense than speculation.

The Buddhist tradition teaches the truth of impermanence, or the transitory nature of things. The past is gone and the future has not yet happened, so we work with what is here—the present situation. This actually helps us not to categorize or theorize. A fresh, living situation is taking place all the time, on the spot. This noncategorical approach comes from being fully here, rather than trying to reconnect with past events. We don't have to look back to the past in order to see what people are made out of. Human beings speak for themselves, on the spot.

Sometimes, however, people are obsessed with their past, and you might need to talk with them about that somewhat in order to communicate with them. But it should always be done with a present orientation. It is not purely a matter of retelling stories in order to reconnect to the past, but rather it is a question of seeing that the present situation has several levels: the basic ground, which could be in the past; the actual manifestation, which is happening now; and where the present is about to go. So the present has three facets. Once you begin to approach a person's experience in that way, it comes alive. At the same time, it is not necessary to try to reach a conclusion about the future. The conclusion is already manifest in the present. There might be a case history, but that history is already dying. Actual communication takes place on the spot. By the time you sit down and say hello to the patient, that person's whole history is there.

You see, we are not trying to figure people out based on their past. Intead, we are trying to find out their case history in terms of who they are *now*, which is really the point. I always do that in interviews with my students. I ask them how old they are, whether they have been outside of America, whether they have been to Europe or Asia, what they have done, what their parents are like, and all the rest of it. But that is based on *this* person rather than on *that* person. It is quite straightforward. The people we are working with might be dwelling in the past, but we as their helpers have to know where they are *now*, what state of mind they are in at the moment. This is very important. Otherwise we may lose track of who a person is now and think of him as someone else, as if he were another personality altogether.

Patients should experience a sense of wholesomeness vibrating from you. If they do, they will be attracted to you. Usually, insanity is based on aggression, rejecting oneself or one's world. People feel that they have been cut off from communication with the world, that the world has rejected them. Either they have isolated themselves or they feel that the world is isolating them. So if there is some compassion radiating from your very presence when you walk into a room and sit down with people, if there is gentleness and willingness to include them, that is the preliminary stage of healing. Healing comes from a simple sense of reasonability, gentleness, and full human-beingness. That goes a long way.

So the first step is to project ourselves as genuine human beings. Then beyond that, we can help others by creating a proper atmosphere around them. I am speaking literally here, extremely literally. Whether someone is at home or in an institution, the atmosphere around them should be a reflection of human dignity, and it should be physically orderly. The bed should be made, and good meals should be prepared. In that way, the person can cheer up and be able to relax in his environment.

Some people may regard the little details of the physical environment as mundane and unimportant. But very often, the disturbances people experience come from the atmosphere around them. Sometimes their parents have created chaos—a pile of dishes in the kitchen, dirty laundry in the corner, and half-cooked food. Those little things may seem incidental, but they actually affect the atmosphere a great deal. In working with people, we can present a contrast to that chaos. We can manifest an appreciation of beauty, rather than just pushing the crazy person into a corner. The appreciation of the environment is an important part of Tibetan and Zen Buddhist practice. Both traditions consider the atmosphere around oneself to be a reflection of one's individuality, and so it should be kept immaculate.

The conventional therapeutic approach is to try to straighten out people's minds first, then give them a bath, and finally help them get dressed. But I think that we have to work with the whole situation at once. The environment is very important, and yet it is often overlooked.

If the patient is presented with a good meal and is acknowledged and received as a special guest, which is what he or she deserves, then we can work from there.

We are talking about creating an ideal, almost artificial life for seriously ill people, at least in the beginning, until they can pull themselves together. We may actually bathe them and clean their rooms, make their beds and cook nice meals for them. We can make their lives elegant. The basis of their neurosis is that they have experienced their lives and their world as being so ugly, so full of resentment, so dirty. The more resentful and ugly they become, the more that attitude is reinforced by society. So they never experience an atmosphere of compassionate hospitality. They are regarded as nuisances. That attitude doesn't help. People are not really nuisances at all. They are just being themselves given their circumstances.

Therapy has to be based on mutual appreciation. If people feel it is just your "trip," they may not like the environment you create for them. You may present them with a nice tray of food, but still they may be outraged if they know that your attitude is not genuine, if they feel your generosity is hypocritical. If your approach is completely unified, if you treat your patients like princes or princesses in the fullest sense, then they may want to respond. They may actually cheer up and begin to extend themselves. They may begin to appreciate their bodies, their strength, and their existence as a whole. It is not so much a matter of finding techniques that will cure people so that you can get rid of them. Rather, it is a matter of learning how to actually include them as part of a good human society. It is important for the therapist to create an atmosphere that makes people feel welcome. That attitude should infuse the whole environment. That is the point.

The ability to work with another person's neurosis, or even their craziness, ultimately depends on how fearless you are when you deal with them or how inhibited you feel. It depends on how much you are embarrassed by somebody or how much you can actually extend yourself. In the case of a mother's relationship to her infant, there is no problem because the mother knows that the child will grow up and one day become a reasonable person. So she doesn't mind changing diapers and doing all sorts of things for her child. Whereas if you are dealing with people who are already grown up, there is some kind of basic embarrassment which has to be overcome. That embarrassment has to be transformed into compassion.

Crazy people in particular are very intuitive. They are somewhat brilliant and they pick up messages very easily, even just the flicker of your thoughts, and that goes a long way with them. Usually they chew it, or they swallow it, or they throw it out. They will make a lot out of it. So it is a question of your basic being and how open you are in those situations. You can at least make an attempt to be open at that moment, which is a tremendous commitment to training and educating yourself. Then there is the possibility of developing fearlessness.

It is necessary to work patiently with others, all the time. That is what I do with my students: I never give up on them. No matter what problems they come up with, I still say the same thing: just keep going. If you have patience with people, they slowly change. You do have some effect on them if you are radiating your sanity. They will begin to take notice, although of course they don't want to let anybody know. They just say, "Nothing has changed. I have the same problems going on all the time." But don't give up. Something happens—if you take your time. It works!

Just do what you have to do to keep them going. They will probably keep coming back to you. You are their best friend anyway, if you don't react too neurotically. For them, you are like a memory of eating in a good restaurant. You remain the same, and they keep coming back to you. Eventually you become very good friends. So don't jump the gun. It takes time. It is an extremely long process, but if you look back at it, it is very powerful. You have to cut your own impatience and learn to love people. That is how to cultivate basic healthiness in others.

It is very important to commit yourselves to your patients fully and not just try to get rid of them after they have been cured. You shouldn't regard what you are doing as ordinary medical work. As psychotherapists you should pay more attention to your patients and share their lives. That kind of friendship is a long-term commitment. It is almost like the student-teacher relationship on the Buddhist path. You should be proud of that.

FIFTEEN

Creating an Environment of Sanity

WESTERN PSYCHOLOGY and the Buddhist tradition have had an interesting history together. Western psychologists first studied Buddhist philosophy as a "second thought"—or secondary interest. But at the beginning of the twentieth century, as Zen and Theravadin Buddhist meditation began to be more widely practiced rather than purely studied, psychologists became interested in these disciplines and in further aspects of Buddhism, particularly the Tibetan vajrayana tradition. In fact, we could say that the hospitality created by the interest and efforts of Western psychologists is what has made it possible for us now to present a proper and full understanding of Buddhism on this continent. In particular, the interaction between Buddhist and Western psychology has provided fertile ground for the establishment of Buddhism in the West.

In this article I would like to present Buddhist psychology and practice in further detail and also mention briefly some differences and similarities between the Western psychological disciplines and the Buddhist approach to working with people. Both the Western psychological tradition and the Buddhist tradition place great emphasis on the importance of upbringing and environment in determining the way people develop psychologically. We could say quite safely that, from the Buddhist point of view, people's basic psychological problems come from neglect in their early years or from the fact that their environment wasn't adequate. This is one of the key places where people develop psychological

143

problems. A whole range of psychological problems comes from individuals being mismanaged by their parents or by their teachers in school. In most cases, parents and teachers have good intentions, but often the environment they create for children is not adequate because of lack of money or lack of skillful means in handling situations. There is some shortcoming in the environment.

This is not to say that parents or teachers or uncles and aunts have to be rich. But they can be skillful enough to provide some psychological hospitality in the early stages of child rearing. There should be a basic sense of welcome, a basic sense of health in the child's environment. There should be some goodness. On the whole, there should be no lying or twisting of logic or pretending that things are other than what they are. If those types of distortion are allowed to build up, then children—who, by the way, are extremely intelligent—begin to see through the deception around them and the unskillfulness that pervades their upbringing. But even though they may see through what is happening, nonetheless, they become victims of their upbringing and are affected by it in later life. This can produce inferiority complexes or some kinds of schizophrenia when the children become adults. Worst of all is the basic attitude of hatefulness and resentment toward individuals; and as adults, children brought up in an atmosphere of hatefulness will direct that hatefulness toward their children. Whenever there is aggression and disliking in any aspect of the environment as you are growing up, that is the ground of insanity, from the Buddhist point of view.

Insanity does not usually come from passion; it usually comes from aggression, from resentment and disliking. By *insanity* here we mean hurting others and hurting yourself, so that there is no gentleness and no sense of helping others. So insanity and aggression are closely connected.

The point of aggression is to keep yourself intact. You refuse to deal with anybody else at all. In fact, if anybody touches you, you want to attack them. It is very straightforward, in that sense. You don't want to take part in the world. That is the problem of aggression. So insanity based on aggression comes from the fact that a person doesn't want to relate with the world because the world has been too punishing to them, particularly in their early years. In some cases, too much hospitality is a form of aggression: it can make people claustrophobic, as well. Hospitality becomes smothering: parents want to impose too much hospitality on their children. In that case, the situation is still unbalanced; there is still a lack of sensitivity in the environment.

Environment is extremely important, not only in how you treat your children but in how you treat yourself. It includes both animate and inanimate situations: your physical living situation as well as the people around you—your parents, teachers, students, maids, governesses, or whatever. Environment includes your relationship with your business partners, your driver, your waitress, whomever you meet. To be sane and to provide a ground of sanity for others, you need to be sensitive to environment. If you create an unbalanced or aggressive environment, it will produce a sense of separation between you and others— you and your world. Then you tend to blame everything on somebody else, which in turn brings blame onto yourself as well, at the same time.

Western education has taught us to think of ourselves as free men and women, which can be distorted into thinking that we have a perfect right to do anything we want. If anything goes wrong, we feel that we can blame somebody else, rather than ourselves. Similarly, Western psychological theories of ego have sometimes been used by psychologists to tell patients and students that they should build up their egos in such a way that they blame somebody else when things don't go their way. This is not at all being sensitive to environment.

The Western tradition has taught us that we have a tremendous personal dignity and confidence. The distortion of this is to feel that if anything goes wrong, we can find a scapegoat somewhere outside of ourselves. We say, "This went wrong; it must be somebody's fault." When people do that consistently, then it can lead to demands for rights, riots, and all sorts of complaints, which are always based on blaming somebody else. But we never blame "me." The extreme outcome of this approach is that we feel we want to rule the world, and in doing that, we display a tremendous personal ego. Ultimately, we could become someone like Hitler or Mussolini. These people represent the ego of an entire nation, which says, "It's not our fault. It is our nation's pride; we have our pride and glory and dignity. We are in the right." It is a gigantic ego world based on a fundamental separation from our environment. This is an extreme example, but distorting dignity into egotism can have these results.

The question for us as psychologists is how to work with people who have been brought up, to some degree, in this way of thinking, and who have developed deep mistrust and resentment of the world. How can we help them to let go of their aggression, which is self-aggression as well as aggression toward the world?

The key point in overcoming aggression is to develop natural trust in yourself and in your environment, your world. In Buddhism, this trust in yourself is called maitri. Maitri is natural gentleness and friendliness to yourself, which very much includes gentleness and absence of aggression in relating with the world. Maitri can actually be cultivated in yourself and in other people; you can cultivate gentleness and warmth. When you express kindness to others, then they in turn begin to find natural warmth within themselves. So the Buddhist approach to working with people—especially those who have been brought up in bad environments—is to provide a gentle, accommodating environment for therapy and teaching.

According to the Buddhist teachings, although we acknowledge that people's problems may have been caused by their past upbringing, we feel that the way to undo problems is to cultivate that person's maitri on the spot. This is done by working with the person's immediate environment rather than by delving into his or her past. Buddhism does not use the Western analytical approach of tracing back to the roots of neurosis in a person's past. Neither are such things as encounter therapy or primal therapy used. Buddhist psychology works with cultivating good behavior patterns, rather than trying to analyze the person's problems. At the same time, we could say that any capable Buddhist master, or teacher, including the Lord Buddha himself, acts in the best sense as a psychologist. However, instead of attempting to analyze a person's problems in terms of his or her internal psychology, a Buddhist teacher might be more apt to try to improve his student's table manners. So the Buddhist psychological approach looks at a person's state of mind in terms of a person's behavior and the larger world around the person. When a student has bad table manners, that usually reflects a general lack of environmental awareness. This is usually corrected directly, either by means of the sitting practice of meditation or else by teaching the student to be generally more mindful of what he is doing.

This approach is similar to that of the early Buddhist monastic tradition. The monks and nuns were supposed to have thirteen articles or possessions when they took ordination, and they were supposed to keep those thirteen articles clean and good. Those thirteen possessions were everything they had; they were not supposed to lose any one of them or mismanage any one of them. The point of those rules was to teach them how to become sane by dealing with the environment—and dealing with your own state of mind comes naturally out of that.

A story is told about Ananda, the Buddha's personal attendant, who had the desire to engage in a long period of fasting. He began to grow feeble and weak; he couldn't sit and meditate, so finally the Buddha told him, "Ananda, if there is no food, there is no body. If there is no body, there is no dharma. If there is no dharma, there is no enlightenment. Therefore go back and eat." That is the basic logic of the Buddhist teachings and of Buddhist psychology. We can actually be decent and sane on the spot, not through extreme measures but by managing our life properly, and thereby cultivating maitri.

One of the fundamental problems seems to be that people feel they are unable to be gentle and relate with the world, with their environment. At Naropa Institute in the psychology program, our foundation is that we can trust our own basic goodness. Human beings are capable of expressing maitri. They are capable of opening themselves up. Basic goodness is the potential that every human being has to express gentleness and warmth in themselves. Basic goodness is not necessarily *solid* goodness, but just *basic* goodness, unconditional goodness. If people can experience that personally, then they find they really don't have any fundamental argument or resentment. We *can* be open to situations; we can relate with our environment, our world, in that way. And from that, the neurosis in the world can be reduced: because *we* don't put aggression out into the world, therefore the world does not feed back any further aggression toward us.

As psychologists, we have to realize this for ourselves first; then we can work with others in this way as well. We can provide a gentle, nonaggressive, warm environment for disturbed individuals. It is a question of feeling a fundamental connection to others. You have to be a people-loving person to begin with. That means you have to love yourself as well, which is maitri: you don't just regard psychology as a J-O-B. You don't say, "I have to go to my job, my work, and suffer sweat and tears." Rather you just do your work with people as if you were cooking for yourself, as if you were peeling potatoes and cooking vegetables and boiling your rice, chopping your meat. When you prepare a good meal, you don't regard that activity as a J-O-B.

Approaching your livelihood as purely a "job" is particularly a problem in American culture. People regard their work and their family life, home life, as very separate. But if you like people, then you like to work with them. And if you like them, you can help them to like themselves. You find that you miss them; you actually want to be with them. They might be quite demanding, but still you are not tired of them. Liking others is also based on maitri: because you like yourself, therefore you like other people, and you are willing to open yourself and invite everybody in. That brings tremendous fresh air into your system. So it is very important to develop friendliness toward yourself, or maitri; then you like others, and you can proceed along.

There are no tricks involved. We are not trying to talk people out of or into anything. We are not trying to talk people out of their insanity or talk them into sanity. In any therapy session, if the therapist feels he has the answer, and he is going to tell it to the patient who doesn't have it, that is a problem. On the other hand, we are afraid to say to somebody, "I think you need to shape up!" We think we should have all the answers, but at the same time, we are afraid to tell the simple truth. We try everything so that we don't have to tell the truth.

The main point is to learn to tell the truth to your patients. Then they will respond to you, because there is power in telling the truth rather than bending our logic to fit their neurosis. Truth always works.

There always has to be basic honesty; that is the source of trust. When someone sees that you are telling the truth, then they will realize further that you are saying something worthwhile and trustworthy. It always works. There are no special tips on how to trick people into sanity by not telling the truth. I don't think there can be such a thing at all. At least I haven't found it in dealing with my own students. Sometimes telling the truth is very painful to them, but they begin to realize it is the truth, and they appreciate it sooner or later.

It is also important to realize that you don't have to have control over others. You see, that is exactly the truth situation: you do not have all the answers; you are not assuming control over people. Instead, you are trying to tell the truth—in the beginning, in the middle, and at the end. You may hope that you can produce results, that there will be some progress from telling the truth, but it is important to relate openly with a person, without expectations. To begin with, you can say things like, "How are you? Who are you? How are you behaving yourself?" That is important, rather than what results you get.

This is not a linguistic twist of any kind: just be honest and straight-forward—and be good at it. In some ways, disturbed people are the most intelligent people. They can tell right from left the minute you open your mouth. Right away, they have an idea about you, they know you, and usually they are extremely accurate—and they are profound. So you have to learn to trust their intelligence as well. You can't think that somebody is just crazy, and therefore you have to reshape him and make him into an acceptable person in society. The enlightened approach is to work with patients, channel them, *as they are.* The approach is to respect their ability to express accuracy. Sometimes, when people have psychological problems, they give up on conventional logic and come up with their own neurotic logic. Nevertheless, there is still truth in them. They are very accurate. It is very stunning sometimes: you wonder who is sane, who is not sane. You have to trust and be willing to let go and take a chance.

If you are not willing to open yourselves fully in dealing with the neurosis of the world, then you begin to develop a system to put people into pigeonholes. It is very dangerous for a therapist, or for anybody who is working with psychological situations, to put people in pigeon-holes. "If patients shake, that means this. If they stutter, that means that." Pigeonholing behavior patterns in people is not helpful. Instead you should look into a person's basic healthiness; you should look for a person's basic goodness. You should ask, where is that? You should look into where the patient's *health* is coming from. No matter how energetic and crazy a person is—where is that energy coming from? Someone might be acting paranoid and critical, but where is that accuracy coming from? They could be extremely neurotic and destructive, but where is the basic pinpoint of that energy? If you can look at people from that point of view, from the point of view of basic goodness, then there is definitely something you can do to help others.

One method of working with basic healthiness that is used in the Buddhist tradition is to give people meditation instruction. This can be a very good technique for helping people with psychological problems, depending on the severity of their disturbance and whether they are open to meditation. Through meditation, you are trying to help people ride on the energy of their minds, which is very, very powerful. If you can tell them how to do it properly, it can be fantastic. But without proper training, introducing the technique of meditation can be problematic. So you should be very careful that you don't become gurus to your patients. However, I think that introducing the sitting practice of meditation is an excellent idea in many cases.

The point of introducing sitting practice to a person is that there is always *some* little connection to basic goodness that a person can contact on the simple level of their sense perceptions. Even without meditation practice, that contact can be made. If our patients are artists, musicians, or connoisseurs of food, or if they even like food or like buying clothes, there is something to work with. As long as there is a connection through any sense perception, any touching of any kind, it involves the person with the world, with their environment. This is the basic approach we discussed earlier: cultivating people's awareness of their environment in which they can learn to appreciate themselves. Everyone has some connection with his or her environment, and any connection they may have to the world should be cultivated and awakened further.

In the early level of therapy, we cannot work only with the emotions. We have to work with a person's connection with the real world, with the environment. For example, people's relationship with their husband or their wife can be approached in terms of how they touch their husband, how they touch their wife, how they kiss, how they hug, rather than how you as the therapist can transform or solve the problems in their relationship. Just work at the concrete level. You might even talk to someone about how she takes her husband's shirt to bed and how she smells it, how she feels it. Anything—as long as it is concrete.

Basic sanity applies to every person, no matter how disturbed he or she may seem. It is not true that, if someone has seemingly gone too far into neurosis, we can't do anything. We *can* help people, even those who have gone too far, beyond the regular channels of communication. The basic point is to evoke some gentleness, some kindness, some basic goodness, some contact. When we set up an environment for people to be treated, it should be a wholesome environmental situation. A very disturbed or withdrawn patient might not respond right away—it might take a long time. But if a general sense of loving-kindness is communicated, then eventually there can be a cracking of the cast-iron quality of neurosis: it can be worked with. This can be arduous. But it is possible, definitely possible.

One basic point is, obviously, to not go along with people's craziness, although you appreciate them. You can't go along with craziness of any kind at all, even the slightest bit, even your *own* craziness. You do not have to be heavy-handed, particularly, but as we have said, you can work with whatever connection a person may have, any little simple thing. Try to work with the pinpoint of the situation by being very practical and ordinary. Working with environment basically means bringing people down to earth. If a person suddenly loses his gravity and floats up to the moon, he wants to come back to earth: he may be willing to become sane. At that point, you can teach him something. He will be so thankful to feel the gravity on the earth. You can use that logic in every situation. Earth is good. If somebody is dancing in the sky and breathing air, that is worse than if he is sitting on the earth, eating dirt—which has more potential. It's as simple as that! But at the same time, as therapists, we also have to ground ourselves first. Otherwise, we become more patient than therapist, which doubles the confusion. So we have to come down to earth. Then we can work with others.

SIXTEEN

Attitude toward Death in the Healer-Patient Relationship

IN DISCUSSING SICKNESS, whether physical or mental, we should recognize the importance of our sense of survival. We want to survive, and when we talk about healing, we are talking about how to survive. Viewed from another angle, our strategy of survival is the pattern of our reaction to the fact of death.

One's attitude toward death is central to any healing process. Although it is frequently ignored it is always in the background. No one actually wants to face the possibility of death, or even the idea of death. Even a mild sickness points to the possibility of nothingness: we might lose control of our physical or mental situation; we might become lost in midair. Since as healers we are dealing constantly with the fear of loss, we should actually bring that possibility into the picture. Facing it will not exactly solve the problem, but, to begin with, the problem should at least be faced.

Many people are confused in their attitude toward death and toward dying persons: should we try to conceal the situation or should we talk about it? Sometimes we do not want to talk about what is happening because it seems that to do so would be to suggest that something is basically wrong. Because of such attitudes there is often a loss of spirit on the part of both the patient and the physician. But when we are willing to acknowledge what is really happening, we pick up spirit, or buoyancy. One could even go so far as to say that by such acknowledgment some kind of sanity develops. So I think it is very important to present the possibility to people that they might have to face some kind of loss, some sense of bewilderment. In fact, the vanguard of death is uncertainty and complete bewilderment. It would be much healthier and more helpful to relate directly to this possibility, rather than just ignoring it. The healer should encourage people who are sick to confront their uncertainty. Such open communication will allow a real meeting to take place, an honest relationship.

We do not have to try to conceal the unspeakable; on the other hand, we do not have to push it to the extreme. At the least, we should help a person to have some understanding of the idea of loss—of the possibility of nonexistence and of dissolving into the unknown. The whole point of any relationship is to share some degree of honesty and to explore how far we can go with it. In that way relationships can become extremely powerful and intense, and beautiful. Sometimes we might only be able to get a hint of this intensity; we might only open up to just the bare minimum. Still, even then it is worthwhile. It is a step in the right direction.

In the healer-patient relationship, we are not concerned with trying to change people, particularly. Sickness and health are not black-and-white situations, but are part of an organic process. We are simply working with sickness and the potential of death, rather than relying on any particular doctrine. We are not talking about converting people. Nevertheless, the materials we have to work with are very rich; as we go along we can see the seed changing into a flower. We do not really change people; they simply grow. Encouraging patients to accept death or uncertainty does not mean that they have to face the devil. Instead such acceptance is something positive in people's lives; conquering the final fear of the unknown is very powerful.

Some people talk about healing in a magical sense, as when so-called healers put their hands on a sick person and miraculously heal them; others talk about the physical approach to healing, using drugs, surgery, and so forth. But I think the important point is that any real healing has to come out of some kind of psychological openness. There are constant opportunities for such openness—constant gaps in our conceptual and physical structures. If we begin to breathe out, then we create room for fresh air to rush in. If we do not breathe, there is no way for the fresh air to enter. It is a question of psychological attitude rather than of being taken over by external powers that heal us. Openness seems to be the only key to healing. And openness means we are willing to acknowledge that we are worthy; we have some kind of ground to relate with whatever is happening to us.

The role of the healer is not just to cure the disease; it is to cut through the tendency to see disease as an external threat. By providing companionship and some kind of sympathy, the healer creates a suggestion of health or underlying sanity, which then undermines naive conceptions of disease. The healer deals with the mishandling of the gaps that occur in one's life, with one's losses of spirit.

People tend to feel that their particular sickness is something special, that they are the only person with such an illness. But in fact, their illness is not so special—nor so terrible. It is a question of acknowledging that we are born alone and that we die alone, but that it is still okay. There is nothing particularly terrible or special about it.

Often the whole notion of sickness is taken as a purely mechanical problem: something is wrong with one's machine, one's body. But somehow that is missing the point. It is not the sickness that is the big problem, but the psychological state behind it. We could not have gotten sick in the first place without some kind of loss of interest and attention. Whether we were run down by a car or we caught a cold, there was some gap in which we did not take care of ourselves—an empty moment in which we ceased to relate to things properly. There was no ongoing awareness of our psychological state. So to the extent that we invite it to begin with, all sicknesses—and not just those diseases traditionally considered to be psychosomatic—are psychological. All diseases are instigated by one's state of mind. And even after we have dealt with the disease and the symptoms have disappeared, by pretending that the problem is over we only plant seeds for further neurosis.

It seems that we generally avoid our psychological responsibility, as though diseases were external events imposing themselves upon us. There is a quality of sleepiness, and of missing the gaps in the seemingly solid structure of our lives. Out of that sense of carelessness comes an immense message. Our bodies demand our attention; our bodies demand that we actually pay attention to what is going on with our lives. Illness brings us down to earth, making things seem much more direct and immediate.

Disease is a direct message to develop a proper attitude of mindfulness: we should be more intelligent about ourselves. Our minds and bodies are both very immediate. You alone know how your body feels. No one else cares; no one else can know but you. So there is a natural wakefulness about what is good for you and what is not. You can respond intelligently to your body by paying attention to your state of mind.

Because of this the practice of meditation may be the only way to really cure ourselves. Although the attempt to use meditation as some sort of cure may seem materialistic, the practice itself soon cuts through any materialistic attitude. Basically, mindfulness is a sense of composure. In meditation we are not accomplishing anything; we are just there, seeing our lives. There is a general sense of watchfulness, and an awareness of the body as an extremely sensitive mechanism which gives us messages constantly. If we have missed all the rest of the opportunities to relate with these messages, we find ourselves sick. Our bodies force us to be mindful on the spot. So it is important not to try to get rid of the sickness but to use it as a message.

We view our desire to get rid of disease as a desire to live. But instead it is often just the opposite: it is an attempt to avoid life. Although we seemingly want to be alive, in fact we simply want to avoid intensity. It is an ironic twist: we actually want to be healed in order to avoid life. So the hope for a cure is a big lie; it is the biggest conspiracy of all. In fact, all entertainment—whether it is the movies or various programs for so-called self-growth—lures us into feeling that we are in touch with life, while in fact we are putting ourselves into a further stupor.

The healing relationship is a meeting of two minds: that of the healer and patient, or for that matter, of the spiritual teacher and student. If you and the other person are both open, some kind of dialogue can take place that is not forced. Communication occurs naturally because both are in the same situation. If the patient feels terrible, the healer picks up that sense of the patient's wretchedness: for a moment he feels more or less the same, as if he himself were sick. For a moment the two are not separate and a sense of authenticity takes place. From the patient's point of view, that is precisely what is needed: someone acknowledges his existence and the fact that he needs help very badly. Someone actually sees through his sickness. The healing process can then begin to take place in the patient's state of being, because he realizes that someone has communicated with him completely. There has been a mutual glimpse of common ground. The psychological underpinning of the sickness then begins to come apart, to dissolve. The same thing applies to meetings between a meditation teacher and his or her student. There is a flash of understanding—nothing particularly mystical or "far out," as they say—just very simple, direct communication. The student understands and the teacher understands at the same moment. In this common flash of understanding, knowledge is imparted.

At this point I am not making any distinction between physicians and psychiatrists: whether we are dealing at the psychological or the medical level, the relationship with one's patient has to be exactly the same. The atmosphere of acceptance is extremely simple but very effective. The main point is that the healer and the patient are able to share their sense of pain and suffering—their claustrophobia or fear or physical pain. The healer has to feel herself to be part of that whole setup. It seems that many healers avoid that kind of identification; they do not want to get involved in such an intense experience. Instead they try to play extremely cool and unconcerned, taking a more businesslike approach.

We all speak the same language; we experience a similar type of birth and a similar exposure to death. So there is bound to always be some link, some continuity between you and the other. It is something more than just mechanically saying "Yes, I know; it hurts very badly." Rather than just sympathizing with the patient, it is important to actually feel her pain and share her anxiety. You can then say "Yes, I feel that pain" in a different way. To relate with total openness means that you are completely captured by someone's problem. There may be a sense of not knowing quite how to handle it and just having to do your best, but even such clumsiness is an enormously generous statement. So, complete openness and bewilderment meet at a very fine point.

There is much more involved in the healer-patient relationship than just going by the books and looking up the appropriate medicine. According to Buddhism, the human essence is compassion and wisdom. So you do not have to acquire skillful communication from outside yourself; you have it already. It has nothing to do with mystical experience or any kind of higher spiritual ecstasy; it is just the basic working situation. If you have an interest in something, that is openness. If you have an interest in people's suffering and conflicts, you have that openness constantly. And then you can develop some sense of trust and understanding, so that your openness becomes compassion.

It is possible to work with sixty people a day and have something click with each of them. It requires a sense of complete dedication, and a willingness to stay alert, without trying to achieve a specific goal. If you have a goal, then you are trying to manipulate the interaction and healing cannot take place. You need to understand your patients and encourage them to communicate, but you cannot force them. Only then can the patient, who is feeling a sense of separation, which is also a sense of death, begin to feel that there is hope. At last someone really cares for him, someone really does listen, even if it is only for a few seconds. That allows intense, very genuine communication to take place. Such communication is simple: there is no trick behind it and no complicated tradition to learn. It is not a question of learning *how* to do it, but of just going ahead with it.

Psychiatrists and physicians, as well as their patients, have to come to terms with their sense of anxiety about the possibility of nonexistence. When there is that kind of openness, the healer does not have to solve a person's problem completely. The approach of trying to repair everything has always been a problem in the past; such an approach creates a successive string of cures and deceptions, which seem to go hand in hand. Once the basic fear is acknowledged, continuing with the treatment becomes very easy. The path comes to you: there is no need to try to create the path for yourself. Healing professionals have the advantage of being able to develop themselves by working with the great variety of situations that come to them. There are endless possibilities for developing one's awareness and openness. Of course, it is always easier to look down on your patients and their predicament, thinking how lucky you are that you do not have their diseases. You can feel somewhat superior. But the acknowledgment of your common ground— your common experience of birth, old age, sickness, and death, and the fear that underlies all of those—brings a sense of humility. That is the beginning of the healing process. The rest seems to follow quite easily and naturally, based on one's inherent wisdom and compassion. This is not a particularly mystical or spiritual process; it is simple, ordinary human experience. The first time you try to approach a person in this way it may seem to be difficult. But you just do it on the spot.

And finally, what do we mean when we say that a patient has been healed? To be healed, ironically, means that a person is no longer embarrassed by life; she is able to face death without resentment or expectation.

SEVENTEEN

Intrinsic Health

A CONVERSATION WITH HEALTH
PROFESSIONALS

I HAVE NOT BEEN to medical school myself, or been a nurse or doctor, but I would like to indicate, from the Buddhist point of view, how to become a helper and a useful person in relating with other people.

Health

The dictionary definition of *health* is, roughly speaking, "freedom from sickness." However we could look at it as something more than that. According to Shambhala tradition, people are basically and intrinsically good; or in Buddhist terms, people inherently possess Buddha nature. That is, from these points of view, health is intrinsic. That is, health comes first; sickness is secondary. Health *is.* This attitude is one of being fundamentally wholesome, with body and mind synchronized in a state of being which is indestructible and good. This attitude is not recommended exclusively for the patients or for the helpers or doctors. It can be adopted mutually because intrinsic goodness is always present in any interaction of one human being with another.

Faith

A second consideration, which comes out of the first, is faith. Commonly, faith means having religious conviction or having trust in someone who has proved himself to be good. But in this case, faith is based on a recognition of the intrinsic goodness of the helpers and the helpees, which exists constantly. When we communicate with anyone at all, there is a ground of trust, faith, or mutual inspiration which comes from acknowledging each other's basic goodness. Because of that faith, individuals can begin to learn to help themselves, work with themselves, and take some pride in their existence. Such pride is not on the level of vanity or one-upmanship, but it is the general sense of physical well-being. If there is not that sense of physical well-being, then when you get sick, things get much worse. You actually want to be sick, want to die, and you begin to give up. So a general sense of physical well-being from both helper and helpee's point of view seems to be very desirable and even necessary. By physical well-being I'm not talking about extravagance—buying expensive clothes, for instance—but about paying attention to your existence. There should be some sense of discipline throughout the day for both helpers and helpees. Because of this, nothing is done haphazardly. The minute you get up, you take a certain attitude in facing your world in the way you take a shower, brush your teeth, shave, wash your hair, and choose what to wear. In getting ready to leave your home and in just being yourself, some kind of tremendous dignity and elegance could take place. You could begin to "taste" your own mind and your own body. In that way, you are not working with a particular medical technique alone, but with the creation of an entire atmosphere; how you set up the room, how you handle yourself, how you *are*.

Working with Sickness

A lot of upsets are invited by inattention and by being unnecessarily cranky, unnecessarily slothful. The feeling is that you couldn't care less, you are just strung out, voluntarily in many cases. You may begin to develop a sense of protest against the world of health. So you invite all the worms, germs, and flies by being sloppy. There is no dignity, no intrinsic goodness in that. However, if the helpers have created a sense of well-being in their own lives, this could help to inspire the helpees. In that regard, "tasting" one's mind and body is very important.

The actual application of these principles is based on the bodhi-sattva vow, in which you are willing to become anything to serve anybody. You're willing to become a bridge, a ship, a train, a motorcar, chopsticks, knives and spoons, a comb. Anything that anybody uses, you are. You become a vehicle for people's well-being. Anybody's well-being. All sentient beings' well-being. With this attitude, you are not there only when someone is sick, shying away when they are not sick.

Taking care of sick people in their homes is a good example. Whether things go well or not, you are always available. The idea is one of taking a human being, responding and working with that person, whether that person is doing fine or experiencing terrible turmoil. There is some kind of even-temperedness and a natural sense of working together, which is the bodhisattva ideal. That bridge can be crossed by anybody, anytime, all the time, whether people are happy or sad, desperate or relaxed. It serves to bind them all together.

Madness

Our last issue is madness. Even though you cure a person of a particular disease, or particular problems, you still could be propagating each other's madness. When your health is good and you are highly fit, then you might be even more well equipped to conduct your madness, to propagate your madness any way you can. The minute you get hit by sickness, inconvenienced physically, you feel, "Maybe I'm doing something wrong." But when you have been cured, you may feel that you are okay. Then you can once again propagate all sorts of madness. So in being cured or in the process of curing, or being helped or in the process of helping, it is always necessary to take on the greater responsibility of not creating the fundamental disease, or madness. Madness is the result of not being able to synchronize body and mind together properly. Our goal is to create "Great Eastern Sun vision," which is the synchronizing of body and mind to uncover our basic health and to overcome madness.

QUESTION: There are times when we may see someone who has multiple complaints. We check him out and find there's nothing physically wrong. We don't necessarily want just to give him pills, and we are faced with the situation of realizing that the best thing he could probably do would be to sit, to meditate. Should we go ahead and . . .

CHÖGYAM TRUNGPA RINPOCHE: I would leave it up to you. That's why you are there. You see, people have to change their cultural preconceptions: doctors have a particular label, and psychotherapists have a particular label, and there's nothing in between the two so far in this society. So people jump back and forth between those two roles. Our role is definitely to create some kind of intermediate situation in which we could accommodate both practices without becoming extreme. You don't have to create an encounter group while having your teeth fixed. You just relate with what's needed. At the same time, there has to be some attention to space and to the physical atmosphere, including how the doctors and nurses look, and how they conduct themselves in that particular atmosphere. When patients come into a treatment situation, they may have a sense of anxiety, a sense of hope, or a sense of complete negativity. It is a very sensitive matter to bring them into the right situation and work with them. The main point is that they are not stuck with their sickness. If a person regards sickness as an enemy, then his body has no working basis to be well. He thinks his body is invaded by enemies and he goes to the doctor to get rid of these foreigners occupying his castle. And once that's taken care of, it's all over. So no relationship is established. There is another problem which goes back even further—the concept of death as the archenemy, where we try to avoid death every minute, every second. There has to be more emphasis on creating an atmosphere of help. Sickness is a message, and it can be cured if the right situation is created.

Q: In working with people in a professional practice, is there a way to help people develop more psychological space?

CTR: This might seem like a very simple-minded approach, but in working with people, I think that the physical environment is extremely important. I mean the actual furniture and decoration in the room, as well as the way you are dressed, the way you smell. There should be some sense that the ground, or the environment, has been conquered, so that when the patient and doctor meet, there is what might be called sacredness involved with the whole situation. That is very important. Mind reflects body, and body is affected by the atmosphere. The idea is *recovering* rather than being *cured of* a particular disease. This approach could also be used with older people who are dying. In the process of dying they are uncovering some kind of sanity. So they could approach their death peacefully.

Q: In a life-death situation, you may have to decide whether to let someone die or stay alive. I just wonder how much karma is involved in that. It would seem as if a bodhisattva approach would always be to keep the person alive. And yet at the same time, there's also some point where you have to let them go.

CTR: I think it is a very individual matter. You can't make a blanket policy or write a statement saying, "The Buddhists say . . ." Sometimes it would be much more helpful for them to go; and sometimes they should stick to it so they can experience a more fundamental feeling, or taste, of their mind and body. It's very individual.

Basically, what we have been talking about is a general sense of healthiness, or intrinsic goodness, in your state of mind. There is some sense of not giving up on life, but viewing every day as a constant journey and a constant challenge, and at the same time a constant celebration. I shouldn't say too much. It is better to experience it yourself.

EIGHTEEN

Maitri Space Awareness in a Buddhist Therapeutic Community

This article was written in the early 1970s, when Chögyam Trungpa and his students were at the beginning stages of creating a therapeutic community, the Maitri community, that would use Maitri Space Awareness as the focal point for therapy with highly disturbed individuals. The community changed its focus quite early on to concentrate on training the staff and ceased to be a facility for people with acute psychological problems. This article does not reflect the change in emphasis. Nevertheless, it provides a provocative introduction to Maitri Space Awareness and the relationship of the five buddha families to the development of ego and working with one's own confusion and underlying wisdom.

THE CREATION OF MAITRI, a Buddhist community working in a semi-clinical situation with Western neurosis, is a landmark in the growth of Tibetan Buddhist teachings in America. It marks a practical and potentially valuable application of the insights of vajrayana Buddhism to emotional disorders prevalent in American society. The Tibetan vajrayana teachings on the development of ego and the ego's relationship to space have found fertile soil here. Though many people think Buddhism is concerned mainly with some kind of mystical enlightenment, the true ground for Buddhism is confusion, neurosis, and pain, as Buddha emphasized in his four noble truths. It is from the ground of neurosis that Buddhist psychology has developed. An understanding of this psychology as it has developed in Tibet is essential to understanding the work we are doing at Maitri.

In contrast to the traditional medical model of disturbances, the Buddhist approach is founded on the belief that basic sanity is operative in all states of mind. One could say, that is, that confusion is not exactly ignorant; it is actually very intricate and detailed; the confusion has a particular style that may differ from person to person. More important, confusion is two-sided: it creates a need, a demand for sanity. This hungry nature of confusion is very powerful and very important. The demand for relief or sanity that is contained in confusion is, in fact, the beginning point of Buddhism. That is what moved Buddha to sit beneath the bodhi tree twenty-five hundred years ago—to confront his confusion and find its source—after struggling vainly for seven years in various ascetic yogic disciplines.

Basically we are faced with a similar situation now in the West. We are confused, anxious, and hungry psychologically. Despite a physically luxurious prosperity, there is a tremendous amount of emotional anxiety. This anxiety has stimulated a lot of research into various types of psychotherapy, drug therapy, behavior modification, and group therapies. From the Buddhist viewpoint, this search is evidence of the nature of basic sanity operating within neurosis; almost an ape instinct to find an answer to our confusion. This confusion is the situation in which various psychotherapy efforts are growing today, and appropriately, it is the basic ground of Buddhism and Buddhist psychology.

The approach of tantric Buddhism or vajrayana Buddhism, however, is not one of looking for a way out of this confused or neurotic situation. Instead, we stop our motion toward finding cures and examine our present state of being and work backward, looking closely at the sources of our very desire for a cure. We must, therefore, start with what we are and why we are searching.

The Structure of Ego:
The Five Skandhas

Buddhist psychology works with the psychological awareness of the space between the perceiver and the perceived. It is the distortion of this space by various types of ego fixation which leads to neurotic patterns of perception of the external world and thence to neurotic behavior which is more or less dysfunctional. In order to understand what is meant by psychological space and its neurotic distortions, it is worthwhile looking at the structure of ego according to Buddhist psychology. Ego is seen as a kind of filter network through which energy is constantly being channeled and manipulated rather than being able to flow freely in unrestricted space. It is not a solid entity but a moment-to-moment process of birth, evolution, and death. In Buddhist terminology, this evolutionary process of the ego is divided into five stages known as the five skandhas.

1. FORM

Psychologically, the background from which ego arises is a basic feeling of spaciousness which contains energy and is not limited by any boundaries. There is a sense of being able to move around, of an open gap. It appears as a question which already contains the answer. This openness is basic intelligence, boundless and unlimited by ego. On the most profound level, it questions the very existence of ego, but openness and the sense of insecurity and doubt which goes with it should be said to be the mark of intelligence on any level. However, while openness is intelligence, it is also confusion. We recognize that there is doubt and insecurity, and panic arises. Maybe there is no answer to our problem. At this point we freeze, trying to make something solid and definite. We refuse to make any further move or even to bother with the question anymore. Having established ourselves on solid and familiar ground as a definite and well-known "I," we now solidify our immediate environment as well and cultivate a sense of familiarity toward that. It is very self-satisfying, yet flat and uninspired.

2. FEELING

This solidification of ourselves and our environment is the fundamental distortion of perceptual space. However, it is at a very primitive level. There is still a large area of insecurity, and the ego has to develop further structures in order to control these areas. At the next stage, there is tremendous pride at having thoroughly established ourselves and our basic territory. But it is a shaky, adolescent pride. It feels fundamentally poor and weak. It therefore sends out tentacles of numbness, not really wanting to feel the situation it is in. Out of its sense of poverty, it also grasps whatever seems to feed it and repels whatever seems to attack it. The entire psychological space, rather than being perceived equally in all directions, is seen purely in terms of its friendly or hostile qualities; there is a bloated feeling of the richness of these qualities.

3. PERCEPTION-IMPULSE

Feeling the situation in terms of friendly or hostile is not quite enough. A more definite sense of the center is needed. Self-consciousness develops and everything is perceived in relation to the center. We validate the basic feeling through criteria—everything is perceived as big or small, negative or positive, in relation to "me." The sense of the poverty of the center leads to an emphasis on surface qualities and a constant attempt to magnetize whatever is perceived as potentially nourishing. Neutral space takes on the qualities of potential pleasure; every corner holds a promise. Creative energy is constantly being diverted to feed our sense of ourselves.

4. INTELLECT

At this stage, the need to control our overwhelming hopes and wants brings in the intellect. A sense of power begins to develop because we can name our feelings and thereby manipulate them. At the same time, naming brings the possibility of comparison. We need to get to the top, comparatively speaking, so that there will be no one above us with whom we can be compared unfavorably. A competitive spirit develops which creates tremendous psychological speed in an attempt to cover all possibilities of attack. There is a highly efficient awareness of the tiny details, which gives the sense of complete control of the situation. At the same time, the lack of any wider view gives the sense of a tremendous need to get above these details. The feeling of openness at this point closes down to a totally narrow view in terms of up or down, higher or lower.

5. Consciousness

The final stage of ego is known as consciousness. It is the limited form of consciousness whose function is purely to preserve the facade of ego. It has a sharp, aggressive quality to penetrate to even the smallest crack in this facade. It is the circulatory system of ego which links together all the fragments into a logical whole, which must be invincible, since any failure would be a weakening of the defense. It is therefore prepared to argue endlessly its own point of view and to give meaning to every perception in accordance with its own system. This need to give its own meaning to everything leads the ego to fragment space and therefore to feel a tremendous need to make new connections.

Consciousness solidifies ego's belief in the separateness of self and projections. This quality of separation could be seen as a wall. The wall is, of course, illusory. The problem is that we don't see that, but we believe the wall is real and begin to react to our own projections. The direction of the reaction always seems to be toward the survival of the personal ego or the solidification of the wall of ignorance from imaginary to real. As the wall becomes more solid, we begin to feel imprisoned by it because there is no possibility of ventilation. The air within the prison of our ego becomes very stuffy. It is too much our own and has lost the freshness of the original open dance. It becomes extremely painful just being ourselves. We begin to struggle to break out of the scheme we have created, but in doing so only further entrap ourselves.

This whole problem develops out of our forgetting the fact that we made the wall in the first place. While the wall seems solid, it is never

totally so because we simply cannot maintain the wall at all times. There
are always gaps in it. If we could give up the struggle and look plainly at
the wall, we could see its gaps, allowing us an appreciation of the open
quality of the actual situation. There is joy in the energy of the wall
itself.

The Five Buddha Families

This joy is seeing the spaciousness of energy. To understand this, we
must first describe energy in more detail. Energy falls into five general
patterns called buddha families. Various combinations of these families
constitute all of existence. Each family is a particular form of the
primordial intelligence that is the basis for confusion that can be transformed into wisdom. We can find examples of these energies every-
where. They are associated with colors, elements, landscapes, seasons,
and personality types. Each personality type has a sane and a neurotic
way of manifesting. The neurotic manifestation is connected with the
distortion of space, which we discussed in the description of the five
skandhas. The buddha families are named buddha, ratna, padma,
karma, and vajra.

1. BUDDHA

Buddha family is associated with the elements of basic space, the ground
which sustains all things. The symbol of the family is the wheel. It is
self-contained, not motivated to relate with things outside itself. It is
limited space considering itself to be ultimate. But there are gaps in this
smug situation just as there are gaps in the ego. Ignoring these gaps is
similar to ignoring the gaps in the ego, which is the basis for the first
skandha. This quality of ignorance in the buddha family is the basis for
the confused aspect of the other four families, just as the ignorance of
the first skandha pervades the last four.

There is inherent in this situation the flicker of doubt that can acti-
vate the intelligence in the buddha family by sensing the gaps and realizing the transparency of the limited viewpoint. Thus there can be a sense

of existence but with an attitude of spaciousness rather than selfishness. This is the wisdom of the Buddha, which is the basis for the realization of wisdom in all the other families. It is called the wisdom of all-encompassing space.

2. RATNA

Padma and ratna families are associated with passion or the idea of attraction. Ratna is the sense of indulging yourself in those attractions. The symbol for ratna is the jewel. Ratna is associated with the element earth and a sense of solidity. This is not only physical solidity but a quality of peace. Whatever happens to earth, it remains basically the same. Whatever ratna indulges in is accepted equally without any idea of rejection. It is very generous and secure. But when the element of ignorance is present, there is the sense of *feeling* secure rather than *being* secure. This leads to pride in that security, but because of this pride there is a feeling that the security is not complete. Whatever one has, one needs more. This is the confused aspect of ratna, which is pride. Without the element of striving to become secure, this energy is transmuted into the wisdom of equanimity. There is the original security but no fear of its loss. Everything is open and free. Ratna relates to the second skandha, feeling.

3. PADMA

Padma is associated with the element fire. The symbol is the lotus. It has a very seductive quality which draws things to itself. When the quality of ignorance is present, the state of *being* united is ignored, and there is a striving toward *becoming* united. In this way, passion is self-defeating. When the energy of padma is transmuted, striving is unnecessary because there is appreciation of the existence of union. This realization is the appreciation of individuality rather than its loss and is thus the working ground for real communication. This occurs through the precise seeing of "this" and "that" without the purpose of self-maintenance. Thus the transmuted energy of padma is called the wisdom of discriminating awareness. The padma family corresponds to the third skandha, perception-impulse.

4. KARMA

Karma family is associated with aggression. In this case, there is not only knowing clearly, but also a desire to execute that knowledge. The symbol for karma is the sword.

Karma is associated with the element wind. Wind has the quality of naturally being active, blowing, and always only in one direction at a time. But when this natural quality is ignored, then effort seems to be required in the blowing. Once there is effort in action, there always seems to be more to do. A person not only seems unable to accomplish all he wants, but others are found to accomplish more. Thus envy develops, and in its full state, the confused aspect of karma is a sense of extreme paranoia that one will never be able to act in any way.

In the transmuted aspect of karma, there is a sense of action, but no paranoia about its accomplishment. Thus the action is like wind, which naturally blows and touches everything in its path. It always takes the appropriate course. This is the wisdom of all-accomplishing action. Karma is associated with the fourth skandha, concept.

5. VAJRA

Vajra is also associated with aggression. This is a type of aggression that holds things at a distance or repels them. The result of this is freedom from emotional involvement, allowing nothing to interfere with the appraisal of the situation. Everything is seen very clearly and precisely. The symbol is the thunderbolt or scepter. Vajra is associated with the element water. Water is clear and impartial. It relates fully with the texture of a situation. But if the seeing is ignored, and there is a striving to see, then water can become turbulent, rushing currents. This confused aspect of vajra is anger. The transmuted energy is like the clear, luminous nature of water. This is called mirrorlike wisdom. Vajra corresponds to the fifth skandha, consciousness.

* * *

The five neurotic manifestations of the five buddha families relate to the three psychosomatic diseases of Tibetan medicine: the diseases of passion, aggression, and ignorance. The Buddha neurosis is associated with ignorance disease which, in a way, is the basic problem or source of the other four styles of neurosis. Ignorance disease affects the internal organs, glands, and nervous system on the physical level. Padma and ratna are associated with passion disease and psychologically with the activity of seduction. There are physical symptoms of insomnia, dizziness, and circulatory problems. Vajra and karma are associated with aggression disease, which may produce symptoms of nervousness, ringing in the ears, kidney problems, lack of appetite, headaches, or general body aches.

Space Therapy

Each of these neurotic styles presents a different way of relating to space, which influences how one relates to a situation. The object of the space therapy we have developed is to increase the energy of a person's neurosis by having a patient lie in a posture particular to his diagnosed neurotic style. The patient is asked to lie in this posture in a room designed to reflect the traits of the buddha family involved. For example, a person with a vajra neurosis is asked to lie in the vajra posture in a vajra room. The patient must remain in the room for two forty-five-minute periods each day, with a short break between periods, together with one of the staff. The result is an increase of energy which makes the neurosis more direct and easier to work with.

For example, the style of a vajra person in his relationship to space is that he wants to see everything, take in all the details. In the vajra posture, the patient lies on his stomach on the floor with the legs together and arms out at right angles to the body, palms pressed against the floor slightly, and the head turned to the side. The position tends to precipitate the basic vajra neurosis because the patient is down on the ground and his vision is very limited. The desire to be in touch with everything visually is denied by this particular physical situation. Everything you would like to see is behind you or above you where you cannot see it. The tendency of a vajra type to fragment space is accentuated by placing many small windows randomly in the room. At first this situation might seem extremely irritating or threatening to the patient, precisely because he feels threatened by his own style of relating to space.

The difference between a person whose neurosis has caused him to become dysfunctional and an ordinary person who may be neurotic but still functional is exactly this threatening quality of his own style. As the therapy continues, the patient's relationship to space in the therapy room becomes less threatening; he can become familiar with it. This corresponds to a change in attitude to his neurosis. Thus the goal of space therapy is not a cure in the sense of a change from a preconceived notion of "unhealthy" to one of "healthy" but rather for the patient to see even his own style as workable, just as it is.

The Maitri program consists of relating to daily domestic situations in a communal environment and using the technique of space therapy. The communal environment, with a minimal hierarchical structure, cuts through the conventional role-playing of a traditional therapeutic situation. Everyone is equally responsible for the work of the community. The demands of this simple domestic situation provide an organic discipline that cannot easily be evaded. Constant reminders from the community environment and from each community member point out the necessity of mutual responsibility. Along with this sense of discipline, there is an emphasis on friendliness toward oneself. The daily routine of communal living provides a background for relating to neurosis directly, through space therapy.

Although the background of Maitri is Buddhist and the staff members are each involved in meditation practice under my guidance, Maitri is nondoctrinal in the sense that the patient is not expected or encouraged to assume a Buddhist point of view. Nor is he specifically given instruction in Buddhist psychology or the theory of space therapy. In this way, the relation with the postures and rooms is direct, not mediated by any preconceptions. We would like to discourage a dependency on the community. So when he has finished his course of training, the patient is asked to leave as soon as it seems possible for him to make independent decisions concerning his life and to function in a regular environment.

Our situation at Maitri is a unique one and, at this stage, somewhat experimental. In the history of Buddhist countries, there is no record of an equivalent to a Buddhist mental hospital. Though the first hospitals of the world had a Buddhist origin under the reign of King Ashoka in India, they were limited mainly to physical diseases. Perhaps because of the very low incidence of advanced psychosis and schizophrenia in Buddhist countries in the Orient, applications of Buddhist psychology have been limited to the scholastic study, meditation practice, and other disciplines of Buddhist monasteries. Maitri, then, is a very recent meeting point of Tibetan Buddhism and American clinical psychology.

A great deal of credit should be given here to the late Suzuki Roshi for the inspiration for a Buddhist community working with American neurosis. It was during a meeting I had with him in May 1971, at Zen Center in San Francisco, that he expressed the need he saw for this type of situation. It was a point of immediate agreement between us that we should try to develop a therapeutic community—a joint effort of our two schools of Buddhism. Suzuki Roshi's death in December of 1971 prevented his participation in the actual work of Maitri as it exists now near Elizabethtown, New York, but he retains an important place in Maitri's development.

NINETEEN

From a Workshop on Psychotherapy

CHÖGYAM TRUNGPA RINPOCHE: We have a tendency in our lives to seek some kind of eternity, to confirm the seeming continuity of our past and future, so perhaps we could discuss the question of eternity and nowness. We want to stretch out the sense of a solid situation. This attempt to keep on top of the situation all the time makes us anxious, since we continually have to struggle to maintain our goal. In the practice of meditation we may discover that eternity does not exist as a long-term situation. We may discover a sense of presentness or nowness.

QUESTION: Could you discuss the differences between meditation and psychotherapy?

CHÖGYAM TRUNGPA RINPOCHE: The difference is in the individual's attitude toward undergoing the disciplines of meditation and psychotherapy. In the popular therapeutic style, the individual's attitude is one of trying to recover from something. He looks for a technique to help him get rid of, or overcome, his complaint. The meditative attitude accepts, in some sense, that you are what you are. Your neurotic aspects have to be looked at rather than thrown away. Actually, in popular Buddhism, meditation is sometimes regarded as a cure, but that's myth; nobody knows what's going to be cured, what's going to happen. When you meditate properly, the notion of cure doesn't come into the picture. If it does, then meditation becomes psychotherapy.

Q: How do you relate that to the use of the term *neurotic?*

CTR: The neurotic aspect is the counterpart of wisdom, so you cannot have one without the other. In the ideal case, when enlightenment is attained, the neuroses are still there but they have become immense energy. Energy is the euphemism for neurosis from that point of view.

Q: In psychoanalysis and Reichian character analysis, the practitioners claim to alter the fundamental character structure and eliminate the continuation of neuroses. You seem to be saying that the neuroses, even in an enlightened being, will continue. That seems to be distinctly different.

CTR: The basic idea is that mind cannot be altered or changed, only somewhat clarified. You have to come back to what you are, rather than reform yourself into something else. Reformation seems to be going against the current, from a Buddhist point of view.

Q: Do you think that if therapy was done with the idea of helping someone become more aware of themselves it would then be consistent with the Buddhist point of view?

CTR: Basically, yes, since there is a sense of self-dislike and not wanting to see oneself, so the idea is to project a sense of friendliness to oneself. The role of the teacher or therapist is to help someone make friends with himself. That's why our psychology program is called Maitri, which means friendliness.

Q: In the Maitri experience you talk about transmuting energies, taking neurotic qualities, solid qualities, things that make one anxious and transmuting them, making them finer, giving them clarity. It seems, in psychotherapy, when one is experiencing negative feelings, that one is encouraged to express them, and in the expression there is some type of release. I am wondering how you see that in relation to say, just being in the Maitri postures, just being with the negativity and watching it. It seems to be two different ways to be with the energy.

CTR: The idea is to be able to actually see the texture, the quality, the rising and the falling of emotion. At first, we are not particularly concerned with what we are going to do with it. We just examine the whole thing. Before we do anything, we have to make a relationship with our emotional energy. Usually, when we are talking about expressing our energies, we are more concerned with the expression than with the energy itself which seems to be rushing too fast. We are afraid that it will overwhelm us. So we try to get rid of it by action.

Q: You're not saying to suppress our feelings, are you?

CTR: No, you don't keep them down. Suppressing them is also doing something with them. Suppression involves a separation between you and your emotions, and therefore you feel that you have to do something with them. When energy is related to properly, it rises, peaks, and then returns back to one's energy bank. A recharging process takes place.

Q: Is that the transmutation process?

CTR: Yes, transmutation is turning the lead into gold.

Q: In Reichian or primal therapy they encourage people to let out all their anger or hatred. Their theory is that the reintegration of the ego will come by the expression of these energies. From your point of view, by merely relating to the energies, not expressing or repressing them, by just being with them, that a certain kind of change . . .

CTR: Once you have developed a harmonious relationship with your energy, then you can actually express it, but the style of expression becomes very sane, right to the point. The idea is that expressing energy properly is the final crescendo, the final power; it is at the level of tantra. So from the Buddhist point of view, skillful, accurate expression is the culmination of one's development. To do this you have to have a harmonious relationship to your energy, to be completely in your own energy. If you try to release your energy at an earlier point, you are wasting a lot of valuable material.

Q: So in the meantime, while we are trying to make the relationship, do we just sit with anger if it comes up?

CTR: Not necessarily. The question is whether the anger is part of you or something separate. You have to make a greater connection between the anger and yourself. So even just sitting with it is not enough. It could still be like a bad marriage where there is no relationship. Emotions are part of you, your limbs. If you don't have energy or emotion, there is no movement, no way to put things into effect. You have to regard emotions as part of you to begin with.

Q: There is a school of Western psychotherapy that doesn't believe in expressing feelings. You just experience them and talk about them. And the interpersonal relationship with a therapist is very important in the process. I don't see any conflict with your ideas and what they are saying.

CTR: It's not a doctrinal problem. It is a matter of how people actually relate to their emotions and each other.

Q: How can I be graceful and totally aware all the time? It seems impossible.

CTR: Awareness does not mean beware, be careful, ward off danger, you might step into a puddle, so beware. That is not the kind of awareness we are talking about. We are talking about unconditional presence which is not expected to be there all the time. In fact, in order to be completely aware, you have to disown the experience of awareness. It cannot be regarded as yours—it is just there and you do not try to hold it. Then, somehow, a general clarity takes place. So awareness is a glimpse rather than a continuous state. If you hold on to awareness, it becomes self-consciousness rather than awareness. Awareness has to be unmanufactured; it has to be a natural state.

Q: What is enlightenment?

CTR: The Buddhist method is to first find out what isn't enlightenment. You begin to peel off all the skins and then you probably find that in the absence of everything, some sort of essence exists. The basic idea of enlightenment is the Sanskrit word *bodhi*, which means "wakeful." Ultimately, it is an unconditional state of wakefulness, which happens to us occasionally. Intelligence is present all the time, but it gets over-crowded. So one has to peel off the excess layers to allow it to shine through.

Q: The initial impact, other than Maitri, which is a whole develop-ment of the application of Buddhism on therapy, will simply be the effect of Buddhist practices on the therapist and then maybe something will slip through no matter what the context is. Whether you are a behavior modification therapist or you're a psychoanalyst, it doesn't make any difference; it could have a really powerful effect.

CTR: I don't see any particular problems here. At this point we are talking about taking an attitude that is based on Buddhist experience. Out of that, any kind of style or technique will be used, as long as the presentation doesn't become too dogmatic. In any case, in therapeutic situations you can't always go by the books; you have to improvise a great deal when you are working with somebody else. So I think we are not so much talking about "should be doing this" or "should be doing that," cookery book style. We are talking about developing some kind of insight. I think an understanding of the ideas of impermanence and ego is a very important contribution. Then everything is an individual application. Problems could occur if there is no relationship between the patient and the doctor. If there is no relationship, then all you can do is go along with the books, what the original prescriptions were. That seems like a second-rate therapy. If a real relationship takes place and everything becomes a part of one's journey, then I don't see any problems.

Q: Could I add another word to that? My hope when I think of what Buddhism can contribute is that it will soften or lessen the need that therapists I know seem to have, which is to have a changing effect on their patients or clients. I think that is the most important part of the message. It goes along with everything you've said: you were spelling it out and I was generalizing it in terms of the tremendous pressure that the client and the therapist bring to the situation, to have something to change. And that is absolutely not what is necessary.

I was first drawn to you when I read one of your books, in which there was a voice saying just that: "Look at it, don't try to change it." It seems to me that Western therapy could go back to that. That's what I think Freud was standing for in the first place. Freud was basically an investigator, he was much less interested in curing than in finding out. If we could only encourage our colleagues to go back to that position in itself, that would be a tremendous change in a very subtle way.

CTR: Precisely.

TWENTY

Is Meditation Therapy?

WE ARE GOING TO DISCUSS the relationship between therapy and meditation. Is meditation therapy?

As we advance on the physical-technological level, spiritual advancement also should take place at the same time. But that has become purely an idea—what has actually happened is that we have become technologically highly advanced, but at the same time we have a problem with spiritual advancement. That seems to be the problem that has developed. The notion of meditation and the notion of therapy and the notion of sanity become big issues at this point.

Can the practice of meditation play as important a part in our society as therapy or as technological advancement? The question here is not so much the value of practicing meditation versus the value of technology and therapy, as such. Maybe the title of this article is deceptive. As soon as you use a question mark and some phrase like "Is meditation therapy?" that automatically involves evaluating which of those is better, as if they were going to compete with each other. So the question we are discussing is not which is more worthwhile, which is more expansive or gives the most direct result, but we are talking about the general situation in our society, the national psychology.

Due to enormous scientific advancement in this country and in the West in general, we have involved ourselves in looking for further advancement and looking for a sort of mechanical spiritual process which has caused spiritual materialism. Maybe we could learn certain yogic tricks and manage to slow down our heartbeat or stand on our heads without using our hands for forty-five hours a day. Maybe we can learn to barely levitate by holding our breath—like a helicopter. When tricks like that are involved, then we are still concerned with collecting gadgets rather than experiencing reality, I'm afraid. Meditation practice is not regarded as another gadget, but it is regarded as a practice—a real practice.

We need to discuss the meaning of the word *practice*—what do we mean by practice? What does practice mean? Practice or discipline is a particular involvement or interest that allows us to let go. I do not mean letting go in the sense of becoming solemn, but letting go in the sense that there is something that we can work with. That working situation is largely based on the notion of cutting through all kinds of expectations and preconceptions about what things might be or which things might answer our question. So letting go is largely based on cutting through preconceptions. When we talk about cutting through preconception, it sounds good, it sounds quite nice. The idea that we would like to cut through our preconceptions sounds *great*. But at the same time, cutting through preconceptions involves cutting through our expectations and our pains and pleasures. Cutting through preconceptions quite possibly could bring us to an enormous state of boredom rather than entertainment. The whole thing doesn't sound very attractive or entertaining or particularly encouraging.

The practice of meditation is largely based on some kind of sacrifice, some kind of openness. Such sacrifice is necessary and has to be personally experienced. Ordinarily we might sacrifice something on behalf of or for the sake of developing goodness, or because we are willing to suffer on behalf of humanity. But those sacrifices are—pardon the expression—bullshit. The sacrifice which has been recommended, prescribed in the Buddhist tradition, is to sacrifice something without any purpose. Now that's outrageous, that's terrible. Does that mean you are going to be a slave? No, not unless you're going to turn yourself into a slave. Sacrificing something without any purpose is outrageous and precisely heroic and fantastic; it is outrageous and very beautiful.

Such a sacrifice without purpose can take place by not regarding any form of therapy as a way of saving yourself from pain, feeling that you will be finally saved or that you have managed to get away with using some method to save yourself from seeing reality. The practice of meditation is sacrifice without techniques, without means, without gloves or pliers or hammers. You have to use your bare hands, bare feet, bare head, to relate with the whole thing.

The notion of reality and reward can become a problem. Basically, fundamentally, there is no reality and there is no reward, and we are not trying to get anything out of this life at all. That is why the notion of freedom is important. Freedom—unexpected, undemanded freedom. Freedom cannot be bought or bartered for. Freedom doesn't come cheap or expensive. It just happens. It is only without any reference point that freedom can evolve. That is why it is known as freedom— because it is unconditional.

From that point of view, we could say that meditation is not therapy. If there is any notion of therapy involved in the spiritual journey, or in any kind of spiritual discipline, then it becomes conditional. You might ask then how we could use our talent, our patience, our discipline, and everything as part of our journey. Well, that particular journey, those particular talents, that evolutionary organic process, also have to be an expression of unconditional freedom. If there is no freedom, complete freedom, then there's no answer to that question, there's no hope at all.

So, it is our duty—in fact, we might even go as far as to say it is the purpose of our life—it is our heroic duty to encourage the notion of freedom as it is, without contamination by any further pollution of this and that and that and this. No bargaining. Truth and honesty are discussed in the, so to speak, military schools or the highly conservative, disciplined training grounds. If there were no concern for truth and honesty, then there could be flexibility in relating with freedom. Suppose we found our death. Then what would happen? Would we be saved? No. We would still keep our allegiance to unconditional freedom. We have to maintain ourselves in an erect posture in order to work with freedom. The practice of meditation in the Buddhist tradition is extremely simple, extremely erect, and direct. There is a sense of pride in the fact that basically you are going to sit and practice meditation. When you sit and practice meditation, you don't do anything at all. You just sit and work with your breathing, your posture; you just sit and let all these thoughts come alive. You let your hidden neurosis come through. Let the discipline evolve itself. That is far from therapy, absolutely far from therapy.

Therapy involves the notion of testimony and support, enormous support: "When I was involved with this particular meditation practice three years ago, three months ago, I was saved. Now I can meditate. I can do a beautiful job with myself; I'm a good general, I am a good busboy, a good postman. I find that my intelligence has been sharpened when I work on Madison Avenue lately," or whatever. The reason why the practice of meditation is not therapy is because it does not particularly provide or even ask for support or testimony about anything at all. When you begin to ask for testimony, that is a sign of weakness; you feel that you need support. *You* need support, the personal support that somebody else is doing it and that person is doing okay, so therefore you can do it. That is the approach to therapy.

But meditation experience is personal experience, extremely personal experience, real experience. You begin to feel alone because you are what you are. You don't feel alone in the sense that you feel that you need somebody else's support. Rather, you can do it yourself. Being alone and being lonely is not a big problem anymore. You begin to feel delight in being alone, as a matter of fact. Aloneness is part of not needing support or testimony. You do not need therapy; you just need your life. There is a new dimension to practicing meditation from that point of view. There is a sense of openness and a sense of not needing further support—you can do it yourself, you're working with yourself, fundamentally, basically. It is up to you, but it is also your own creation at the same time. When we begin to relate with that principle of aloneness, the notion of independence, of freedom, becomes extraordinarily powerful, extraordinarily interesting, and highly creative. We do not ask questions about the nature of reality, about what is going to be good and bad for us, but we begin to pick and choose in accordance with our own dimensions, our own experience of freedom, of loneliness. You know that you are lonely already, alone already. You know that you are with nobody but yourself. Even the phenomenal world does not help.

And because of that loneliness and aloneness you are able to help other people, of course. Because you feel so lonely, so alone, the rest of the world, humanity, your friends, your lovers, your relatives and parents are part of your life, because they are the expression of loneliness at the same time.

So there can be a sense of enormous openness, which largely depends upon you being open, free, and highly disciplined. Therefore, precisely, meditation is not therapy. It goes beyond therapy, because therapy involves conforming to some particular area of relative reference. The practice of meditation is the experience of totality. You can't regard it as anything at all, but it is completely universal. It covers all areas of your life: domestic, emotional, economic, and social situations, whatever there may be.

The notion of unconditional freedom is the notion of meditation from that point of view, and therefore freedom cannot be said to be therapy. If we regard the notion of freedom as therapy, we are already in trouble, because "I am supposed to get out of this mess." So if the very meaning of therapy is regarded as freedom or the very meaning of freedom is regarded as therapy, then you are kidding yourself or somebody else is kidding you. It is like someone saying, "I tell you that you are free from now onward," and then later they tell you, "What I said to you was therapy." You feel that you have been completely deceived. You are no longer free at that point, because that approach of therapy is just purely trying to cheer you up so that you will get more involved in the mess, and you will have no hesitation about getting into the mess of confusion.

So therefore, if we say that meditation is therapy, that is an enormous disservice to the intelligence of the universe, to universal consciousness. If we say that meditation is not therapy, then we are contributing something to understanding the notion of unconditional freedom. Freedom in itself is not regarded as therapy, but it is regarded as the expression of openness and potentiality.

QUESTION: I was interested in your saying that therapy could cheer you up, only to make you get more involved in the mess. You do prescribe seeing your neurosis though. So, in that sense, how is therapy a problem?

CHÖGYAM TRUNGPA RINPOCHE: What do you mean by therapy?

Q: Something that makes you a more open person. You said that therapy could cause you to have more confidence—so that you would get into the mess more.

CTR: You could get into all kinds of trouble when you begin to use therapeutic practice. Often, when we use the term *therapy*, we are talking about how we can save ourselves from our problems. We are confronting our problems by using some kind of technique or medium. Could we wear plastic gloves, or could we use anesthetics so that we don't have to face our problems? We are afraid to relate with what we are and what our problems are. We are embarrassed to work with all that or to confront it. Such an approach is the wrong usage of the word *therapy*. It is a kind of linguistic problem. Viewing it in such a way, if we are involved in therapy, that automatically means that we don't have to face our wife or our husband. Instead, we go to a therapist who is going to create a kind of numbness between us. We begin to lose the sharpness we experience with our husband or wife, the sharpness and irritation. We would like therapy to help us to get together by putting some kind of numbness or lozenge between those sharp edges. We would like therapy to numb us to that sharpness we are experiencing so intensely, so that we never have static. We would like to join together with our husband or wife, but at the same time we would like the physician to put us on anesthetics so that we don't have to go through the pain of being joined together. Then we could wake up very happy and feel ourselves already sewn together. It could work out and we could feel happy ever after. That approach has been the problem, I'm afraid. The word *therapy* has come to mean the notion of being joined together by anesthesia.

On the other hand, the word *therapy* could be used as skillful means or application for how certain parts of a jigsaw puzzle could fit together. Then therapy has the sense of application or method. In that sense, therapy should not become anesthesia, but instead is a method of sharp precision. It is the way you get yourself together, rather than a way of being anesthetized. The desire for anesthesia seems to be the problem, whether we use the term *meditation* or *therapy*. That attitude always becomes a problem.

In the true sense, therapy is not anesthesia but actual experience. That is very important. We should experience our own embarrassment, or whatever it may be, and try to link together another embarrassment, which is what the world is relating to us, rather than using any anesthetic or numbing agent to solve our problems. There's no particular hospitality involved from that point of view. To be willing to experience our world directly is the mark of our courageousness, our openness—which actually means freedom. So in other words, we could say quite seriously that freedom cannot be bought by anesthetics.

GLOSSARY

ABHIDHARMA (Skt.): The systematic and detailed analysis of mind, including both mental processes and contents. Also, the third part of the Tripitaka, the "three baskets" of early Buddhist scripture.

ALAYA (Skt.): The fundamental unbiased ground of mind.

ALAYAVIJNANA (Skt.): The eighth consciousness. Arising from the ground of alaya, alayavijnana is the point at which subtle seeds of bias or duality begin to appear. As such it is the root of samsara.

ASURA (Skt.): A jealous god, in one of the six realms of existence. The asura mentality is based on paranoia and competition, always trying to one-up a situation.

AVIDYA (Skt.): *A* means "negation," and *vidya* means "intelligence" or "wisdom." So *avidya* refers to "un-intelligence," or ignorance. In this case, it is ignoring the fundamental space or the wisdom inherent in oneself and one's experience. It is connected with the first stage, or skandha, in the development of ego. *See also* rikpa.

BASIC GOODNESS: Unconditional goodness of mind at its most basic level. The natural goodness of alaya. Sometimes used as a synonym for *bodhichitta* (awakened heart) or *tathagatagarbha* (buddha nature).

BODHICHITTA (Skt.): "Mind/heart of awakening." Sometimes called buddha nature, it is the awakened heart and mind inherent in all human beings. Bodhichitta is discussed in terms of absolute and relative, although these two aspects are inseparable. Ultimate, or absolute, bodhichitta is the union of emptiness and compassion, the essential nature of awakened mind. Relative bodhichitta is the tenderness arising from a glimpse of ultimate bodhichitta that inspires one to train oneself to work for the benefit of others.

BUDDHA (Skt.): Literally, "awake." One who has won the victory over ignorance and attained enlightenment. Shakyamuni Buddha is the historical buddha of this age, according to Buddhist belief. Also, one of the five buddha families.

EGO: In Chögyam Trungpa's use of this term, ego refers to an illusory belief in the solid existence of a self. The belief in a separate self or ego is the fundamental source of suffering and anxiety. It is contrasted with one's basic goodness and buddha nature, which are the genuine ground of self-confidence.

FIVE BUDDHA FAMILIES: Five basic qualities of energy in the tantric tradition. The five families refer to the mandala of the five buddhas, or tathagatas, and the five fundamental principles of enlightenment they represent. In the mandala of enlightenment, these are five wisdom energies, but in the confused world of samsara, these energies arise as five confused emotions.

The following list gives the name of each family, its buddha, its wisdom, its confused emotion, and its direction and color in the mandala: (1) vajra (adamantine or diamond), Akshobhya, mirrorlike wisdom, aggression, east, blue; (2) ratna (jewel), Ratnasambhava, wisdom of equanimity, pride, south, yellow; (3) padma (lotus), Amitabha, discriminating-awareness wisdom, passion, west, red; (4) karma (action), Amoghasiddha, all-accomplishing wisdom, jealousy, north, green; (5) buddha, Vairochana, all-pervading wisdom, ignorance, center, white. Some qualities differ slightly in different tantras.

FIVE SKANDHAS: *See* skandha.

FIVE TATHAGATAS (Skt.): The five types of awakened being. *See also* five buddha families.

KARMA (Skt.): Literally, deed or action. The universal law of cause and effect. The basic samsaric or volitional action of karma can be defined as "karmic chain reactions." In the vajrayana teachings, the four karmas (pacifying, enriching, magnetizing, and destroying) refer to enlightened actions associated with the accomplishment of yogic discipline. Karma is also the name of one of the five buddha families.

LODRÖ (Tib.; Skt. *mati*): Intellect and the application of intellect, in the sense of having a great thirst and capacity for learning and knowledge.

MAGNETIZING: One of the four karmas (*see* karma). More generally, the quality of drawing in and attracting things to oneself.

MAHAMUDRA (Skt., great symbol or seal): The central meditative transmission of the Kagyü lineage. The inherent clarity and wakefulness of mind, which is both vivid and empty.

MAITRI (Skt., loving-kindness, friendliness): In connection with compassion, or karuna, maitri refers to the process of making friends with oneself as the starting point for developing compassion for others.

MAITRI SPACE AWARENESS: A practice developed in the early 1970s by Chögyam Trungpa, which incorporates postures, often done in specially constructed rooms, that accentuate different psychological approaches to perceiving and interacting with the world. Maitri Space Awareness uses the five buddha families, fundamental styles of relating to space, that in vajrayana Buddhism describe both the five wisdoms as well as the energy of confused emotions. Initially, based on discussions with Shunryu Suzuki Roshi, Chögyam Trungpa developed this approach to working with people with severe psychological problems. The postures were intended to be practiced in a therapeutic community designed for the treatment of mental illness. Maitri Space Awareness is now mainly used in workshops and in the contemplative psychology program at Naropa University, as a means for anyone to explore different qualities, or styles, of fundamental confusion and sanity.

MINDFULNESS: The practice of bare attention connected with shamatha meditation. More generally, the quality of paying attention to the details of one's life.

NEUROSIS: As used by Chögyam Trungpa, this term refers to the fundamental distortion that arises from the illusory belief in a solid, separate self or ego. In this sense, neurosis is the universal experience of beings caught in the web of samsaric mind, the world of duality.

NIRVANA (Skt.): The idea of enlightenment according to the hinayana. It is the cessation of suffering and freedom from ignorance and conflicting emotions and therefore freedom from compulsive rebirth in samsara.

PADMA (Skt., lotus flower): One of the five buddha families.

PRAJNA (Skt.): "Transcendent knowledge" or "perfect knowledge." This knowledge is called transcendent because it sees through the veils of dualistic confusion. It is also sometimes called discriminating awareness or insight, and in a general sense it refers to applying the basic sharpness or intelligence of mind to understanding the world and oneself in a precise and detailed fashion. *Prajna* can also mean wisdom, understanding, or discrimination. At its most developed level, it means seeing things from a nondualistic point of view.

PRAJNAPARAMITA (Skt.): The application or development of prajna, or discriminating awareness.

RATNA (Skt., jewel): One of the five buddha families.

RIKPA (Tib.; Skt. vidya): All-pervading sense of wakefulness or intelligence. Rikpa may be associated with the larger sense of wisdom and being. On a more domestic level, the term refers to the basic analytical aspect of mind.

SAMADHI (Skt., meditation, concentration): A state of total meditation in which the mind is at rest and the content of the meditation and the meditator's mind become one.

SAMSARA (Skt.): The vicious cycle of confused existence; the world of struggle and suffering that is based on ego-clinging, conflicting emotions, and habitual patterns. Its root cause is ignorance of our true nature, which is openness beyond the duality of self and other.

SEM (Tib.; Skt. *chitta*, mind): The quality of mind related to keeping track of, or minding, everything in one's experience. The quality of mind that distinguishes "this" from "that," on a simple, everyday level. Sem is sometimes described as the basic capacity for duality.

SHAMATHA (Skt.; Tib. *shi-ne*): Mindfulness practice, a basic meditation practice common to most schools of Buddhism, the aim of which is to tame the mind. The Tibetan *shi-ne* means "dwelling in peace."

SHAMBHALA (Skt.): The name of an ancient mythic kingdom in Central Asia where the Buddha is said to have taught the *Kalachakra Tantra*, which contains some of the most advanced teachings within the vajrayana, or tantric, tradition. Chögyam Trungpa often referred to Shambhala as an inner experience: residing in the heart rather than somewhere externally. He also connected Shambhala with many teachings he gave on basic goodness and the warrior tradition of human wakefulness.

SHAMBHALA TRADITION: "The Shambhala teachings are founded on the premise that there is *basic* human wisdom that can help to solve the world's problems. This wisdom does not belong to any one culture or religion, nor does it come only from the West or the East. Rather it is a tradition of human warriorship that has existed in many cultures throughout history."—Chögyam Trungpa.

SHILA (Skt.): Discipline. Usually associated with the application of discipline in the context of meditative or monastic training. *Shila* can relate to the general sense of being disciplined or dedicated in one's practice as well as to following specific rules, or disciplines, that are part of the practice.

SIX REALMS: The six realms are associated with Buddhist teachings on the wheel of life, which describes all aspects of samsaric existence. The realms can be understood literally as defining a realm such as heaven, or they can be understood more psychologically, in terms of states of mind. They are the realm of the gods, the realm of the jealous gods (asuras), the human realm, the animal realm, the realm of hungry ghosts (pretas), and the hell realm. There is a buddha who teaches in each of the six realms, relieving the suffering of beings in each of them. Chögyam Trungpa related the six realms to emotional and psychological states of mind.

SIX SENSE CONSCIOUSNESSES: Sight, smell, taste, hearing, touch, and mind (Tib. *yi*).

SKANDHA (Skt.): Group, aggregate, or heap. The five skandhas are the five aggregates or psychophysical factors that make up what we generally understand as personality or ego. The five skandhas are form, feeling, perception (or impulse), concept (or intellect), and consciousness.

SUTRA (Skt.): Sutra refers to the hinayana and mahayana texts or teachings attributed to Shakyamuni Buddha. A sutra text is usually a dialogue between the Buddha and one or more of his disciples, elaborating on a particular topic of dharma.

TANTRA (Skt.; Tib. *rgyud*): *Tantra* literally means "continuity" or "thread." It is used as a synonym for *vajrayana*, the third of the three main yanas, or "ways," that make up the Buddhist path. *Tantra* refers both to the root texts of the vajrayana and to the systems of meditation they describe. *See also* vajrayana.

TATHAGATAGARBHA (Skt.): "Buddha nature." The enlightened basic nature of all beings. *Tathagata* means "thus come" or "thus gone" and is an epithet for the Buddha; and *garbha* means "womb," or "essence." *See also* bodhichitta.

VAJRA (Skt.): Literally "diamond." The quality of complete indestructibility; the capacity for cutting through neurotic emotional tendencies. Symbolized by the vajra scepter (Tib. *dorje*). Vajra is also one of the five buddha families.

VAJRAYANA (Skt.): "Indestructible vehicle" or "indestructible way." The third of the three yanas (ways or vehicles) of Tibetan Buddhism, connected with tantra. The vajrayana emphasizes the attainment of vajra nature, or indestructible wakefulness, and its indivisibility from compassion. The practice of vajrayana emphasizes devotion to the guru, or vajra master. In the vajrayana, buddhahood is presented as already existing, available to be actualized through the application of the vajrayana teachings. The vajrayana is characterized by a great deal of discipline. The tantric, or vajrayana, discipline of life refers both to ongoing discipline in one's life and to the discipline of recognizing one's perceptions as sacred on the spot.

VIDYA (Skt.): *See* rikpa.

VIPASHYANA (Skt., insight): Awareness practice; "seeing things as they are." With shamatha, one of the two main modes of meditation common to most forms of Buddhism. According to Chögyam Trungpa, vipashyana develops naturally out of the experience of shamatha. Also connected with a general sense of wakefulness and with the development of intellect.

YI (Tib.; Skt. *manas*, mind): The mind or mental sensitivity, one of the six sense consciousnesses. Itself the sixth sense consciousness, yi coordinates impressions from the other five into a coherent whole of experience.

SOURCES

Prelude. The Meeting of Buddhist and Western Psychology: Reprinted from *The Collected Works of Chögyam Trungpa*, vol. 2 (Boston & London: Shambhala Publications, 2003), pp. 538–546. Originally published in *Buddhist and Western Psychology*, edited by Nathan Katz (Boulder: Prajña Press, 1983), pp. 1–7. © 1982, 2003 by Diana J. Mukpo.

1. Taming the Horse, Riding the Mind: Reprinted from *The Collected Works of Chögyam Trungpa*, vol. 2 (Boston & London: Shambhala Publications, 2003), pp. 454–457. Originally published in *Naropa Magazine* 1 (February 1984). © 1984, 2003 by Diana J. Mukpo.

2. Discovering Basic Goodness: Reprinted from *The Collected Works of Chögyam Trungpa*, vol. 8 (Boston & London: Shambhala Publications, 2004), pp. 25–30, *Shambhala: The Sacred Path of the Warrior*, 35–41. © 1984, 2004 by Diana J. Mukpo.

3. The Four Foundations of Mindfulness: Reprinted from *The Collected Works of Chögyam Trungpa*, vol. 3 (Boston & London: Shambhala Publications, 2003), *The Heart of the Buddha*, chap. 3, "The Four Foundations of Mindfulness," pp. 329–348. Based on material originally published in *Garuda IV* (Boulder: Vajradhatu Publications, 1976) and remarks on meditation practice at the 1973 Vajradhatu Seminary. © 1991, 2003 by Diana J. Mukpo.

4. An Approach to Meditation: A Talk to Psychologists: Reprinted from *The Collected Works of Chögyam Trungpa*, vol. 2 (Boston & London: Shambhala Publications, 2003), pp. 441–453. Originally published in *Journal of Transpersonal Psychology* 5, no. 1 (1973): 62–74. © 1973, 2003 by Diana J. Mukpo.

5. Natural Dharma: Reprinted from *The Collected Works of Chögyam Trungpa*, vol. 2 (Boston & London: Shambhala Publications, 2003), pp. 586–

588. Originally published in *Speaking of Silence: Christians and Buddhists on the Contemplative Way*, edited by Susan Walker (Mahwah, NJ: Paulist Press, 1987), pp. 200–202. © 1987, 2003 by Diana J. Mukpo.

6. Mind: The Open Secret: Reprinted from *The Collected Works of Chögyam Trungpa*, vol. 3 (Boston & London: Shambhala Publications, 2003), *The Heart of the Buddha*, chap. 3, "The Four Foundations of Mindfulness," pp. 324–329. Based on material originally published in *Garuda IV* (Boulder: Vajradhatu Publications, 1976) and remarks on meditation practice at the 1973 Vajradhatu Seminary. © 1991, 2003 by Diana J. Mukpo.

7. The Spiritual Battlefield: Reprinted from *The Collected Works of Chögyam Trungpa*, vol. 2 (Boston & London: Shambhala Publications, 2003), pp. 461–468. Originally published in *Shambhala Sun* 1 (January/February 1993): 36–39. © 1993, 2003 by Diana J. Mukpo.

8. The Birth of Ego: Reprinted from *The Collected Works of Chögyam Trungpa*, vol. 2 (Boston & London: Shambhala Publications, 2003), pp. 469–473. Originally published in *The Halifax Shambhala Centre Banner* 8 (Summer 1994): 1, 26–27. © 1994, 2003 by Diana J. Mukpo.

9. The Development of Ego: Reprinted from *The Collected Works of Chögyam Trungpa*, vol. 3 (Boston & London: Shambhala Publications, 2003), *Cutting Through Spiritual Materialism*, pp. 93–102. © 1973, 2003 by Diana J. Mukpo.

10. The Basic Ground and the Eight Consciousnesses: Reprinted from *The Collected Works of Chögyam Trungpa*, vol. 2 (Boston & London: Shambhala Publications, 2003), *Glimpses of Abhidharma*, "Form," pp. 239–243. © 1975, 2003 by Diana J. Mukpo.

11. Intellect: Reprinted from *The Collected Works of Chögyam Trungpa*, vol. 2 (Boston & London: Shambhala Publications, 2003), *Glimpses of Abhidharma*, pp. 266–278. © 1975, 2003 by Diana J. Mukpo.

12. The Six Realms: Reprinted from *The Collected Works of Chögyam Trungpa*, vol. 3 (Boston & London: Shambhala Publications, 2003), *The Myth of Freedom and the Way of Meditation*, "Styles of Imprisonment," pp. 202–213. © 1976, 2003 by Diana J. Mukpo.

13. The Five Buddha Families: Reprinted from *The Collected Works of Chögyam Trungpa*, vol. 4 (Boston & London: Shambhala Publications, 2003), *Journey without Goal*, pp. 77–85. © 1981, 2003 by Diana J. Mukpo.

14. Becoming a Full Human Being: Reprinted from *The Collected Works of Chögyam Trungpa*, vol. 2 (Boston & London: Shambhala Publications, 2003), pp. 532–537. Originally published in *Awakening the Heart: East/West Approaches to Psychotherapy and the Healing Relationship*, edited by John Welwood (Boston & London: Shambhala Publications, 1985), pp. 126–131. Based on an article by the same title previously published in *The Naropa Institute Journal of Psychology* 1, no. 1. (1980): 4–20. © 1980, 2003 Diana J. Mukpo.

15. Creating an Environment of Sanity: Reprinted from *The Collected Works of Chögyam Trungpa*, vol. 2 (Boston & London: Shambhala Publications, 2003), pp. 547–555. Originally published in *The Naropa Institute Journal of Psychology* 2 (1983): 1–10. © 1983, 2003 by Diana J. Mukpo.

16. Attitude toward Death in the Healer-Patient Relationship: Reprinted from *The Collected Works of Chögyam Trungpa*, vol. 3 (Boston & London: Shambhala Publications, 2003), *The Heart of the Buddha*, chap. 9, "Acknowledging Death," pp. 449–455. Based on a 1973 seminar in Barnet, Vermont, "The Meaning of Death." © 1991, 2003 by Diana J. Mukpo.

17. Intrinsic Health: A Conversation with Health Professionals: Reprinted from *The Collected Works of Chögyam Trungpa*, vol. 2 (Boston & London: Shambhala Publications, 2003), pp. 556–560. Originally published in *Journal of Transpersonal Psychology* 11, no. 2 (1979): 111–115. © 1979, 2003 by Diana J. Mukpo.

18. Maitri Space Awareness in a Buddhist Therapeutic Community: Reprinted from *The Collected Works of Chögyam Trungpa*, vol. 2 (Boston & London: Shambhala Publications, 2003), "Space Therapy and the Maitri Community," pp. 566–575. Article written in 1974. © 2003 by Diana J. Mukpo.

19. From a Workshop on Psychotherapy: Reprinted from *The Collected Works of Chögyam Trungpa*, vol. 2 (Boston & London: Shambhala Publications, 2003), pp. 561–565. Reprinted with permission from *Loka: A Journal from Naropa Institute*, edited by Rick Fields (Garden City, NY: Anchor Books, 1975), pp. 71–73. © 1975 Nalanda Foundation/Naropa Institute.

20. Is Meditation Therapy?: Reprinted from *The Collected Works of Chögyam Trungpa*, vol. 2 (Boston & London: Shambhala Publications, 2003), pp. 526–531. Originally published in *Journal of Contemplative Psychotherapy* 6 (1989): 3–10. © 1989, 2003 by Diana J. Mukpo.

ACKNOWLEDGMENTS

The Sanity We Are Born With: A Buddhist Approach to Psychology is made up of material from many sources. I would like to thank everyone who played a role in the editorial preparation of the original publications, including Susan Szpakowski, Judith Lief, Sonja Margulies, Sherab Chödzin Kohn, John Baker, Marvin Casper, the late Rick Fields, the late Dr. Edward Podvoll, and undoubtedly others whom I may have forgotten or of whom I am not aware. Thanks also to the original audio engineers and transcribers who recorded many of these lectures and to the Shambhala Archives, where they are now preserved.

Naropa Institute (now Naropa University) and its contemplative psychology program provided many opportunities for Chögyam Trungpa to refine and communicate his ideas about psychology and working with others. I would like to thank two people who taught there who were pivotal in the development of Chögyam Trungpa's work in this area. The first, Marvin Casper, has for many years worked with the Maitri Space Awareness teachings. In the early days, even before the founding of Naropa, Marvin worked closely with Trungpa Rinpoche on the articulation and application of space awareness. From 1977 to 1990, Dr. Edward Podvoll was the chairman of the Department of Psychology at Naropa, and in that capacity he worked closely with Chögyam Trungpa on many aspects of the program and the teachings presented there. Ed really transformed the program at Naropa, helping to deepen it and bring it to maturity. He left Naropa to devote himself to the practice of the Buddhist teachings, and he spent many years in retreat in France. Just a few years ago, he left retreat and began working once again in the field of psychology, as well as presenting Buddhist teachings to interested students. He and I spoke about his contributing a foreword to this volume. He seemed excited by this possibility and sent me some articles he had written recently to give me an idea of the direction his work was taking. Unfortunately, he died at the end of 2003 before he had time to complete a foreword. I regret very much that he was unable to contribute something new for *The Sanity We Are Born With*, but in a very real sense, he made a great contribution to this book, both through his work with Chögyam Trungpa in the 1970s and '80s and through his dedication to applying basic sanity in his own life. He helped a lot of people, and I am very grateful to him.

Dr. Kidder Smith, professor of Asian studies at Bowdoin College, transformed this book when he suggested a title for it. Thank you Kidder for giving this book its true name: *The Sanity We Are Born With*. And thanks as well for the provocative and heartfelt foreword, which spurs us to go further with this material. For me, it communicates a deep quality of relaxation, based on the insight of someone well practiced in and dedicated to this view of inherent sanity.

Many thanks as well to Daniel Goleman, Ph.D., the well-known author on psychology and meditation, who very kindly contributed a foreword to the book. I very much appreciate him sharing his early discussion of Buddhism and psychology with Chögyam Trungpa.

I would also like to thank Dr. Alexis Shotwell and Bonnie Rabin for taking the time to read and comment on the manuscript.

Thanks as well to Dr. Jeffrey Fortuna, who studied with Ed Podvoll at Naropa and became his colleague, for sending me material on the current work of Windhorse Community Services to review for the preparation of this volume.

Kendra Crossen Burroughs, my editor at Shambhala, has provided a sane reference point for this project and a keen editorial eye. I am, as always, so appreciative for her involvement. Thanks also to Peter Turner, president of Shambhala Publications, for helping to refine the original proposal and to Eden Steinberg, who served as the editor in the earliest stages of the project. Appreciative thanks as well to Liz Shaw for additional editorial help, to L. S. Summer for the index, and to Graciela Galup for the design of the book.

Diana J. Mukpo has kindly allowed me to compile and present this book of teachings by her late husband. I am indebted to her for her unflagging commitment to the publication of Chögyam Trungpa's work.

Chögyam Trungpa himself spoke the words that appear here, for which many thanks are due. Beyond that, his luminous mind and his extraordinary kindness and care for beings pervade these teachings. I hope that these qualities are able to shine forth from these pages so that we truly can recognize the sanity we are born with and our responsibility to share this buddha mind with others. Thanks also to the other "old ones": R. D. Laing and Shunryu Suzuki Roshi, ancestors who helped this material to take form.

Finally, I would like to thank all those who work in the fields of psychology, healing, and the health professions in general. This is important work, the stuff of life and death, and all of us are affected and helped by what you do. May this book be of service to you and to all of its readers.

CAROLYN ROSE GIMIAN
Trident Mountain House
April 30, 2004

FURTHER READINGS BY CHÖGYAM TRUNGPA

Additional discussion of the practice of meditation overall and an in-depth treatment of mindfulness and awareness (shamatha and vipa-shyana) meditation is provided by Chögyam Trungpa in *The Path is the Goal: A Basic Handbook of Buddhist Meditation* (Shambhala Publications, 1995). The discussion of awareness practice is particularly well developed in this small manual on Buddhist practice.

Cultivating loving-kindness and compassion toward all beings is at the root of Chögyam Trungpa's approach to working with others in general and to healing and the work of health professionals in particular. *Training the Mind and Cultivating Loving-Kindness* (Shambhala Publications, 1993) presents fifty-nine slogans, or aphorisms related to medita-tion practice, that show a practical path to making friends with oneself and developing compassion for others.

For readers interested in an overview of the Buddhist path, the fol-lowing volumes are recommended: *Cutting Through Spiritual Material-ism* (Shambhala Publications, 1973), *The Myth of Freedom and the Way of Meditation* (Shambhala Publications, 1976), and *The Essential Chögyam Trungpa* (Shambhala Publications, 2000). Each of these books demon-strates how specific teachings presented in this volume connect to a broader perspective.

The Shambhala path of warriorship offers heartfelt advice on trans-forming fear and anxiety into gentle bravery, so that one develops con-fidence and skill in working with others. These teachings on basic goodness and how to be more self-assured, yet genuine and vulnerable, in one's life are available in *Shambhala: The Sacred Path of the Warrior* (Shambhala Publications, 1984) and *The Great Eastern Sun: The Wisdom of Shambhala* (Shambhala Publications, 1999). *The Shambhala Warrior Slogans: 53 Principles for Living Life with Fearlessness and Gentleness* (Shambhala Publications, 2004) provides a small handbook and a group of slogan cards that can be used to contemplate these teachings on working with oneself and others.

RESOURCES

For information regarding meditation instruction or inquiries about a practice center near you, please contact one of the following:

Shambhala International
1084 Tower Road
Halifax, NS
Canada B3H 2Y5
Telephone: (902) 425-4275, ext. 10
Fax: (902) 423-2750
Website: www.shambhala.org (This website contains information about the more than 100 meditation centers affiliated with Shambhala, the international network of Buddhist practice centers established by Chögyam Trungpa.)

Shambhala Europe
Annostrasse 27
50678 Cologne, Germany
Telephone: 49-0-700-108-000-00
E-mail: europe@shambhala.org
Website: www.shambhala-europe.org

Dorje Denma Ling
2280 Balmoral Road
Tatamagouche, NS
BoK 1Vo Canada
Telephone: (902) 657-9085

Fax: (902) 657-0462
E-mail: info@dorjedenmaling.com
Website: www.dorjedenmaling.com

KARMÊ CHÖLING
369 Patneaude Lane
Barnet, VT 05821
Telephone: (802) 633-2384
Fax: (802) 633-3012
E-mail: karmecholing@shambhala.org

SHAMBHALA MOUNTAIN CENTER
4921 Country Road 68C
Red Feather Lakes, CO 80545
Telephone: (970) 881-2184
Fax: (970) 881-2909
E-mail: shambhalamountain@shambhala.org

SKY LAKE LODGE
P.O. Box 408
Rosendale, NY 12472
Telephone: (845) 658-8556
E-mail: skylake@shambhala.org
Website: http://sky-lake.org

DECHEN CHÖLING
Mas Marvent
87700 St Yrieix sous Aixe
France
Telephone: 33 (0)5-55-03-55-52
Fax: 33 (0)5-55-03-91-74
E-mail: dechencholing@dechencholing.org

Audio and videotape recordings of talks and seminars by Chögyam Trungpa are available from:

KALAPA RECORDINGS
1678 Barrington Street, 2nd Floor
Halifax, NS
Canada B3J 2A2
Telephone: (902) 421-1550
Fax: (902) 423-2750
E-mail: shop@shambhala.org
Website: www.shambhalashop.com

For publications from Shambhala International, please contact:

VAJRADHATU PUBLICATIONS
1678 Barrington Street, 2nd Floor
Halifax, NS
Canada B3J 2A2
Telephone: (902) 421-1550
E-mail: shop@shambhala.org
Website: www.shambhalashop.com

For information about the archive of the author's work—which includes more than 5,000 audio recordings, 1,000 video recordings, original Tibetan manuscripts, correspondence, and more than 30,000 photographs—please contact:

THE SHAMBHALA ARCHIVES
1084 Tower Road
Halifax, NS
Canada B3H 3S3
Telephone: (902) 421-1550
Website: www.shambhalashop.com/archives

The *Shambhala Sun* is a bimonthly Buddhist magazine founded by Chö-gyam Trungpa. For a subscription or sample copy, contact:

SHAMBHALA SUN
P. O. Box 3377
Champlain, NY 12919-9871
Telephone: (877) 786-1950
Website: www.shambhalasun.com

Buddhadharma: The Practitioner's Quarterly is an in-depth, practice-oriented journal offering teachings from all Buddhist traditions. For a subscription or sample copy, contact:

BUDDHADHARMA
P. O. Box 3377
Champlain, NY 12919-9871
Telephone: (877) 786-1950
Website: www.thebuddhadharma.com

Naropa University is the only accredited, Buddhist-inspired university in North America. For more information, contact:

NAROPA UNIVERSITY
2130 Arapahoe Avenue
Boulder, CO 80302
Telephone: (303) 444-0202
Website: www.naropa.edu

A BIOGRAPHY OF
CHÖGYAM TRUNGPA

THE VENERABLE CHÖGYAM TRUNGPA was born in the province of Kham in eastern Tibet in 1940.* When he was just thirteen months old, Chögyam Trungpa was recognized as a major tulku, or incarnate teacher. According to Tibetan tradition, an enlightened teacher is capable, based on his or her vow of compassion, of reincarnating in human form over a succession of generations. Before dying, such a teacher may leave a letter or other clues to the whereabouts of the next incarnation. Later, students and other realized teachers look through these clues and, based on those plus a careful examination of dreams and visions, conduct searches to discover and recognize the successor. Thus, particular lines of teaching are formed, in some cases extending over many centuries. Chögyam Trungpa was the eleventh in the teaching lineage known as the Trungpa Tulkus.

Once young tulkus are recognized, they enter a period of intensive training in the theory and practice of the Buddhist teachings. Trungpa Rinpoche, after being enthroned as supreme abbot of Surmang Monastery and governor of Surmang District, began a period of training that would last eighteen years, until his departure from Tibet in 1959. As a Kagyü tulku, his training was based on the systematic practice of meditation and on refined theoretical understanding of Buddhist philosophy.

---

*There has been some confusion about Chögyam Trungpa's precise date of birth. His memoir, *Born in Tibet*, gives it as the full-moon day of the first month of the Earth Hare year, 1939. Other autobiographical sources, including an important doha (song) that he wrote in Tibet, suggest that he was born in the year of the Iron Dragon, 1940. Later in his life, Chögyam Trungpa himself considered 1940 to be his birth year.

One of the four great lineages of Tibet, the Kagyü is known as the practicing (or practice) lineage.

At the age of eight, Trungpa Rinpoche received ordination as a novice monk. Following this, he engaged in intensive study and practice of the traditional monastic disciplines, including traditional Tibetan poetry and monastic dance. His primary teachers were Jamgön Kongtrül of Sechen and Khenpo Gangshar—leading teachers in the Nyingma and Kagyü lineages. In 1958, at the age of eighteen, Trungpa Rinpoche completed his studies, receiving the degrees of kyorpön (doctor of divinity) and khenpo (master of studies). He also received full monastic ordination.

The late 1950s were a time of great upheaval in Tibet. As it became clear that the Chinese communists intended to take over the country by force, many people, both monastic and lay, fled the country. Trungpa Rinpoche spent many harrowing months trekking over the Himalayas (described later in his book *Born in Tibet*). After narrowly escaping capture by the Chinese, he at last reached India in 1959. While in India, Trungpa Rinpoche was appointed to serve as spiritual adviser to the Young Lamas Home School in Delhi, India. He served in this capacity from 1959 to 1963.

Trungpa Rinpoche's opportunity to emigrate to the West came when he received a Spaulding sponsorship to attend Oxford University. At Oxford he studied comparative religion, philosophy, history, and fine arts. He also studied Japanese flower arranging, receiving a degree from the Sogetsu School. While in England, Trungpa Rinpoche began to instruct Western students in the dharma, and in 1967 he founded the Samye Ling Meditation Center in Dumfriesshire, Scotland. During this period, he also published his first two books, both in English: *Born in Tibet* (1966) and *Meditation in Action* (1969).

In 1968 Trungpa Rinpoche traveled to Bhutan, where he entered into a solitary meditation retreat. While on retreat, Rinpoche received*

---

*In Tibet, there is a well-documented tradition of teachers discovering or "receiving" texts that are believed to have been buried, some of them in the realm of space, by Padmasambhava, who is regarded as the father of Buddhism in Tibet. Teachers who find what Padmasambhava left hidden for the beings of future ages, which may be objects or physical texts hidden in rocks, lakes, and other locations, are referred to as tertöns, and the materials they find are known as terma. Chögyam Trungpa was already known as a tertön in Tibet.

a pivotal text for all of his teaching in the West, *The Sadhana of Mahamudra*, a text that documents the spiritual degeneration of modern times and its antidote, genuine spirituality that leads to the experience of naked and luminous mind. This retreat marked a pivotal change in his approach to teaching. Soon after returning to England, he became a layperson, putting aside his monastic robes and dressing in ordinary Western attire. In 1970 he married a young Englishwoman, Diana Pybus, and together they left Scotland and moved to North America. Many of his early students and his Tibetan colleagues found these changes shocking and upsetting. However, he expressed a conviction that in order for the dharma to take root in the West, it needed to be taught free from cultural trappings and religious fascination.

During the seventies, America was in a period of political and cultural ferment. It was a time of fascination with the East. Nevertheless, almost from the moment he arrived in America, Trungpa Rinpoche drew many students to him who were seriously interested in the Buddhist teachings and the practice of meditation. However, he severely criticized the materialistic approach to spirituality that was also quite prevalent, describing it as a "spiritual supermarket." In his lectures, and in his books *Cutting Through Spiritual Materialism* (1973) and *The Myth of Freedom* (1976), he pointed to the simplicity and directness of the practice of sitting meditation as the way to cut through such distortions of the spiritual journey.

During his seventeen years of teaching in North America, Trungpa Rinpoche developed a reputation as a dynamic and controversial teacher. He was a pioneer, one of the first Tibetan Buddhist teachers in North America, preceding by some years and indeed facilitating the later visits by His Holiness the Karmapa, His Holiness Khyentse Rinpoche, His Holiness the Dalai Lama, and many others. In the United States, he found a spiritual kinship with many Zen masters, who were already presenting Buddhist meditation. In the very early days, he particularly connected with Suzuki Roshi, the founder of Zen Center in San Francisco. In later years he was close with Kobun Chino Roshi and Bill Kwong Roshi in Northern California; with Maezumi Roshi, the founder of the Los Angeles Zen Center; and with Eido Roshi, abbot of the New York Zendo Shobo-ji.

Fluent in the English language, Chögyam Trungpa was one of the first Tibetan Buddhist teachers who could speak to Western students directly, without the aid of a translator. Traveling extensively throughout North America and Europe, he gave thousands of talks and hundreds of seminars. He established major centers in Vermont, Colorado, and Nova Scotia, as well as many smaller meditation and study centers in cities throughout North America and Europe. Vajradhatu was formed in 1973 as the central administrative body of this network.

In 1974 Trungpa Rinpoche founded the Naropa Institute (now Naropa University), which became the first and only accredited Buddhist-inspired university in North America. He lectured extensively at the institute, and his book *Journey without Goal* (1981) is based on a course he taught there. In 1976 he established the Shambhala Training program, a series of seminars that present a nonsectarian path of spiritual warriorship grounded in the practice of sitting meditation. His book *Shambhala: The Sacred Path of the Warrior* (1984) gives an overview of the Shambhala teachings.

In 1976 Trungpa Rinpoche appointed Ösel Tendzin (Thomas F. Rich) as his Vajra Regent, or dharma heir. Ösel Tendzin worked closely with Trungpa Rinpoche in the administration of Vajradhatu and Shambhala Training. He taught extensively from 1976 until his death in 1990 and is the author of *Buddha in the Palm of Your Hand*.

Trungpa Rinpoche was also active in the field of translation. Working with Francesca Fremantle, he rendered a new translation of *The Tibetan Book of the Dead*, which was published in 1975. Later he formed the Nālandā Translation Committee in order to translate texts and liturgies for his own students as well as to make important texts available publicly.

In 1979 Trungpa Rinpoche conducted a ceremony empowering his eldest son, Ösel Rangdröl Mukpo, as his successor in the Shambhala lineage. At that time he gave him the title of Sawang ("Earth Lord").

Trungpa Rinpoche was also known for his interest in the arts and particularly for his insights into the relationship between contemplative discipline and the artistic process. Two books published since his death—*The Art of Calligraphy* (1994) and *Dharma Art* (1996)—present this aspect of his work. His own artwork included calligraphy, painting, flower arranging, poetry, playwriting, and environmental installations. In addition, at the Naropa Institute he created an educational atmosphere that attracted many leading artists and poets. The exploration of the creative process in light of contemplative training continues there as a provocative dialogue. Trungpa Rinpoche also published two books of poetry: *Mudra* (1972) and *First Thought Best Thought* (1983). In 1998 a retrospective compilation of his poetry, *Timely Rain*, was published.

Shortly before his death, in a meeting with Samuel Bercholz, the publisher of Shambhala Publications, Chögyam Trungpa expressed his interest in publishing 108 volumes of his teachings, to be called the Dharma Ocean Series. "Dharma Ocean" is the translation of Chögyam Trungpa's Tibetan teaching name, Chökyi Gyatso. The Dharma Ocean Series was to consist primarily of material edited to allow readers to encounter this rich array of teachings simply and directly rather than in an overly systematized or condensed form. In 1991 the first posthumous volume in the series, *Crazy Wisdom*, was published, and since then another seven volumes have appeared.

Trungpa Rinpoche's published books represent only a fraction of the rich legacy of his teachings. During his seventeen years of teaching in North America, he crafted the structures necessary to provide his students with thorough, systematic training in the dharma. From introductory talks and courses to advanced group retreat practices, these programs emphasized a balance of study and practice, of intellect and intuition. *Trungpa* by Fabrice Midal, a French biography (available in English translation under the title *Chögyam Trungpa*), details the many forms of training that Chögyam Trungpa developed. Since Trungpa Rinpoche's death, there have been significant changes in the training offered by the organizations he founded. However, many of the original structures remain in place, and students can pursue their interest in meditation and the Buddhist path through these many forms of training. Senior students of Trungpa Rinpoche continue to be involved in both teaching and meditation instruction in such programs.

In addition to his extensive teachings in the Buddhist tradition, Trungpa Rinpoche also placed great emphasis on the Shambhala teachings, which stress the importance of meditation in action, synchronizing mind and body, and training oneself to approach obstacles or challenges in everyday life with the courageous attitude of a warrior without anger. The goal of creating an enlightened society is fundamental to the Shambhala teachings. According to the Shambhala approach, the realization of an enlightened society comes not purely through outer activity, such as community or political involvement, but from appreciation of the senses and the sacred dimension of day-to-day life. A second volume of these teachings, entitled *Great Eastern Sun*, was published in 1999.

Chögyam Trungpa died in 1987, at the age of forty-seven. By the time of his death, he was known not only as Rinpoche ("Precious Jewel") but also as Vajracharya ("Vajra Holder") and as Vidyadhara ("Wisdom Holder") for his role as a master of the vajrayana, or tantric teachings of Buddhism. As a holder of the Shambhala teachings, he had also received the titles of Dorje Dradül ("Indestructible Warrior") and Sakyong ("Earth Protector"). He is survived by his wife, Diana Judith Mukpo, and five sons. His eldest son, the Sawang Ösel Rangdröl Mukpo, succeeds him as the spiritual head of Vajradhatu. Acknowledging the importance of the Shambhala teachings to his father's work, the Sawang changed the name of the umbrella organization to Shambhala, with Vajradhatu remaining one of its major divisions. In 1995 the Sawang received the Shambhala title of Sakyong like his father before him and was also confirmed as an incarnation of the great ecumenical teacher Mipham Rinpoche.

Trungpa Rinpoche is widely acknowledged as a pivotal figure in introducing the buddhadharma to the Western world. He joined his great appreciation for Western culture with his deep understanding of his own tradition. This led to a revolutionary approach to teaching the dharma, in which the most ancient and profound teachings were presented in a thoroughly contemporary way. Trungpa Rinpoche was known for his fearless proclamation of the dharma: free from hesitation, true to the purity of the tradition, and utterly fresh. May these teachings take root and flourish for the benefit of all sentient beings.

INDEX